Refractions of Violence

Refractions of Violence

Martin Jay

Routledge
Taylor & Francis Group
New York London

First published in 2003 by
Routledge
711 Third Avenue,
New York, NY 10017
www.routledge-ny.com

Published in Great Britain by
Routledge
2 Park Square, Milton Park,
Abingdon, Oxon, OX14 4RN
www.routledge.co.uk

This edition published 2012 by Routledge

Routledge
Taylor & Francis Group
711 Third Avenue
New York, NY 10017

Routledge
Taylor & Francis Group
2 Park Square, Milton Park
Abingdon, Oxon OX14 4RN

Routledge is an imprint of the Taylor & Francis Group.

Library of Congress Cataloging-in-Publication Data

Jay, Martin, 1944–
Refractions of violence / Martin Jay.
p. cm.
Includes bibliographical references and index.
ISBN 0-415-96665-5 (HB : alk. paper) — ISBN 0-415-96666-3 (PB : alk. paper)
1. Violence. 2. Civilization, Modern—20th century. I. Title.
HM1116.J39 2003
303.6—dc21

2003006445

For Frances

CONTENTS

ACKNOWLEDGMENTS

There can be few gestures less violent than exposing to visibility the hidden presences of the many friends and colleagues whose efforts to solicit, criticize, and improve the following essays I can only acknowledge with unalloyed gratitude. Despite my fear that I must be slighting others whose names deserve inclusion, let me single out the following people for their contributions, of whatever kind, to the making of this book: John Rundell, Michael Ure, Robert Pippen, Emmanuel Sivan, Jay Winter, Sarah Harasym, Hal Foster, Lynda Nead, Costas Douzinas, Ken Goldberg, Ales Erjavec, Richard Shusterman, Froma Zeitlin, Robert Barsky, Eric Méchoulan, Ieme van der Poel, Sophie Bertho, Helga Geyer-Ryan, Susan Buck-Morss, Beatrice Hanssen, Miriam Hansen, David Hollinger, David Henkin, Susanne Lowenthal, Chungmoo Choi, John Efron, and Richard Wolin. I was also helped by the excellent research skills of Andrew Jainchill, John Abromeit, Benjamin Lazier, and Vincent Cannon.

Special thanks go to Robert Boyers, the editor of *Salmagundi* in whose pages many of the essays first appeared, Toru and Yu Oba Tani, whose inspiration to publish a Japanese collection of my recent essays led to its English counterpart, and to the staff at Routledge, William Germano, Damon Zucca, and Gilad Foss, who guided the book through the treacherous shoals of the publishing process. I have also been helped in too many ways to acknowledge by the light emanating from my daughters, Shana Lindsay and Rebecca Jay, now themselves pursuing careers in the visual arts. Special thanks to Becca for preparing the index. As always, my greatest debt is to my wife, Catherine Gallagher, through whose refracting intelligence I have the great good fortune to pass all my texts before they see the light of day.

INTRODUCTION

During the first decade of the terrible twentieth century, the French social theorist Georges Sorel issued a clarion call for revolutionary violence as an antidote to the flaccid, morally compromised society he saw around him. Deeply pessimistic about the exhaustion of the vital forces in European culture and anxious to jolt it out of its decline, he advocated the intensification of the class struggle rather than its peaceful resolution. Hopeful of generating moral fervor through the deliberate fostering of a new myth, Sorel hit on the apocalyptic "general strike" as a way to bring the current order to its knees. "It is to violence," his book ended rhapsodically, "that Socialism owes those high ethical values by means of which it brings *salvation* to the modern world."[1] The redemptive goal, which at the time he identified in syndicalist terms with a classless society of producers, was in fact less important than the means invoked to realize it. And so, not surprisingly, his advocacy of violence could easily be turned to other ends, as it soon was by Mussolini and the fascists, who claimed him as one of their inspirations.

Reflections on Violence, as his book was called, seems light years away from us today at the dawn of another century. Written before the two World Wars, before the Armenian genocide and the Holocaust, before the Gulag and the "killing fields" of Cambodia, before Hiroshima and Rwanda, and before countless other now emblematic instances of a violence that has proven anything but redemptive, its reckless insistence that ethical benefits would flow from the intensification of struggle seems naive at best, and deeply culpable at worst. And yet, the temptations of violence remain powerful even with these horrors registered on our consciousness, and our power to resist them is far too weak. Indeed, with the multiplier effect of technology operating to exacerbate the problem, the twenty-first century threatens to outdo its bloody predecessor.

We are, I think it fair to say, all hovering nervously in the shadow of that threat, which preoccupies us in so many different ways. And therefore I suppose it should be no wonder that without any conscious intent, my own work in the past few years has gravitated, if fitfully and without any systematic ambition, towards the question of violence. To be sure, the ostensible subject of that work often seemed to stem from the aftereffects of an earlier project, which had explored the issue of visuality, or more precisely, the French critique of "ocularcentrism."[2] That is, the extraordinary efflorescence of interest in visual culture in all of its myriad forms compelled me to return again and again to considerations of one aspect of that theme or another. But often just beneath the surface, and only really apparent in retrospect, was an inclination to mix questions of visuality with those of violence. Although not all of the texts collected in this volume are equally devoted to the interactions of these two themes, most—to my retrospective surprise—do.

Together, they provide what can justifiably be called "refractions on violence." That is, rather than self-conscious reflections on that theme in Sorel's sense or merely ruminations about visuality or violence in themselves, each essay more or less refracts one theme through the other, bending it as a ray of light is bent when it passes through one medium to another of a different density. Insofar as we live in a world increasingly saturated with images and simulacra, the ways in which actual violence often comes to us are precisely through such visual refractions. The domination of the eye as the most hegemonic sense has, of course, often been seen as a source of a violence all its own; it may well be possible to speak, as Derrida does in his early essay on Levinas, of "the violence of light" itself.[3] The fact that we live in an increasingly ocularcentric world means that we are sometimes inclined to believe that the evil eye can be taken as more than just an antiquated superstition. That is, there may be a kind of distanced violence in the penetrating stare or withering gaze that is more than a metaphorical analogue of its more proximate tactile counterpart. The underlying aggression in the photographer's "shot" has also not gone unnoticed.

Images of violence—whether produced by such technologically mediated "shots" or by the painter's hand—have often been the source of considerable controversy. As Paul Crowther notes, "the representation of violence is a source of enduring pleasure and fascination in our culture."[4] It has, of course, been no less a source of guilt and anxiety, as evidenced in periodic bouts of iconoclastic fervor, which can unleash a counterviolence in the service of purification or expiation (aimed, to be sure, at other types of images as well). Often the rhetoric of antipornography is employed to stigmatize such images still further, or more precisely to stigmatize those who find them fascinating. In so doing, it testifies to the often erotic charge intensifying our feelings about violence, either pro or con, as well as our ambivalence about the "lust of the eye."[5]

Even when seemingly benign images are employed as public icons, they can elicit powerful feelings of anger as well as veneration. As W. J. T. Mitchell has noted, "the association of public art with violence is nothing new. The fall of every Chinese dynasty since antiquity has been accompanied by the destruction of its public monuments, and the long history of political and religious strife in the West could almost be rewritten as a history of iconoclasm."[6] Here what might be called a closed circuit of violence is created in which the offending image is itself violated, caught in an economy of violence and visuality in which there is no complete outside. It may well be, as Derrida argued in the essay cited above, that "if light is the element of violence, one must combat light with a certain other light, in order to avoid the worst violence, the violence of the night which precedes or represses discourse. This *vigilance* is a violence chosen as the least violence by a philosophy which takes history, that is, finitude, seriously."[7]

The essays in this collection were written with a keen awareness that we do indeed live in such a finite economy in which utter redemption *from* violence is as utopian as redemption through it. The "fall" into history or finitude, whatever else it may mean, signifies a loss of prelapsarian grace and a hope for a peaceful kingdom that will be infinitely delayed. And yet, the essays also betray a belief that some countervailing light can be shed on the sources of the worsening violence that threatens our existence. As thorny as the problem of violence may seem, the following discursive refractions will, I hope, help shine a few rays of that "certain other light" to which Derrida refers.

In introducing a heterogeneous collection of occasional pieces like this one, it is best to be candid about the variations in tone and ambition that set some apart from others. Half of the essays were solicited for scholarly conferences or journals and have all of the normal apparatus and constrained style that characterize that genre. The other half were originally prepared for the biannual "Force Fields" column I have been contributing since 1987 to the general humanities journal *Salmagundi.* Often more colloquial in tone and personal in perspective, they provide an opportunity to touch on issues less suited for a formal scholarly presentation to an audience of experts. And even though their themes are often weighty, some are written in a cheekier and less solemn voice. No writing, to be sure, cancels out the mediation of its author's sensibility and normative intuitions, but the columns make no attempt to disguise them behind the rhetoric of scholarly objectivity. The result will, I hope, be taken as exploratory forays into territory—or rather, many different territories—for which no map, no systematic survey, has been provided.

The first essay, "Against Consolation: Walter Benjamin and the Refusal to Mourn," was generated by an invitation to speak to the inaugural meeting of the International Walter Benjamin Society in 1997 in Amsterdam. It was later refined at the gathering of contributors assembled by Jay Winter and Emmanuel Sivan in Chinchon, Spain for the volume on *War and Remembrance in the Twentieth Century* published in 1999.[8] Although there were still residues of Sorel's apocalyptic evocation of violence in the young Benjamin, he intransigently refused to condone the slaughter of the First World War and was unwilling to countenance consoling gestures of reconciliation after it. In visual terms, this meant he resisted architectural manifestations of national unity or positive monuments to the fallen, which were symbolic vehicles of a premature mourning that needed to be forestalled. Instead, he favored a jagged aesthetic of allegory, montage, and juxtaposition, which violated the ideological sublimation of still festering wounds, an aesthetic that would come into its own with the "dialectical images" he sought to produce in his unfinished *Arcades* project. In the spirit of Derrida's pitting of "a certain other light" against its hegemonic opposite, Benjamin refused to "work through" his anger and grief and accept the dominant discourse of completed mourning, which served to legitimate "sacrifice" for an allegedly higher cause. Like the Berlin Dadaists and French Surrealists of his day, he understood the dangers of integrated images of formal closure and resolution, preferring to remain unconsoled and melancholic until genuine transformation might occur.

After exploring so saturnine a sensibility as Benjamin's and empathizing with his resolute refusal to mourn, it may seem trivializing to turn to another, less serious moment in the German response to war, that occasioned by my participation in the founding of the Peace University in Berlin in 1995. The *Salmagundi* column I wrote on the subject, facetious as its tone may be, nonetheless touches on an important issue: can all the well-meaning, "spiritually" infused pacifist intentions in the world really do anything to temper the violence unleashed by the modern state? Here the question of vision appears largely in metaphoric terms as I express my reluctance to play the role of "visionary" assigned me in the spectacle of the University's founding ritual. Despite all my skepticism, I should report that the University's leaders have continued to solicit my thoughts on their projects and taken no umbrage at my reluctance to do so. And there are, as I indicate in the column, lots of worse causes that might be pursued by people with the entrepreneurial talents of the University's founders.

The essay that follows, "Fathers and Sons," also contributed to *Salmagundi* as a column, focuses on the intersection between collective and personal violence, dealing as it does with the traumatic ordeal of a contemporary figure in Germany, Jan Philipp Reemtsma. The penitent son of a Nazi industrialist who has dedicated his life to progressive causes, Reemtsma was also the victim of a shocking kidnapping in 1996. Kept in a darkened cellar for a month before his miraculous release, Reemtsma wrote a powerful account of his confinement, which only ended with the payment of an enormous ransom. Contrasted with the darkness of his underground prison, it might be argued, was the light his Institute for Social Research in Hamburg has tried to shed on the complicity of the German Wehrmacht during the Holocaust. The traveling exhibition they mounted to document the criminal deeds of ordinary German soldiers was met with enormous controversy, stirred still further when some of its images were shown to be misleadingly labeled and attributed (this happening after my column had appeared).[9] After some initial hesitation, Reemstma withdrew and remounted the exhibition, taking into account the accusations of his detractors, but maintaining the larger argument presented visually by his photographs and documents. In an era when the trustworthiness of what we see is rendered ever more suspect by the spread of ever more effective simulacral techniques, the demand to use visual material as historical documentation with utmost care has rarely been as explicitly presented as in this extremely fraught case. It is a mark of Reemstma's integrity that he responded constructively to the challenges to certain images and was willing to remount the exhibition to take new evidence into account.

The next essay recounts an uncomfortable personal story of an historian—to be precise, this historian—feeling violated by posthumous revelations of disdain for him on the part of two of his most admired subjects, Theodor W. Adorno and Gershom Scholem. "The Ungrateful Dead" doesn't deal directly with the issues of violence and visuality, except in the sense that it foregrounds the power of idealizing images in our intercourse with the past and the costs of the historian's transferential investments. When this *Salmagundi* column was translated in the *Frankfurter Rundschau*, it solicited a wave of consoling letters from German friends, including a well-intentioned, if somewhat deflating, comment from Jürgen Habermas, who recalled that Adorno had never mentioned me to him at all!

A far less trivial issue is raised in the following piece, which was prepared for the Biderman Lecture at Princeton in the spring of 2002 and a forthcoming volume of essays on the Holocaust and objectivity edited by Sarah Harasym. As the controversy roused by the misattributed images in Reemtsma's exhibition on the Wehrmacht's role in the Holocaust shows, the validity of visual evidence remains very much a contested dimension of our struggle to remember, understand, and prevent the recurrence of unfathomably terrible events. Without coming to any definitive answers, "When Did the Holocaust End? Reflections on Historical Objectivity" explores the limits of an objective historical account that depends on conceptual and representational strategies that go beyond any simply fidelity to discrete "facts." Even the seemingly straightforward films of the liberation of the camps, it turns out, need to be understood as mediated documents rather than merely indexical traces of real events.

Moving back to a much more personal level, the next essay, "The Conversion of the Rose," speculates on the implications of the astounding and entirely unexpected deathbed profession of a new faith on the part of the British philosopher and Frankfurt School expert, Gillian Rose. Violence was, in fact, one of the constant themes of her remarkable work, as it was in subtle ways in her turbulent life, including what she called "violence-in-love."[10] The issues of mourning and melancholy, raised so powerfully in Benjamin's oeuvre, were also ones she probed, albeit ultimately coming to a different, more positive conclusion. In retrospect, it is possible to understand her deathbed conversion to Anglicanism as an enactment of her challenge to what she condemned as his "*aberrated mourning*, and the yearning for invisible, divine violence."[11] In embracing the visibility of her new religion's incarnationist theology, Rose sought to affirm creation, contradictions and all, rather than remain frozen in a melancholic posture of permanently delayed consolation.

The next essay, "Pen Pals with the Unicorn Killer," also prepared for *Salmagundi*, is perhaps the most troubling of the entire collection because it touches on a freshly committed, monstrous crime and the flight of the man who committed it. My own, totally contingent link to the murder it involves came unexpectedly through a letter sent in response to "The Conversion of the Rose" by the fugitive, using a pseudonym, who was only shortly thereafter discovered in his French hideout. Ira Einhorn, having lost his battle against extradition to the United States, was subsequently retried and found guilty again in September

2002.[12] A while after my column appeared and when he was still in French custody, I received several extensive e-mail messages from Einhorn, protesting his innocence and trying to persuade me to join the campaign to exonerate him. Although I did respond to the first one or two entreaties, I found myself reluctant to be drawn deeper into a story whose competing versions I had no objective way of adjudicating, and so let the correspondence lapse. While no longer hoping that the exhortation I permitted myself in the column will have an effect, I followed the playing out of this miserable tale with grim fascination.

Visuality and violence are more intimately intertwined in the next chapter, a former *Salmagundi* column entitled, "Kwangju: From Massacre to Biennale," which chronicles a visit to the South Korean city where "Unmapping the Earth," an international art exhibition and accompanying conference were held in 1997.[13] Once again the issue of how to memorialize past victims of violence came to the fore, as did the difficulties of drawing new cultural maps in a rapidly changing world. But perhaps the most powerful lesson of the trip, which is drawn at the essay's conclusion, concerns the yawning gap between local or even national democratization and economic globalization. How to "represent" the people is more than just an aesthetic question when it is not clear what institutions exist to transmit a discursively generated popular will into political action. The simulacral nature of so much contemporary democracy is particularly painful to acknowledge at a time when countries like South Korea have cast off their authoritarian past and are searching for ways to achieve meaningful political reform.

If politics and visuality are intimately intertwined, no less imbricated are images and the law. In "Must Justice Be Blind?," prepared for a conference at the Tate Gallery in London organized by Costas Douzinas and Lynda Nead in 1996,[14] I attempted to tease out the implications of the blindfolding of the statue of Justitia, which began in the fifteenth century. Acknowledging that the putative impartiality of justice is neatly symbolized by the goddess's covered eyes, the article also explores the costs of denying sight to a female viewer, able to discern the differences between individual cases. What has been called the violence of conceptual subsumption, in which equivalence is forced on the nonidentical, finds here a certain visual expression. But the essay concludes that such violence may be useful in checking the countervіolence of a singular, nonrule-bound judgment that pretends it can be certain about the guilt or innocence in concrete, incommensurable cases. It concludes with a plea for a negative dialectic of the two judicial imperatives, brilliantly symbolized by a sixteenth-century image of justice with two heads, one blindfolded and one not.

Prepared for a conference organized by Robert Pippin called "After the Beautiful: Politics and Modernism" at the John M. Olin Center at the University of Chicago and published in the inaugural issue of the new Australian journal *Critical Horizons* in 2000, the next essay speculates about the transformation of spectatorship at the end of the twentieth century.[15] As indicated by its title, "Diving into the Wreck" focuses on the fascination with simulated disasters and vicarious traumas in the popular media, which, borrowing Hans Blumenberg's metaphor, collapses the distance between spectators and shipwrecks. Arguing for the preservation of a certain visual distance against the proximate kinaesthetic thrills of the culture industry, it voices concern for the anaesthetic implications of excessive virtual immersion in pseudodisasters, which effaces the contemplative distance that is needed for not only aesthetic, but also political judgment.

Distance and virtuality are also the themes of the next essay, which was first presented at a conference organized by the French Department of University College, London, at the Tate Gallery, in 1997, and then published in a remarkable collection edited by my Berkeley colleague Ken Goldberg on *The Robot in the Garden*.[16] Examining the consequences of the discovery of the speed of light in the seventeenth century by the Danish astronomer Ole Roemer for our understanding of the temporal dimension of visual experience—in particular the deep time revealed by what the essay calls "astronomical hindsight"—I argue that our current world of virtual simulation is itself haunted by residues of its origins in a past reality. The result is that the apparent self-sufficiency of the virtual world, stressed by commentators like Jean Baudrillard and Paul Virilio, is disrupted by the flickering remnants of a past that is not entirely effaced in a timeless present. As in the case of the entertainment industry examined in the previous essay, the claims of absolute virtualization are challenged by the return of a real—traumatic or not—that escapes being absorbed without remainder into a world of simulacra "all the way down."

Although the issue of violence is less on the surface in the next essay, which was initially prepared for a conference in Amsterdam in 1994 on "France–USA Transatlantic Exchange of Ideas," it nonetheless is not far beneath.[17] Trying to explain the extraordinarily receptive response to the French critique of ocularcentrism in America, "Returning the Gaze" focuses on the ways that the hegemony of vision has been associated with aggression and domination in modern society. Although the French were perhaps the first to make these connections a target of sustained analysis, as I had tried to demonstrate in *Downcast Eyes*, Americans sympathetic to postmodernist critiques of high modernist art and modern rationalized society soon found that analysis equally persuasive.

A similar curiosity about the ways that American intellectuals refracted ideas from France motivated the subsequent essay, which was delivered to a conference organized by Robert Barsky at University College, London, Ontario on the theme "Paris-Substance-America: The Passage of Literary and Cultural Criticism" in 1999, and published in *Substance* three years later.[18] It focuses on the attempt made by the editors of a series of books published by Princeton University Press and called "New French Thought" to substitute a fresh pantheon of Parisian intellectuals for the post-structuralists discussed in the previous essay. Neoliberal for the most part, these thinkers stress the importance of human rights and the sanctity of the individual as a bulwark against unjust state power. But a closer look at the content of their thought shows no consensus about the origin, justification, or extent of those rights, leaving us with the nagging doubt that the challenge to their transcendent foundation provided by French critics of Enlightenment notions of reason, humanism, and the subject still needs to be met.

The next essay looks for inspiration from American rather than French theory, finding in the "somaesthetics" of John Dewey and Richard Shusterman a suggestive source of new ideas about the relationship between art and democracy. Written for a conference on that theme organized by Herman Pfütze and Karlheinz Lüdeking for the Deutsche Gesellschaft für Aesthetik in Berlin in 2002, the essay explores a version of transgressive body or performance art ignored by the American Pragmatists, but which may have something useful to tell us about the ways that art and democracy refract each other. The tradition is one in which violence towards the artist's body, as well as towards the aesthetic sensibility of the audience and its expectations of visual pleasure, raises uncomfortable questions about the fragility and vulnerability of the body in the modern world. As a counterpoint to the popular manipulation of traumatophilia discussed in "Diving into the Wreck," "Somaesthetics and Democracy" comes to the paradoxical conclusion that this more esoteric and elite art may ultimately better serve democratic ends.

The final two essays, both *Salmagundi* columns, can be understood in retrospect as unintended book-ends around the most violent and visually spectacular act of the twenty-first century: the destruction of the World Trade Center on September 11, 2001. Written the summer before and aimed at the pious claim of Senator Joseph Lieberman that religion is the basis for morality, "The Paradoxes of Religious Violence" explores the intimacy of violence and religious faith, which often suspends ethical commands in the name of a higher calling. Although the examples come from sacrificial violence in the pagan, Jewish and Christian traditions, their Islamic counterpart was frighteningly apparent shortly after the column appeared. The final essay, "Fearful Symmetries: 9/11 and the Agonies of the Left," was written in its shattering aftermath and seeks to rescue some lessons from the tradition of negative dialectics associated with Theodor Adorno for dealing with its implications.

We appear, alas, very much on the threshold of an age of increasing opacity and incoherence, in which many of our earlier narrative tools and analytical strategies seem inadequate to the challenges that face us. Violence, no matter how one defines, measures, justifies, or condemns it, looms ever larger as a feature of human interaction. However bright the searchlight we shine on its causes and remedies, it baffles our attempts to contain it. After the horror of 9/11 and against the anticipation of even worse to come, Sorelian threnodies to its redemptive power seem more obscenely misplaced than ever. All we can do, it seems, is hope that some dim light can still be cast by refractions of a violence that has proven more refractory than the champions of enlightenment had ever imagined in their most vivid nightmares.

1

AGAINST CONSOLATION
Walter Benjamin and the Refusal to Mourn

In August, 1914, Walter Benjamin, along with many other twenty-two-year-old German men, volunteered for the Kaiser's army. He acted, however, according to his friend Gershom Scholem, "not out of enthusiasm for the war but to anticipate the ineluctable conscription in a way that would have permitted him to remain among friends and like-minded people."[1] Benjamin was, as it happened, refused, and when it came the turn of his age group to be drafted that fall, he faked palsy and was able to postpone induction until another order arrived to report in January, 1917. Again he was able to avoid conscription by trickery, undergoing hypnosis to simulate the symptoms of sciatica.[2] Shortly thereafter, Benjamin left Germany for Bern, Switzerland with the hypnotist, who was also his new wife, Dora Kellner. This was Benjamin's first emigration from his native country in a period of crisis, but not his last. After the armistice, following a short stay in Austria, the Benjamins returned to Berlin in March 1919, where he spent the turbulent years of the Weimar Republic until forced to flee to Paris in 1933.

Walter Benjamin was thus spared the glory and misery of the *Fronterlebnis*, the community of the trenches that so powerfully marked his generation for the rest of their lives, if they were lucky enough, that is, to survive it. But he did not, in fact, escape the violence caused by the war. Indeed, it might be said to have sought him out immediately after the hostilities were declared. On August 8, 1914, two of his friends, the nineteen-year-old poet Friedrich (Fritz) Heinle, to whom he was passionately devoted, and Heinle's lover, Frederika (Rika) Seligson, the sister of one of Benjamin's closest comrades in the Youth Movement, Carla Seligson, committed suicide together in Berlin. Their act, carried out by turning on the gas, was designed as a dramatic protest against the war, a war in which lethal gas was, as we know, to take many more victims. Benjamin learned of the news when he was awakened by an express letter from Heinle with the grim message "You will find us lying in the Meeting House."[3] The place of their deaths was not chosen accidentally; "the Meeting House" (*Sprechsaal*) was the apartment Benjamin had rented as a "debating chamber" for his faction of the movement.

All accounts concur that Benjamin was inconsolable for months, and indeed seems never to have fully recovered from the loss of Heinle, to whom he could only bear to refer in later years as "my friend."[4] According to Pierre Missac, who came to know Benjamin in 1937, he was able to overcome his shame at surviving only by "mythologizing the lost friendship."[5] In the quarter century that followed the initial trauma, ended only by his own suicide in 1940, Benjamin composed seventy-three unpublished sonnets, discovered in the Bibliothèque Nationale in 1981. Some fifty-two of these he arranged in a cycle dedicated to Heinle, prefaced by a motto from Hölderlin's *Patmos*, which began: "Wenn aber abstirbt alsdenn/An dem am meisten/Die Schönheit hing (. . .)."[6] His will, which was discovered in 1966, revealed that "my entire estate contains in addition to my own writings primarily the works of the brothers Fritz and Wolf Heinle," the latter having also been a poet and friend, who died prematurely in 1923 at the age of twenty-four.[7] Until the end, Benjamin had hoped to get his friend's own poetry published, a desire that was to remain unfulfilled until many years later.[8]

Although several commentators have shown that Benjamin's disillusionment with the Youth Movement began well before the war, the suicides intensified and brought to a climax his disgust for the devil's pact he saw between the movement's alleged idealism, its celebration of pure *Geist*, and its patriotic defense of the state.[9] With the death of the adolescent Heinle came the end of Benjamin's faith in the redemptive mission of youth itself, although he remained stubbornly wedded to its ideals. In March 1915, he abruptly broke with his mentor in the Youth Movement, Gustav Wyneken, in a harsh letter that detailed his feelings of betrayal.[10] During the rest of the war, Benjamin distanced himself from others who defended it, such as Martin Buber, and brutally dropped old friends from the Youth Movement, such as Herbert Belmore.[11] Instead, he gravitated towards like-minded critics of the conflict, although never himself actively engaging in antiwar agitation, and wrote increasingly apocalyptic treatises on the crisis of Western culture. His estrangement from the German university community, which reached its climax with the now notorious rejection of his *Habilitationsschrift* at the University of Frankfurt in 1925, began with his disgust at the spectacle of so many distinguished professors enthusiastically supporting the so-called ideas of 1914.[12] The empty bombast of their chauvinist rhetoric hastened his abandonment of traditional notions of linguistic communication, as well as whatever faith he may have had left in the German Jewish fetish of *Kultur* and *Bildung*.[13]

It has long been recognized in the extensive scholarship on Benjamin that the war had a decisive effect on all his later work. As one commentator typically put it, "it is the first world war which provides the traumatic background to Benjamin's culture theory, fascism its ultimate context."[14] In particular, it has been acknowledged as a powerful stimulus to his remarkable thoughts on the themes of experience and remembrance, which were to be so crucial a part of his idiosyncratic legacy. One of the most frequently cited passages in his work, from his 1936 Essay "The Storyteller," is often cited to show its relevance. It reads:

> With the [First] World War a process began to become apparent which has not halted since then. Was it not noticeable at the end of the war that men returned from the battlefield grown silent—not richer, but poorer in communicable experience? What ten years later was poured out in the flood of war books was anything but experience that goes from mouth to mouth. And there was nothing remarkable about that. For never has experience been contradicted more thoroughly than strategic experience by tactical warfare, economic experience by inflation, bodily experience by mechanical warfare, moral experience by those in power. A generation that had gone to school on a horse-drawn streetcar now stood under the open sky in a countryside in which nothing remained unchanged but the clouds, and beneath those clouds, in a field of force of destructive torrents and explosions, was the tiny, fragile human body.[15]

The modern crisis of experience, or more precisely of the integrated, narratively meaningful variety known as *Erfahrung* as opposed to mere discontinuous, lived experience or *Erlebnis*, was thus brought to a head, Benjamin tells us, by the war and its aftermath. Despite the efforts by celebrants of the *Fronterlebnis* such as Ernst Jünger to recapture its alleged communal solidarity, Benjamin knew that the technologically manufactured slaughter of the western front was anything but an "inner experience" worth reenacting in peacetime. In his trenchant 1930 review of the collection edited by Jünger entitled *War and Warrior*, he ferociously denounced the aestheticization of violence and glorification of the "fascist class warrior" he saw lurking behind this new cult of "eternal" war.[16] There could be nothing "beautiful" about such carnage.

These aspects of Benjamin's response to the war are well known. What is perhaps less widely appreciated and will thus be the focus of what follows is the fact that Benjamin, never a straightforward pacifist hostile to all violence,[17] also steadfastly defied all attempts to heal the wounds caused by the war. However much he may have lamented, at least in certain of his moods, the lost experience underlying the storyteller's craft, Benjamin resisted short-circuiting the process of recovering the conditions that allowed it to occur—or more precisely, creating the new ones that might allow it to reappear. He refused, that is, to seek some sort of new symbolic equilibrium through a process of collective mourning that would successfully "work through" the grief. Scornfully rejecting the ways culture can function to cushion the blows of trauma,[18] he wanted to compel his readers to face squarely what had happened and confront its deepest sources rather than let the wounds scar over. Rather than rebuilding the psychological "protective shield" (*Reizschutz*) that Freud saw as penetrated by trauma, he labored to keep it lowered so that the pain would not be numbed. For the ultimate source of the pain was not merely the war itself. As Kevin Newmark has noted,

> Benjamin seems, ultimately, to generalize Freud's hypothesis—produced in response to the traumas of World War I—about the destabilizing and repetitive memory-traces left in accident victims into a global economy of modern life. And in so doing, he gives himself the means of repeatedly bemoaning the traumatic loss of "experience" entailed for the subject when the mode of all possible experience is recognized as a recurrent strategy of defense against the "inhospitable, blinding age of large-scale industrialism."[19]

This generalization was evident, inter alia, in his influential discussion of Baudelaire's response to the shocks of modern life. The poet's lyric parrying of distressful stimuli, he argued, was in the service of preventing them from becoming truly traumatic, keeping them, that is, at the level of unreflected episodes with no long-term effect on the mind, which failed to register them beyond the moment of impact.[20] Although he understood the reasons for doing so, Benjamin warned explicitly against such defensiveness, which was of a piece with other techniques of anesthesia developed in the nineteenth century to dull the pain of modern life.[21] Shock-parrying purchases its fragile peace, he claimed, at the cost of a deeper understanding of the sources of the shocks, which might ultimately lead to changing them.[22] Shocks, in short, must be allowed to develop into full-fledged traumas, for reasons that will be clarified later.

In so arguing, Benjamin was profoundly at odds not only with the nineteenth-century culture of anesthesia, but also with the postwar, international "culture of commemoration" that, as George Mosse, Annette Becker, and Jay Winter have recently shown, desperately drew on all the resources of tradition and the sacred it could muster to provide meaning and consolation for the survivors.[23] Rejecting, for example, the cult of nature that led to the construction of *Heldenhaine* (heroes groves) of oaks and boulders in the German forests, Benjamin wrote:

> It should be said as bitterly as possible: in the face of this "landscape of total mobilization" the German feeling for nature has had an undreamed-of upsurge. . . . Etching the landscape with flaming banners and trenches, technology wanted to recreate the heroic features of German Idealism. It went astray. What is considered heroic were the features of Hippocrates, the features of death. Deeply imbued with its own depravity, technology gave shape to the apocalyptic face of nature and reduced nature to silence—even though this technology had the power to give nature its voice.[24]

No pseudoromantic simulation of pastoral tranquility in cemeteries that were disguised as bucolic landscapes could undo the damage. No ceremonies of reintegration into a community that was already deeply divided before the war could suture the wounds.

The same impulse informed Benjamin's celebrated defense of allegory in *The Origin of German Tragic Drama*, which has been recognized by Susan Buck-Morss as "a response to the horrifying destructiveness of World War I."[25] Understood as a dialectic of unmediated extremes, opposed to the mediating power of symbolism, allegory refused to sublimate and transfigure a blasted landscape like that of the war into a locus of beauty, a forest of symbolic correspondences.[26] "Whereas in the symbol destruction is idealized and the transfigured face of nature is fleetingly revealed in the light of redemption," Benjamin argued, "in allegory the observer is confronted with the *facies hippocratica* [death's head] of history as a petrified, primordial landscape. Everything about history that, from the very beginning, has been untimely, sorrowful, unsuccessful, is expressed in a face—or rather in a death's head."[27]

Benjamin's saturnine attraction to *Trauerspiel*, the endless, repetitive "play" of mourning (or more precisely, melancholy), as opposed to *Trauerarbeit*, the allegedly healthy "working through" of grief, was, however, more than a response to the war experience in general. It was, I want to argue, specifically linked to his reluctance to close the books on his friends' antiwar suicides.[28] As he argued in the case of another suicide, that of the innocent Ottilie in Goethe's *Elective Affinities*, the work to which Benjamin devoted a remarkable study in 1922,[29] making sense of such acts in terms of sacrifice, atonement, and reconciliation could only reinforce the evil power of mythic fatalism (and the mythlike social compulsions of bourgeois society).

To understand Benjamin's uncompromising resistance to both the cult of the *Fronterlebnis* and the culture of commemoration, including its pseudopastoral naturalism, it is thus necessary to recall the precise nature of the trauma that he personally suffered in the war. For the suicides of two teenagers vainly protesting the outbreak of hostilities cannot have had the same meaning as the deaths of the soldiers who were assumed to have gallantly fought for their country. Although both could be made intelligible, even ennobled, through a rhetoric of sacrifice, in the case of the former, the cause could be construed as even more of a failure than in that of the latter. It certainly was one little honored in the interwar era. Benjamin's bitterness is evident in the autobiographical "Berlin Chronicle" he composed in 1932, in which he wrote of the obstacles he experienced in attempting to lay Fritz Heinle and Rika Seligson to rest: "Even the graveyard demonstrated the boundaries set by the city to all that filled our hearts: it was impossible to procure for the pair who had died together graves in one and the same cemetery."[30]

But rather than remaining a prisoner of his resentment, Benjamin ultimately made a virtue out of that failure, or at least turned it into a warning against the premature, purely aesthetic smoothing over of real contradictions. It was this intransigence that saved him, however close he may seemed to have come, from wallowing in the self-pitying "left-wing melancholy" of the homeless Weimar intellectuals, as well as from the seductive nostrums offered by those on the right.[31] Unlike the commemorative lyrics filled with the traditional healing rhetoric that has allowed Jay Winter to claim that "a complex process of resacralization marks the poetry of the war,"[32] Benjamin's sonnets to his war dead—or rather antiwar dead—enacted a ritual of unreconciled duality. Here eternal salvation and no less eternal sorrow remained in uneasy juxtaposition, as antinomies that resist mediation. As Bernhild Boie has noted, whereas the nationalist mobilization of religious rhetoric, in the work of, say, Friedrich Gundolf, sacrificed individual souls for the collective good, Benjamin's poems refused to do so: "Because Gundolf pompously sacralized the profane horror of the hour, he robbed conscience of its responsibility. Benjamin had conceptualized his sonnet cycle as the radical antithesis of such violence."[33] Only by a ritualized repetition—the value of ritual, according to Adorno, having been taught to Benjamin by the poetry of Stefan George[34]—could the violence of amnesia be forestalled. Only by refusing false symbolic closure in the present might there still be a chance in the future for the true paradise sought by the idealist self-destroyers buried in their separate and separated graves.

The trope of troubled burial is, in fact, one to which Benjamin returned only a few pages after describing the suicides in the "Berlin Chronicle," where he generalized about the relation between memory, experience, and language. "Language," he wrote,

> shows clearly that memory is not the instrument of exploring the past but its theater. It is the medium of past experience, as the ground is the medium in which dead cities lie interred. He who seeks to approach his own buried past must conduct himself like a man digging. This confers the tone and bearing of genuine reminiscences. He must not be afraid to return again and again to the same matter; to scatter it as one scatters earth, to turn it over as one turns over soil.[35]

Benjamin's own method of digging and redigging his personal past in memoirs like "A Berlin Chronicle" or *Berlin Childhood around 1900* was, of course, generalized into a tool of cultural rediscovery—or rather redemptive reconstellation—in his never completed *Passagenwerk.* It followed the principle he derived from that restless, obsessive returning to the displaced graves he had experienced in his relation to his dead friends: "remembrance must not proceed in the manner of a narrative or still less that of a report, but must, in the strictest epic and rhapsodic manner, assay its spade in ever-new places, and in the old ones delve to ever-deeper depths."[36]

Benjamin's insistence on not letting the dead rest in peace, at least as long as they remained in false graves, was at the heart of his celebrated critique of historicist attitudes towards the past. Whereas historicists assumed a smooth continuity between past and present, based on an Olympian distance from an allegedly objective story, he assumed the guise of the "destructive character" who wanted to blast open the seemingly progressive continuum of history, reconstellating the debris in patterns that would somehow provide flashes of insight into the redemptive potential hidden behind the official narrative.[37] It is hard not to hear echoes of his personal anguish over the suicides of Heinle and Seligson when he remarked in the *Passagenwerk* that the task of remembrance is "to save what has miscarried."[38] The complicated notion of salvation (*Erlösung*) with which he worked, at once theological and political, contained the imperative to rescue what had been forgotten by the victors of history.

As Stéphane Mosès has argued, such an act of total recall—what might be called a benign variant of the malady of memory dubbed "hypermnesia" by the French psychologist Théodule Ribot[39]—was ultimately aimed at an "*un-knotting* of the *aporias* of the present"[40] through the mobilization of the utopian potential of the past for future transformation. Rather than constructing spatial topoi of commemoration, those *lieux de mémoire* or *Kriegerdenkmals* that functioned to solidify national identity in the present and justify the alleged sacrifices made in its name, the explicitly u-topian—in the literal sense of "no place"—and ritualized remembrance of past miscarriages must intransigently resist current consolation.

It would perhaps be exaggerated to claim that Benjamin, like Georges Bataille, the friend who saved many of Benjamin's texts after the Second World War, consistently wrote "against architecture," to borrow the title of the English translation of Denis Hollier's study of Bataille.[41] Benjamin's ambivalent fascination with the glass architecture of complete transparency and public openness promoted by the utopian novelist Paul Scheerbart must, after all, be acknowledged, as must his enthusiasm for the work of Siegfried Giedion and Adolf Loos.[42] But Benjamin did vigorously protest nonetheless against the attempt to embody symbolic fullness in visible, opaque, built forms above the earth, such as the tower, the cenotaph or the pyramid. Even before the war, he was suspicious of this cultural practice. In his *Berlin Childhood Around 1900*, he recalled youthful visits he had made to the triumphal column that had been erected in the capital of a united Germany to commemorate the famous Prussian victory over the French at Sedan. At its base was a galley of murals, from which he had always averted his gaze out of fear that they would remind him of the illustrations from Dante's *Inferno* he had seen in the house of one of his aunts. "The heroes whose deeds glimmered there in the hall of the column," he wrote, "seemed as quietly infamous as the crowds who did penance whipped by whirlwinds, imprisoned in bleeding tree-stumps, or frozen into blocks of ice. So this gallery was the Hell, the counterpart of the circle of grace around the radiant Victoria above."[43] No amount of ceremonial gilding, in short, would efface the grim fate of the victims of even the most famous victory.

As is well known, both Benjamin and Bataille were hostile to the general Hegelian logic of sublimation and sublation that sought to transfigure horror into something culturally elevating. Both were suspicious of calls for a return to a lost *Gemeinschaft* through symbolic restoration in architectural terms.[44] Indeed, as Irving Wohlfahrt has noted, Benjamin's more general relation to the past "marks a clear departure from the

Hegelian digestive system, an encyclopedic, (anal-)retentive, self-interiorizing memory (*Er-Innerung*) which 'preserves and negates' (*aufheben*) the entirety of its prehistory."[45] Such "digestive" remembering can only be premised on a certain forgetting, the forgetting of everything that resists incorporation into its system, such as the suicides of antiwar protestors, which are then abjected as so much unnecessary waste.[46]

In fact, even the war itself, Benjamin once speculated, might be understood on one level as a comparable kind of misconceived struggle to heal the fissures that rent modern life. It had been, he wrote in *One-Way Street* of 1928, a "desperate attempt at a new commingling with the cosmic powers,"[47] which would overcome the gap between man and nature that had disastrously widened since the time of antiquity through the application of technical means. "This immense wooing of the cosmos was enacted for the first time on a planetary scale, that is, in the spirit of technology. But because the lust for profit of the ruling class sought satisfaction through it, technology betrayed man and turned the bridal bed into a bloodbath."[48] Benjamin may have held out hope for a different version of benign technology not in the service of that lust for profit, and thus did not reject the desire for reconciliation between man and nature out of hand. But he was resolutely against the distorted effort that characterized the war, as well as the aestheticization of destructive technology that he saw in the postwar writings of Jünger and other "reactionary modernists."[49]

Only a variant of what Lenin had called "revolutionary defeatism," a willingness to ride the catastrophe until the end rather than stop it prematurely before its full destructive fury could be allowed to do its work, would provide a sober alternative to such aestheticization. The daily catastrophe of even peacetime society had to be understood as such, and this knowledge had to facilitate a more fundamental reckoning with the forces that led to the war in the first place. As he put it at the conclusion of his essay on Jünger's volume on *War and Warrior*, referring to "the habitués of the chthonic forces of terror," they will possess "a key to happiness" only "when they use this discovery to transform this war into civil war and thereby perform that Marxist trick which alone is a match for this sinister runic humbug."[50]

Not surprisingly, Benjamin could not stomach the religious rhetoric of Resurrection employed by certain artists after the war to give meaning to those who died in battle.[51] "Everything saturnine," Benjamin wrote in *The Origin of German Tragic Drama*, "points down into the depths of the earth."[52] Thus, the labyrinth, that subterranean tangle so often evoked in descriptions of the trenches on the western front,[53] was preferable to the monument as a spur to the right kind of remembrance.[54] Although originally an archaic topography, it was revived, Benjamin later argued, in the modern city, the locus of the *flaneur* and the prostitute, where the Minotaur mythically situated at its center embodies the image of "death-dealing forces."[55]

Accordingly, it is only the dead body acknowledged as nothing but the corpse that it has become, only, that is, a melancholy acceptance of the destruction of the organic, holistic, lived body, which prepares the remains for their allegorical and emblematic purposes. "The human body," Benjamin grimly wrote, "could be no exception to the commandment which ordered the destruction of the organic so that the true meaning, as it was written and ordained, might be picked up from its fragments. . . . The characters of the *Trauerspiel* die, because it is only thus, as corpses, that they can enter into the homeland of allegory. It is not for the sake of immortality that they meet their end, but for the sake of the corpse."[56]

Although it is impossible to know for certain that Benjamin's refusal to seek consolation for the trauma of his friends' suicides found an expression in his bleak ruminations on unresurrected, fragmented corpses in his book on Baroque Tragic Drama, the parallel between the two is striking. In both cases, the proper attitude was one of allegorical melancholy rather than symbolic mourning. The restless ghosts of Heinle and Seligson seem to haunt the pages of this book and much else in Benjamin's oeuvre, which one commentator has gone so far as to call a "love affair with death."[57]

Benjamin's morbid preoccupations were thus the opposite of those that fed the widespread revival of spiritualism, which accompanied that superstitious belief in the uncanny presence of lost comrades prevalent among soldiers at the front.[58] For whereas the soldiers yearned for the dead miraculously to return to life and thus end their own grieving, Benjamin, resolutely hostile to vitalism of any kind, sought to keep the grief unconsoled by focusing on the deanimization that had produced the corpse. "Criticism," he was famously to argue in *The Origin of German Tragic Drama*, "means the mortification of the works . . . not then—as the romantics have it—awakening of the consciousness in living works, but the settlement of knowledge in dead ones."[59] Mortification of the nontextual world as well, or at least facing the catastrophe that had already occurred, was preferable to wishing it away. Rather than seek life in death, the animate in the inanimate, it was better to acknowledge the ubiquity of *mementi mori* and decry the false consolations offered by magical thinking.[60] Only in so doing might the utopian hope for an ultimate apokatastasis, the redemption of all the fragments of fallen reality, the admission of all souls into heaven, be maintained.[61] Only then might happen a true awakening from the spell of myth and mystification that produced the conditions that led to the war in the first place.

Benjamin's desperate gamble that such an outcome might possibly follow from the rigorous denial of any consolation in the present has aroused considerable discomfort in many of his commentators. The nihilist streak evident in his antinomian evocation of divine violence and refusal to endorse the humanist pieties of conciliation and communication—as if the promise of the Youth Movement's *Sprechsaal* had been smashed forever by the self-destructive violence committed in its halls—seems to some a literal dead end. According to Gillian Rose, "it is this unequivocal refusal of any dynamic of mutual recognition and struggle which keeps Benjamin's thinking restricted to the stasis of desertion, *aberrated mourning*, and the yearning for invisible, divine violence."[62] His defense of repetitive, never worked through remembrance Rose grounds in the Jewish notion of *Zakhor*, which she claims "has the consequence of devaluating historiographical discernment in different times and places. It encourages eschatological repetition in the place of political judgment. But for Benjamin, all political judgment is melancholic and violent."[63] What she calls "inaugurated" as opposed to "aberrated mourning" contains the potential for forgiveness that Benjamin, with his furious fixation on the injustice of his friends' antiwar suicides, could never realize. As such, Benjamin's position may seem uncomfortably close to what the recent historian of psychoanalysis Peter Homans has called the Nazi's own "refusal to mourn."[64] For, to put it in the vocabulary of Judith Lewis Herman, it favors the maintenance of "traumatic memory," which simply repeats the past, over "narrative memory," which works it through by telling intelligible stories.[65]

Jeffrey Mehlman, from a vantage point far less Hegelian than Rose's, suggests other dangers. Benjamin's insistence on valorizing catastrophe rather than trying to heal it, on "plunging into evil, albeit to defeat it from within,"[66] echoes the Jewish messianic tradition that Scholem had shown often promoted mystical transgression as a means to redemption. It also recalls the tragic episode of the seventeenth-century false messiah Sabbatai Zvi, in which catastrophe was mingled with fraud, an explosive mixture that Mehlman ingeniously discerns in the scripts of Benjamin's radio plays of the early 1930s. Sabbatianism, he notes, rejected the symbolic reading of the world in the earlier Kabbalah in favor of an allegorical one, in which there was no apparent or natural unity between sign and signified. But this dissolution had its great danger. For now, to be a good Jew and to appear to be one were no longer necessarily the same, which opened the door to the possibility of a false messiah, such as the Sabbatai Zvi.

In the case of what he calls Benjamin's "neo-Sabbatianism,"[67] the same dangerous possibility exists. That is, there could be no guarantee that Benjamin's desperate wager on melancholic intransigence and resistance to commemorative healing would ultimately bring about the genuine redemption for which he so fervently yearned. Especially when he yoked his negative theology to the Marxist dream of a classless society, as he did in the final lines of his essay on Jünger's *War and Warrior* when he advocated the transformation of the war into a civil war, the potential for catastrophe to produce fraud rather than salvation was increased still further.[68] When one recalls Benjamin's own willingness to use fraudulent means to dodge the draft during the First World War—one of the few links in the chain left unforged by Mehlman's superheated associative imagination—it may well seem as if he were not above exploiting both catastrophe and fraud for his own dubious redemptive fantasies.

A third critique is made by those who claim that by holding on to such fantasies in whatever form Benjamin drew inadvertently near to the very fascist aestheticization of politics he was ostensibly trying to fight. This is the damning conclusion, for example, of Leo Bersani's *The Culture of Redemption*.[69] From this perspective, Benjamin's apparent resistance to symbolic mourning, his defiance of the imperative to work through his grief, is understood as still in the service of an ultimate reconciliation, which is impossible to attain. Whereas neo-Hegelians like Gillian Rose fault Benjamin for rejecting a good version of mourning—inaugurated rather than aberrated in her vocabulary—anti-Hegelians like Bersani see a desire for *any* version of mourning as problematically holistic and harmonistic, based on a nostalgia for an origin prior to the fall, a state of bliss that never really existed.[70]

What these critics perhaps fail to register is the critical distinction between a refusal to mourn that knows all too well what its object is—in Benjamin's case, the antiwar suicides of his idealist friends—and is afraid that mourning will close the case prematurely on the cause for which they died, and a refusal to mourn based on a denial that there was anything lost in the first place. Whereas Benjamin defended allegorical melancholy to keep the wound open in the hope of some later utopian redemption, understanding ritual and repetition as a placeholder for a future happiness, the Nazis sought symbolic closure without any delay, hoping to fashion a seamless continuity between the revered war dead and their own martyrs.[71] Rather than melancholic, their refusal to mourn was maniacal, in the clinical sense of a mania that giddily denies the reality of the lost object. Melancholy and mania, as Freud famously argued, may be both sides of the same inability to mourn, but in this case, the differences, it seems to me, outweigh the similarities.

What makes Benjamin's hopes for redemption so hard to grasp is that they seem not to have been grounded in a simple desire to undo the trauma of the antiwar suicides and resurrect the dead or even merely to realize the antiwar cause for which they died. Instead, the model of redemption he seems to have favored, I want to suggest, may paradoxically have been based on the lesson of trauma itself. Was he perhaps talking more of himself than of Baudelaire when he wrote in "On Some Motifs in Baudelaire" that "psychiatry knows traumatophile types?"[72] It will be recalled that Benjamin's critique of Baudelaire's poetic parrying of the shocks of modern life was directed at the anesthetic refusal to register the pain of the trauma; it meant keeping the protective shield of the psyche up at all costs. Like the aesthetic response of symbolic sublimation, defensive parrying struggled to regain the subject's mastery over a world that seemed out of control. In a certain sense, both aesthetic and anesthetic responses missed something in their haste to move beyond that pain. Or put differently, both were too hasty in trying to reconcile the irreconcilable. What was irreconcilable about trauma has been noted by Freud, who understood, to cite Cathy Caruth, "that the impact of the traumatic event lies precisely in its belatedness, in its refusal to be simply located, in its insistent appearance outside the boundaries of any single place or time . . . trauma is not simple or single experience of events but . . . events insofar as they are traumatic, assume their force precisely in their temporal delay."[73]

Benjamin's redemptive fantasies, such as they were, were thus not for harmonistic closure and plenitudinous presence. They were u-topian, as we have seen, precisely because they denied a positive place that could be the locus of fulfillment. They were also temporally disjunctive, *pace* his frequent evocation of the mystical notion of *Jetztzeit* (Now-time). Favoring instead what might be called the stereoscopic time of the dialectical image, they incorporated that experience of lag time produced by trauma. They were thus based on a notion of memory that differed from a Hegelian *Erinnerung*, in which the past was digested by the present in a heightened moment of totalizing interiorization. Instead, Benjamin's notion of *Gedächtnis* preserved the very dissociation between past and present, the temporal delay of the trauma itself, that made a constellation—and not a collapse—of the two possible. For only if the distinctness of past and present and the heterogeneity of multiple spaces were maintained could a true apokatastatis, a benign hypermnesia without exclusion and incorporation, be achieved. Only if the intractable otherness of the lost object is preserved and not neutralized through a process of incorporation can the possibility of genuine *Erfahrung* be realized.[74] Thus, in some profoundly paradoxical sense, the catastrophe and the redemption were the same, and the infinite ritual repetition without closure not a means, but an end. The true fraud, *pace* Mehlman, is thus the very belief in the resurrection of the dead, their symbolic recuperation through communal efforts to justify their alleged "sacrifice" and ignore their unrecuperable pain.

It is for this reason that Benjamin's intransigent resistance to symbolic healing and positive commemoration merits continued respect. For even if one is unable to share his belief in utopian apokatastasis, it must be acknowledged that he gave the lie to the assumption that the victims of the war—or more profoundly, of the society ruled by myth and injustice that could have allowed it to happen—could be best understood as heroic warriors who died for a noble cause. This is a lesson that ironically can be learned as well from the fate Benjamin himself suffered on the eve of the Second World War. For his suicide on the French/Spanish border also defied symbolic closure. Indeed, his rest proved as peaceless as those of Fritz Heinle and Frederika Seligson in 1914. As Pierre Missac observed in words that can fittingly serve as the final ones of this paper:

> His body . . . disappeared after his death. We have nothing but one more death without burial among so many others; no name on a common grave, even for someone who, while alive, provided a name for the nameless; not even the white cross of the military cemeteries sprinkled across Europe and the Pacific. All the more reason why no tombeau will evoke Benjamin's memory, only the interminable prose pieces after Babel, among them the present work.[75]

2

PEACE IN OUR TIME

By the time I arrived in late September 1995, most of the major players had already left. The Dalai Lama, Robert McNamara, Oscar Arias, Betty Williams, and the other political celebrities had come and gone; so too had the entertainment stars, among them Patti Smith, Adam Yauch of the Beastie Boys, Vladimir Ashkenazy, and Dmitri, the Russian clown. The opening month of ceremonies, seminars and concerts of the Peace University Berlin '95 was clearly winding down, with the official inaugural ceremony only a few days away.

Not everything, however, had gone as planned, and Uwe Morawetz, the young, entrepreneurial director of the Peace University had a touch of bitterness in his voice as he described to me the drubbing it had received in the German press and from established churches. Accused of being everything from a Moonie front to a cynical New Age scam, the university had suffered cancellations of speakers, broken promises of financial support, and a falling off of attendance. Many of the luminaries who had been expected to come discovered they were booked elsewhere, among them Henry Kissinger, one of the ten Nobel Prize laureates listed on the university's board of sponsors, and Rita Süssmuth, the president of the Bundestag. As a final indignity, the government was threatening to charge them a stiff fee to use the title of university, forcing them to downgrade the operation, at least for the moment, to a mere Peace College.

Still, Morawetz was optimistic that something important had begun and the extraordinary efforts he and his mostly volunteer staff had expended had not been entirely in vain. Some 202 speakers had directed or participated in more than 450 lectures, seminars, panels, and workshops. More than 800 people from 29 countries were involved for at least a week and tickets for individual events reached 12,000 in number. At the stiff price of DM 1,475 ($997) for the month and DM 168 ($114) for a single day, with some reductions for students, the unemployed, and pensioners, enough people had shown an interest to keep the venture afloat, helped by the fact that no honoraria were given to any of the speakers. The foreign press, moreover, had been far kinder than their local counterpart. *The New York Times*, for example, had reported favorably on Anne Halprin's 400-participant "Planetary Dance: A Prayer for Peace" and Oscar Arias's appeal for a global code of conduct for the international arms trade.

Plans for the future were, moreover, well underway, including a summer university to be held in the Bosnian city of Tuzla in 1996. Links with the United Nations Peace University in Costa Rica, the International Peace Research Institute in Oslo, and the Club of Budapest were established and others with universities elsewhere were in the process of being forged. And in Berlin, long-term rights to the elegant Palais am Festungsgraben, off the Unter den Linden in the former eastern sector of the city, had been secured as college headquarters.

Morawetz, nonetheless, was right to be troubled, as the enterprise's first month revealed certain serious, even potentially fatal problems. These became immediately clear to me on the first panel on which I participated, which focused on the issue of interdisciplinarity. Before it began I was taken aside by the other panelist, a distinguished American physicist with a Nobel Prize to his credit, who urged me to talk as long as possible in order to keep questions to a minimum. Try as I might to comply with this request, there was still time for several lengthy, emotionally overwrought interventions from the floor that could only be described as incoherent rants with no relevance to the remarks being made from the podium. Apparently, my co-panelist had already experienced this phenomenon the previous day, and so was better prepared for it than I. He quickly exited when the panel ended, but I was corralled by one of the ranters, who, with eyes flashing like a dragon and breath to match, shared with me his special insight into the way to achieve world peace.

In the interim before my talk that afternoon, I was invited to participate in a small group discussion with ten or so members of the audience. We were all given a quantity of little rocks and told to pass one or more of them to those whose views we most wanted to hear. When things sorted themselves out, the most popular participant turned out to be an American woman with a permanently beatific smile, who lived in a commune in India. She spoke with great fervor of her guru, Baba Virsa Singh Ji, who had predicted that the people of Germany would display great spiritual distinction. And from her brief experience at the Peace University, she was delighted to confirm that they did.

When the rocks came my way, I expressed a certain amount of distrust, as diplomatically phrased as I could manage, for the role of a guru, which seemed a bit too authoritarian for my taste. I also thought it might be a little premature to make judgments about spiritual distinction and national character. When it came time to finish, one of the other participants, a former member of the European Parliament representing the German Green Party, whom I had briefly met during a previous trip to Berlin, went around the room identifying all of the speakers by what she took to be their most salient characteristic. When she got to me, I was somewhat discomforted to discover that I was a sterling example of "critical Jewish intelligence." I suppose she meant well and the description isn't all that far from the mark, but it still was unnerving to be so typified in, of all places, Berlin, especially when nothing I said was remotely connected to my ethnic background. I began to look furtively for the exit.

That evening, after my talk on the theme of experience in a post-subjective era had gone off without a hitch, the pleasant volunteer who had been assigned to watch over me took me to a concert space connected to an artists' commune called UFA Fabrik for an evening of university-related entertainment. When we arrived, I was introduced to various other speakers, including my first Sufi faith healer. The evening began with a dance dedicated to Mahatma Gandhi by a very athletic young Asian man in a loincloth. Although the accompanying musical tape refused to work right, he nonetheless managed to convey, as well as the medium of dance can, his yearning for world peace. An odd slide show followed by a drum recital came next, but I somehow couldn't muster the energy to stay until the end.

The following day's events went smoothly, including the talk I discovered I was scheduled to give on "Learning from the Past: Forming the Future" (luckily I had just finished my column for *Salmagundi* on the concept of the uncanny, so something was rattling around in my mind relevant to the theme). Among those present was Arnold Graf von Keyserling, a large, full-bearded man who turned out to be the son of the Russian-born spiritual teacher whose Darmstadt School of Wisdom vied with Rudolf Steiner's Anthroposophy during the Weimar era for the honor of being the leading fount of a "new *Weltanschauung*." One of his texts had, in fact, found its way into the *The Weimar Republic Sourcebook* I had recently co-edited, and when I asked the current

Count if he were continuing in his father's footsteps, he replied with a twinkle in his eye, "yes, I have joined the family firm."

Spiritualism and commerce have, of course, been very easy bedfellows over the years, and it was quickly becoming obvious to me that the Peace University could be comfortably placed in that great tradition. Peace-mongering, like its bellicose counterpart, could, after all, be a profit-making enterprise. Still, I wanted to withhold final judgment until the inaugural ceremony the final day of my stay in Berlin. Despite all the moments of high silliness, which would have made excellent fodder for David Lodge's next novel, Morawetz had managed to attract many people of talent and good will, who were earnestly seeking solutions to real problems. Although "religiously unmusical," to borrow Max Weber's celebrated self-description, and normally hostile to anything smacking of pseudospirituality, I was not willing to give myself over entirely to cynical condescension.

In fact, in certain respects, I was enjoying the experience, which was a welcome relief from the normal run of academic conferences. Sufi faith healers, after all, never ask the dreaded question "and what are you working on?" My volunteer guide, a high school gym teacher who was astonished to learn that where I came from Jung had a weaker reputation than Freud, had also turned out to be a refreshingly ingenuous and gracious person. It was clear that she and many of the other participants were there for the mood of comradely idealism that had not been entirely crushed by the bad press. Not all were only one step ahead of the cult deprogrammers, but were instead earnest representatives of a cross section of the German population. I was, moreover, fascinated by the audacity of the whole undertaking, which surpassed even the weeklong extravaganza on "Spirit and Nature" organized in Hannover by the Minister-President of Lower Saxony in 1988 to which I had also been invited, along with an international gaggle of speakers ranging from Sir Karl Popper, Ted Turner, and R. D. Laing to sundry Tibetan lamas, Zen masters, and the Maharajah of Kashmir. No one seems to put together these kinds of ecumenical festivals of heightened consciousness and celebrity speakers as well as do the Germans, and it was hard not to go along for the ride.

Still, my "critical Jewish intelligence" genes began to kick in again when I saw the program for the inaugural ceremony, which was to take place on October first in the Renaissance-Theater in the former western part of the city. For I was listed, along with the twenty or so other speakers who were still around, as a "visionary" who would be asked to speak for one minute on world peace. Now, I have been called many things in my career, but visionary has not been among them, and moreover, I wasn't sure how much of a vision I could impart in sixty seconds even if I had one. All sorts of curmudgeonly thoughts came to mind, mostly having to do with the skepticism I felt for the university's fundamental premise, that "outer and inner disarmament" were somehow connected. This may work for the Dalai Lama, I thought of saying, but until we are all angels, outer peace needs to be secured by other means.

It was clear, however, that the mood in the hall was too celebratory to countenance any sour notes. This time even the music for the dance dedicated to Mahatma Gandhi worked right and speaker after speaker extolled the promise of the new venture. Sir Sigmund Sternberg, the chairman of the International Council of Christians and Jews, announced a $5,000 annual prize for contributions to "inner, social and outer peace, disarmament, protection of the environment and human rights." The "scientific director" of the Peace College, Erwin Laszlo, spoke enthusiastically about furthering the evolution of human consciousness. Heitor Gurgulino de Souza, rector of the United Nations University in Tokyo, blessed the new undertaking. An appeal to Jacques Chirac to end nuclear testing in the Pacific was read with great approval from the audience.

I was becoming increasingly desperate as the time to share my own "vision" approached, only a few moments after Count von Keyserling and an American Indian medicine man named Lightening Bear Pushican. Luckily—providentially?—I was given my way out by the sudden appearance of a large and beautiful butterfly in the hall, which flew around the stage and even landed once or twice on delighted speakers. "I am not good at composing inspirational soundbites," I said when it came my time, "but any organization that can train butterflies to alight on its leaders must have a bright future in front of it." And then I quickly sat down to appreciative laughter and tumultuous applause.

The odd symbolism of the day was not yet over, however. Once the ceremony ended and farewells were exchanged, I hurried back to my hotel to retrieve my bag and set out for the train station and my next stop in Poznan, Poland, where I had been invited by the Philosophy Department to talk on less exalted scholarly subjects. My guide drove me through the crowded streets of Berlin until we came up against a seemingly insuperable barrier. The entire Unter den Linden was cordoned off, and there was no way to drive across to my hotel without an impossible detour. It turned out that a mammoth parade celebrating the fifth anniversary of German reunification was in progress. Desperate to make my train, I abandoned the car and my guide and gathering my courage, pushed to the front of the sidewalk crowd. Suddenly, there was a break in the endless succession of marching bands, dignitaries in cars, and floats with happy peasants—or at least people in appropriate costumes—from various German hinterlands. I breathlessly dashed across the Unter den Linden, raced to my hotel, and caught a cab, which got me to the station and my train for Poland without further ado. Not even a reunited Germany exulting in its new role in the world could deter this messenger of peace.

Avoiding a facetious tone in reporting all of this may be difficult, but the issues raised are not trivial ones. It is hard to be unmoved on some level by the idea of an institution in the heart of reunited Berlin—call it a university, a college, or whatever—dedicated entirely to nonviolent solutions to political problems, the reconciliation of different religions and creeds, and an international dialogue on issues of global concern, such as ecology and women's rights. There are many other less laudable goals to which Uwe Morawetz and his colleagues could be devoting their considerable entrepreneurial talents.

Still, there is such a dismal record of piously invoked peace—think of its frequency in the mouths of former leaders of the GDR and other "peace-loving" Communist countries—that some skepticism is in order. As I bluntly told Morawetz when he asked for my reactions, the mixture of serious scholarship and political activism with esoteric spiritualism was doomed from the start. It was clear that the latter had begun to overwhelm the former in at least the public perception of the Peace College. Despite the extraordinary success it had enjoyed in attracting an international group of supporters, once the word was out that it was dominated by faith healers, medicine men, and New Age mystagogues, it would quickly alienate its serious audience. Whether or not Morawetz is ready to move the venture away from that direction—in a subsequent visit to California, he assured me he was preparing to do so—remains to be seen. But without such a resolute decision, all the butterflies in the world won't give the Peace College a chance.

3

FATHERS AND SONS

Jan Philipp Reemtsma and the Frankfurt School

During the Second World War, the cigarette of choice of soldiers in the German Wehrmacht would likely have been manufactured by the Reemtsma Company. Begun in Erfurt on the eve of the First World War by Johann Bernhard Reemtsma (1857–1925), it controlled, by the eve of the Second and its move to Hamburg, some 75 percent of the domestic market. Its guiding lights were by then the founder's sons Philipp Fürchtegott Reemtsma (1893–1959) and Hermann Fürchtegott Reemtsma (1895–1961), with the former the dominant figure in creating one of the great industrial success stories of the century. By shrewdly marketing his product under brand names (such as "R6" and "Gelbe Sorte" before the war, "West," "R1" "Ernte 23" and "Peter Stuyvesant" after it), he created an expectation of standard quality in his customers that translated into ever-increasing sales.

Philipp Reemtsma was also a survivor, who managed to shield his company, which had Jewish employees, against the threat of Ernst Röhm's Sturm Abteilung in 1933. He did so, however, by seeking the aid of a still more powerful protector, with whom he had had the good fortune to fly in World War I, Hermann Göring. The Reichsmarschall took his tribute in the form of a "donation" of some 12 million marks. Reemtsma sacrificed even more to the Third Reich during the war; two sons by his first marriage were killed in the fighting, a third died of polio. When the war was over, his concern was largely in ruins. Because of his bribery of Göring he was ordered to pay a fine of 10 million marks to avoid a jail sentence. But in 1950, Reemtsma was amnestied, and by his death in 1959, his firm once again dominated the German tobacco market.

After the war, Reemtsma was married for the second time to a considerably younger woman. Gertrud Reemtsma (1917–1995) bore him a son and heir in 1952 named Jan Philipp. It is, in fact, his story that concerns us now. For it is a remarkable story that became common knowledge only in the spring of 1996, when the younger Reemtsma, who had always shunned the limelight, was suddenly and brutally thrust into it. On the evening of March 25, he was abducted outside his Hamburg home and held in a cellar, shackled to the wall, for thirty-three days while his wife, the Sinologist Ann Kathrin Scheerer, desperately negotiated his release. With the German press willingly suppressing the story and the police backing off following a number of early missteps, an agreement was finally reached through a series of coded communications disguised as personal ads in the *Hamburger Morgenpost.* After two friends delivered a record-setting ransom—30 million marks, roughly equivalent to 20 million dollars—on April 24, Reemtsma was set free in a forest two days later. Although oddly under-reported by the Anglo-American news media, the kidnapping received the kind of detailed coverage in Germany—a cover story in *Der Spiegel*, for example—reserved for only the most sensational of events.[1] In the spring of 1997, Reemtsma himself published a movingly introspective account of his ordeal, entitled *Im Keller* (*In the Cellar*), which quickly became a best-seller.[2] At this writing, although the police located the place of his captivity and apprehended two of the culprits, the mastermind is still at large and virtually the entire ransom unrecovered.

However dramatic and heart-wrenching such a tale might be, it would not be worth recounting now except for the unusual claim on our attention made by this particular victim. For Jan Philipp Reemtsma is not an ordinary rich man's son who has had the bad luck to pay for his father's worldly success. He is a powerful, politically engaged intellectual in his own right, who, faced with some of the most pressing ethical dilemmas presented by our tormented century, has shown remarkable fortitude and exemplary courage. Like his father a survivor, he has managed to survive precisely the damaging legacy of his father and his generation. In the longer view, his ordeal in the cellar is perhaps best seen as a concentrated version of the trial that he has had to undergo ever since he came to understand the burdens placed on him by his special inheritance.

When his father died in 1959, Reemtsma was only seven. In the years that followed, during the period when the German left was on the ascendant, he grew increasingly troubled as he came to understand the extent of his father's complicity in the horrors of the Third Reich. In 1980, Reemtsma sold his interest in the tobacco company that bears his name for 300 million marks. He leveled his parents' grandiose house and built a more modest compound with two main buildings for work and living. Although he had studied literature at the University of Hamburg, writing his dissertation on the Enlightenment poet Christoph Martin Wieland and championing the contemporary writer Arno Schmidt, he was eager for a more direct political cum intellectual engagement that would help him—and not him alone—work through what was then being called Germany's "unmastered past."

For many on the German New Left, the returning exiles of the Frankfurt School had functioned as surrogate paternal figures, who provided models of uncompromised critical thought and intellectual integrity. Although some of their "children" came to turn against Horkheimer and Adorno during the worst days of "infantile leftist" anti-authoritarianism, Reemtsma seems to have found in them a constant source of inspiration. He supported the creation of a superb archive in Frankfurt for Adorno's *Nachlass* and quietly supported the philosopher's widow Gretel during the final years of her sad life (she had been incapacitated ever since a failed suicide attempt some time after Adorno's death in 1969).

In 1985, Reemtsma met Berkeley sociologist Leo Lowenthal, the last surviving member of the school, who was then spending the year at the Wissenschaftskolleg in Berlin. Lowenthal, as I know from personal experience, performed the role of benign father figure with great skill and tact, and he and Reemtsma quickly became friends, regularly seeing each other on both sides of the Atlantic. When Lowenthal died in January, 1993, Reemtsma paid him the honor of flying to Berkeley (along with Helmut Dubiel, who had conducted the extensive biographical interviews published as *Mitmachen wollte ich nie*),[3] to speak at the memorial service.

As an even greater expression of his dedication to the emancipatory goals of the Frankfurt School, Reemtsma founded an Institut für Sozialforschung in Hamburg in 1984, unabashedly borrowing the name of its illustrious Frankfurt predecessor. The parallel with the generosity of another rich man's son, Felix Weil, who had persuaded his father, the grain merchant Hermann Weil, to support the original institute in 1923, was not lost on German observers. Prominent on the institute's board of directors was the psychoanalyst Margarete Mitscherlich, the widow of Alexander Mitscherlich, who had worked with Horkheimer in 1956 to organize an important celebration of the centenary of Freud's birth and made seminal contributions to the postwar debate over "working through" the German past.[4]

Although the Hamburger Institut's start was troubled—Reemtsma and its designated director, the political scientist Wolf-Dieter Narr, had an early falling out—it has emerged in the past few years to become an increasingly powerful stimulant to investigations of past and present political injustice and violence. Its journal, *Mittelweg 36*, named after the institute's Hamburg address, has published work not only on the Third Reich, but also on the Armenian massacres, the situation in the Middle East, and the dropping of the atomic bomb. Nor has it ignored the current situation in the Balkans or the plight of asylum seekers in unified Germany. Although not as theoretically ambitious or broadly interdisciplinary as Horkheimer's Institut, it has applied its critical spirit to the concrete issues it has chosen to investigate.

Perhaps the Hamburger Institut für Sozialforschung's most ambitious venture has been a traveling exhibition, first mounted before the abduction and continuing after, on the contribution of normal German soldiers to the Nazi terror. Displaying an assortment of documents, images, and paraphernalia, *Vernichtungskrieg: Verbrechen der Wehrmacht, 1941–1945* (War of Annihilation: Crimes of the Wehrmacht, 1941–1945)[5] sought to undercut one of the most cherished myths of the postwar era: that the traditional armed forces had rarely, if ever contributed to the atrocities committed by the SS or the *Einsatzgruppen* (mobile killing units).[6] In the intervals between smoking Reemtsma cigarettes, common German soldiers, it turns out, were engaged in a war against civilians and prisoners of war (who were often executed rather than imprisoned) that went well beyond the defense against partisan resistance that had traditionally been used to justify certain excesses.

Moving from city to city in Germany, the exhibition has attracted large crowds and provoked sharp controversy, especially in locations such as Munich where conservative sentiment remains strong.[7] On March 13, 1997, the Bundestag devoted a day of heated debate to its implications, with one outraged Christian Democrat representative, Erika Steinbach, proposing, ultimately in vain, a counterexhibition to salvage the Wehrmacht's honor. By including images of recognizable faces and letters of specific soldiers, the exhibition made it possible to give the current generation of Germans the unsettling opportunity to look for their grandfathers among the criminals.

Inevitably, Reemtsma has been drawn into the larger debate unleashed in Germany by Daniel Jonah Goldhagen's *Hitler's Willing Executioners*, whose implications were in line with the exhibition's stress on the active role of allegedly uninvolved Germans. Without accepting all of the American political scientist's more extreme claims or explanations, he has sought to salvage the truth at the center of Goldhagen's accusation of widespread criminal complicity and called it a "necessary provocation."[8] *Mittelweg 36* published several essays focusing on the debate itself and the often disturbing subtextual insinuations of Goldhagen's critics. Although Reemtsma has repeatedly repudiated a special responsibility for intellectuals,[9] it is clear that he has aggressively used the opportunities given him to intervene as a concerned citizen in the public sphere.

Among those opportunities, it must be acknowledged, are not only his financial resources, but now also the unintended consequences of the kidnapping. As dreadful as those thirty-three days surely were for him and his family—Reemtsma has forcefully repudiated later press speculation that because he was allowed reading and writing materials, it was somehow a "delux" version of the hostage genre—they have inadvertently given him a new authority and a more self-assured voice. Before March 1996, he had resisted any publicity, refusing to have his picture taken or draw any attention to himself. Although one reason was the prudent—and as it turned out justifiable—fear that he might be a target for either political or financial terrorism, another was the evident ambivalence he felt about the source of his wealth and dilemmas it presented.

The Reemtsma I met in Berkeley in the late 1980s and early 1990s was in many ways an uncomfortable figure, laconic, solemn, impatient with small talk, and ill at ease in his skin. German friends would sometimes say that when he entered a room, it was as if he wanted to blend into the wallpaper. It cannot, after all, have been easy to assume the burdens of a tainted fortune and try to turn it to good use, while at the same time enduring the resentment of those who suspected he was buying his way into a position of influence on the left. The example of Felix Weil, whose generosity was welcomed by the members of the Frankfurt Institute but whose scholarly achievement they privately denigrated, could not have been much of a comfort. "Anyone who says that he suffers under too much money," Reemtsma once sardonically remarked, "is a liar, because he can also throw it away. Money sets nothing in motion; only men do."[10] But whether or not having money can automatically free you from suffering is another story. It certainly led to his abduction, which had no political motivations.

It also, to be sure, ultimately liberated him from his tormentors, but as *Im Keller* eloquently makes clear, the stress of his ordeal endures. The only antidote, he writes, to the degraded intimacy of his captivity may be the publicity that he had once tried so hard to avoid. Building on the scholarly work he had done on violence—ironically, the issue of *Mittelweg 36* that appeared at the time of the kidnapping was largely devoted to trauma studies—Reemtsma meticulously reconstructs and dissects his own personal horror in direct and unmelodramatic prose. Cleverly exploiting the device of using the first person when he discusses his life before and after the thirty-three days and the third person when he describes the ordeal itself, he conveys a powerful sense of the disruption of his prior sense of integrated selfhood. Utterly impotent to control his fate, uncertain at any moment whether he would live or die, anguished by his family's suffering, and even perversely coming to sympathize with the abductors (which he recognizes from his knowledge of previous hostage crises as the so-called Stockholm Syndrome), he comes to realize the impossibility of assimilating the trauma into the narrative of his life. Drawing on a distinction that only German registers between kinds of experience, he explicitly says his was merely an *Erlebnis*, a series of unassimilated shocks, rather than a true *Erfahrung*, "because *Erfahrungen* have something to do with the continuity of life."[11]

And yet, if that continuity has been shattered, it seems not to have produced in Reemtsma a sense of despair or resignation. The final, brilliantly written pages of *Im Keller* describe the contrast he came to perceive between normal being in the world, with all of its quotidian cares and woes, and the far simpler existence of a hostage in a dark hole in the ground, who can focus only on the exigent question of his very survival. Although the normal world no longer has the self-evident solidity it once had—he says it appears as if he were wearing a special pair of glasses that moves everything a half centimeter to one side—and although he understands the horrible lure of an emotional return to the cellar, where complexity is banished, Reemtsma has defiantly chosen a life of public involvement. With only a brief escape to New York after his liberation, he soon resumed with undiminished vigor his intellectual and political pursuits.

In fact, it may be because he himself was thrust so brutally into the role of the victim that Reemtsma can finally free himself from the guilt-ridden identification he previously felt with the victimizers. The doubts about his motives in supporting progressive causes and seeking to educate his countrymen about their traumatic past are now no longer tenable. His voice is that of someone who has personally endured the violence and torment that has been visited on so many others in this cataclysmic century. Although he has, to my knowledge, never sought to exploit the parallel or abuse the status of victim, an easy temptation in our era of competitive victimizations, his objective condition has nonetheless altered. He now has the authority of someone whose suffering is not merely vicarious, whose anguish is not entirely compensatory.

His is also now the voice of someone who has finally laid to rest his need to come to terms with his fathers, both evil and benign.[12] Like a liminal rite of passage, his thirty-three days of hellish torment have been followed by an elevation to a higher status in which he is fully his own man, no longer in the shadow of his elders. He has now fully paid his debts. Some of the most moving pages in *Im Keller*, in fact, involve Reemtsma as a father, writing encouraging and loving letters to his own son Johann, who was thirteen at the time of the abduction. In one letter he promises the boy an around-the-world trip after his high school graduation, listing more than fifty ports of call. Reemtsma is now embarked on an ambitious voyage of his own, which will carry him through the public world well beyond the borders of his native country. As a force for atonement, reconciliation and nonviolence, he has more than monetary capital at his disposal; he now has the moral capital that comes from surviving so woeful an ordeal, or more precisely, from the example of dignified and thoughtful reflection on his misfortune evident in *Im Keller*. It will be a voyage well worth watching as a unified Germany struggles to assume its destined role as a responsible, if much chastened, leader of nations in the twenty-first century.

4

THE UNGRATEFUL DEAD

A few months ago, a massive three-volume set of books arrived in the mail unannounced from Hamburg, courtesy of the publisher Rogner and Bernhard.[1] Edited by Wolfgang Kraushaar and sponsored by the Hamburg Institut für Sozialforschung, it was devoted to a scrupulous recording of the tumultuous relationship between the Frankfurt School and the German student movement. Containing an astonishing wealth of archival documents, including many previously unpublished letters and journalistic ephemera, and lavishly illustrated, the volumes testify to the remarkable persistence of the German fascination with the generation of 1968, even at a time when the page has clearly been turned to a new epoch in German history.

For anyone even indirectly involved with this moment, sharing in its hopes and frustrations, Kraushaar's labors will produce an intense jolt of recognition that goes beyond mere nostalgia. Future historians of the Frankfurt school and its impact on the politics of the Federal Republic will also be forever in Kraushaar's debt for his feats of collection and annotation. For this past historian of the school, however, *Frankfurter Schule und Studentenbewegung* produced another kind of jolt, which is the real stimulus to this column.

Let me backtrack a bit. Having passed through Frankfurt in the winter of 1969 while doing the research for my dissertation and later book *The Dialectical Imagination*, I had made arrangements to interview a number of the school's survivors. Similar opportunities had been enormously productive in the months before I left home, when I had met Herbert Marcuse, Leo Lowenthal, Karl August Wittfogel, and Erich Fromm (as well as ancillary figures in the school's history like

Paul Lazarsfeld). The most important new contact was with Theodor W. Adorno, then the institute's director and a towering figure in European intellectual life. The interviews I had with him in March, 1969 were, however, among the least fruitful and revealing I conducted. Adorno, it soon became apparent, was so preoccupied by vicious controversies with the students that any distraction was unwelcome. The institute had been only recently occupied by radicals led by Hans-Jürgen Krahl, and a planned visit by Marcuse to Frankfurt, unhappy with the way that the occupation had been handled and sympathizing with the students, was causing untold difficulties. Adorno, moreover, was increasingly impatient to return to his still uncompleted *Aesthetic Theory*. What made his unease most palpable to me at the time was a refusal to allow the tape recording of our conversations for fear, as I have recalled on several other occasions, that he would leave "verbal fingerprints." Perhaps the only productive thing that emerged from our two talks was his assertion, often cited in the years since I first quoted it, that "Marx had wanted to turn the world into a giant workhouse."[2]

In any event, I had always felt a sense of disappointment with the way things had gone, especially as Adorno's death in August of that same year made it impossible to know his response to my account of the institute's history. But I was still unprepared for what was waiting for me in the Kraushaar collection. On March 25th, by which time I had left Frankfurt to speak with Max Horkheimer and Friedrich Pollock in Switzerland, Adorno wrote a long letter to Marcuse, which is published here for the first time. Devoted mostly to the aftermath of the occupation and the uncertainty of Marcuse's visit, it included as an afterthought the following paragraph, alluding to my visit: "This Mr. Jay is a horrible guy. Beyond that he has an unerring instinct to direct himself to the dirt (*Unheil*). I've given him as little time as possible. At the moment he is molesting Max in Montagnola."[3]

Coming upon such a withering rant, thirty years after it was written, by a long-dead figure whose intellectual legacy I had spent half my career promoting, came, to put it mildly, as a shock. So this is what Adorno had meant by his famous metaphor of a *Flaschenpost*, a message in a bottle thrown on the waves for future generations to open! Blood draining from one's face, I can now attest, is not merely a figure of speech. Narcissistically wounded, I nonetheless immediately began to wonder what I had done to set him off. If he had said something dismissive about my grasp of his ideas or familiarity with his dauntingly extensive oeuvre, he would have had a point; I was still very much working my way into the labyrinth of Critical Theory. But what dirt had I maliciously tried to uncover? At the time, I had been unaware of Adorno's opportunistic article in *Die Musik* written after the Nazi takeover in which he had sought to curry favor with Baldur von Schirach, so I couldn't have been nosing around in that muck.[4] I was also still in the dark about his ugly falling out with his friend Siegfried Kracauer, which came to light only when I gained access to the newly opened Kracauer archive in the summer of 1973.[5] Nor was I privy to the petty jockeying for power with institute rivals like Leo Lowenthal that I later discovered in that same archive and which I confirmed in conversations with Lowenthal. Perhaps it had been the questions I asked about his relationship with Walter Benjamin and the edition of Benjamin's works that had earned him reproaches from critics on the left (as well as others like Hannah Arendt) in the mid-1960s. Perhaps I had touched a nerve when I cautiously probed the chill in his relationship with Arnold Schoenberg after the publication of Thomas Mann's *Dr. Faustus*, which had drawn on Adorno's advice for the depiction of the twelve-tone row as Adrian Leverkühn's compositional innovation. The notes I made of the interview, now yellowing in the box where they've sat for thirty years, give no other clue as to the provocation. Whatever the cause, what I had thought were the earnest and respectful attempts of a sympathetic twenty-four-year-old graduate student to understand the work and career of an intimidating intellectual giant had produced this monstrous result.

Now, it has long been known that Adorno was not the most accommodating or generous of personalities. Over the years he had rubbed many people the wrong way. A glance, say, at Hannah Arendt's correspondence makes clear her virulent dislike for him; indeed, as early as the 1920s, she told her then husband Günther Stern "that one's not coming into our house!"[6] Similarly, Lotte Lenya's references to Adorno in her letters to Kurt Weill are filled with venom, culminating in her blunt characterization of him in April 1942, as a "paleface, flaming asshole."[7] Over the years I have had conversations with other acquaintances, who were no less critical. The first time I met Sir Isaiah Berlin in 1973, for example, he told me how insufferable he had found Adorno in Oxford in the 1930s; the last time I saw Berlin, a year before his death in 1997, we hadn't finished walking up the stairs to his study when he launched into the same diatribe. Clearly, Adorno's "damaged life" as he had famously called it in *Minima Moralia*, had left some destruction in its wake.

Still, I had always resisted allowing such knowledge, and other less than attractive things I had learned about other members of the school, from interfering with my attempt to do justice to their ideas and careers. A saying of Hegel's had always been my guiding principle:

"No man is a hero to his valet. But that's not because heroes aren't heroes; it's because valets are valets." Trying hard not to be a valet meant working to see past the dirty linen and acknowledge the value of intellectual achievement in its own terms. Now, however, I was not only in the spectatorial valet's role, but also in that of the victim, scorned by Adorno as a muckraking stinker in a posthumously published letter for all the world to see. Such was my reward, I darkly thought, for writing not only my first book, but a good part of a second and the entirety of a third—the Modern Masters volume on Adorno—that helped introduce him to readers in a dozen languages (the Chinese, I waxed wroth, even have a choice between two different translations of my *Adorno*)!

In addition to feeling waves of hurt and indignation, only sporadically relieved by the thought that the letter revealed more about Adorno's suspicious state of mind than my own real transgressions, I nonetheless came to wonder how many other rude surprises there were out there waiting for me. Horkheimer, to be sure, had found my "molestation" in Montagnola agreeable enough to write a generous preface to the book when it appeared, thanking me "in the name of the dead" for my efforts. Marcuse had also sent a very gracious letter, part of which he allowed to be used as a blurb for the paperback, and my subsequent relations with him were always warm. Lowenthal and I became colleagues at Berkeley, indeed intimate friends. But still, I couldn't help feeling a premonition of things to come.

As it turned out, I didn't have to wait very long for a second message to arrive in a bottle from the ungrateful dead. A week after the appearance of *Frankfurter Schule und Studentenbewegung*, a student brought to my attention an article that had appeared in the *Frankfurter Allgemeine Zeitung* in late 1997 entitled "Everything Else is a Swindle: Gershom Scholem Reads the History of the Frankfurt School."[8] Apparently shortly before his death in 1982, an angry Scholem had composed a handwritten screed against what he took to be a vile misrepresentation of the school's history. It had just been discovered in his *Nachlass* in Jerusalem and was reprinted in one of Germany's leading newspapers. The relevant passage reads as follows: "Critical Theory and Marxism—*consciously confused* in representations by people like Lowenthal and Jay. What is claimed here for the special meaning of Critical Theory before 1936/37 is all *nonsense—post facto (nachträglich)* retouching. Three witnesses, who must have known about it and whom I asked, have unanimously confirmed it: *Benjamin, Tillich, and Adorno*. Crit. Th. (sic) was, after the edition in Paris [the institute's journal was published in Paris after 1933] *invented* from above as a solution by

Horkheimer for *political* reasons (*Angst, Angst, Angst*), designed simply as a *code word* and esoteric synonym for Marxism, nothing more. Everything else is a swindle."

Scholem, I recalled, had been upset by the appearance a short while before of Lowenthal's autobiographical reflections, *Mitmachen wollte ich nie*, in which Scholem's account of the institute's allegedly manipulative treatment of Walter Benjamin was disputed.[9] Calling the claim that the institute had "blackmailed" Benjamin into censoring his texts an "infamous distortion,"[10] Lowenthal had noted that Scholem and Arendt, "both of whom I greatly respect," had joined certain East German critics in trying to damage the reputation of his institute colleagues. Affronted, Scholem had sent Lowenthal a sharp letter, which had occasioned a mollifying response. Clearly it had failed to do the job, as the posthumous journal entry now revealed. Rather than fulminating against Lowenthal's lumping him together with communist critics of the Institute, Scholem agreed that they had been right in bemoaning the institute's cautious adoption of aesopian language to disguise their true colors. Oddly, in the light of his own disdain for Marxism and futile struggle to win Benjamin for Zionism, Scholem took umbrage at the tacit attempt to discount the Marxist credentials of his friend. The entry in his *Nachlass*, the reporter for the *Frankfurter Allgemeine Zeitung* insisted, should thus be understood as an example of Scholem's mourning (*Trauerarbiet*) for Benjamin.

Whether or not this attempt to explain the depth of Scholem's fury against the "swindle" he saw perpetrated by Lowenthal and myself is persuasive is not something I want to address in any detail now, although surely Scholem had had ample time and opportunity in the intervening forty years to work through his *Trauer*. Nor am I anxious to debate the charge that a deliberate cover-up of the "real" meaning of Critical Theory was carried out in *The Dialectical Imagination* or Lowenthal's reminisences.[11] Ironically, Scholem himself had written to Benjamin in November, 1938, after a meeting with the institute leaders in New York that he had found all of them "diligent and very outspoken anti-Stalinists, great and small, and I didn't hear a single good thing said about Brecht."[12] Now, however, such discriminations were forgotten and the true Marxist colors of the institute needed to be reasserted against the attempts by Lowenthal and me to put mealy-mouthed euphemisms in their place. In his fury to set the story straight, Scholem had sadly lost sight of precisely what makes the history of the Frankfurt School still interesting: its members' self-lacerating struggle to salvage only certain aspects of a Marxist tradition that was heading for shipwreck, while honoring its critical impulse through an openness to ideas from elsewhere. Recognizing the beginning of this trajectory in Horkheimer's celebrated 1937 essay on "Traditional and Critical Theory," while acknowledging that it was not yet complete, is surely far more than the "swindle" of historical revisionism.

Be that as it may, my real concern in rehearsing all of this is the response elicited by Scholem's tart dismissal of my historical account, coming so close on the heels of reading Adorno's nasty letter to Marcuse. I cannot claim, to be sure, to have spent as much time working on Scholem's ideas as I have on Adorno's, or to have had much of a personal relationship with him. We met once in Jerusalem shortly after my first book appeared; he scolded me for not consulting him about Benjamin, and promised to read anything I wrote on the subject in the future. Taking him up on his offer, I sent a draft of a piece I wrote the following year on the dispute over the Buber-Rosenzweig translation of the Bible, a dispute in which he as well as Benjamin and Siegfried Kracauer had participated.[13] He wrote an extensive, constructive critique, which I found very helpful in revising the article for publication. Although I've been asked over the years to fashion blurbs for two of his books in English translation, which I happily provided, this encounter was really the last we had.

But the point is that, like Adorno, Scholem was one of those figures whose work I have always read with extraordinary admiration and interest. He was one of the giants of the intellectual migration from Germany, whose history I have found so fascinating. So to be rebuked from beyond the grave was, to say the least, not a pleasant experience. But on reflection, it may have proven a healthy one, which is the real reason for this essay.

Writing history, as Dominick LaCapra has recently emphasized, inevitably has a powerful transferential dimension.[14] We always invest our accounts of the past with the desires, fantasies, and memories that shape our normal relations with our contemporaries. However much we disavow our own voice in the construction of allegedly impersonal, objective narratives, it returns to haunt our texts. Whom we chose to study, what stories we decide to tell, and the modes of emplotment, analysis and judgment we apply to them are determined at least in part by psychological processes that we only dimly perceive, if at all. Despite all of our efforts to bracket current prejudices and allow the past to reveal itself to us, we cannot entirely escape the effect of our identifications, idealizations, and demonizations. Indeed, it is precisely because we can become so invested in figures, movements, and events in the past that they invite our interest in the first place; the exigency to remember someone else's things past can only come from somewhere deep within ourselves.

Rarely, however, does the past ever return the favor and indulge in a kind of countertransferential projection on to the historian. In the case of my ungrateful dead, however, something very much like that seems to have occurred. That is, while I was busy heroizing Adorno and (to a lesser extent) Scholem, making every effort to honor their intellectual achievement and contribute to their posthumous glory, they were muttering darkly about how inadequate I was to the task. In some ultimate sense, they were no doubt right about that estimation, as I would be the first to admit. But in both cases, it also seems clear that I served as a kind of screen onto which they were projecting their own anxieties and fantasies, often having to do with their own vexed relationships to Benjamin and his contested legacy. Adorno was caught up in a maelstrom of student protest in 1969 that would culminate in the painful episode a few weeks after I last saw him when bare-breasted women jumped on the podium during one of his lectures to humiliate and demean him—literally enacting the "molestation" he claimed I was then performing on Horkheimer in Montagnola. Any question about ambiguous moments in his past, such as the controversy surrounding his role in the writing of Mann's *Dr. Faustus*, must have seemed of a piece with the assaults he was experiencing from the Frankfurt *enragés*. He thus mistook his confessor for an assassin.

Scholem, still fuming over the injuries that he claimed were dealt to his friend Benjamin by Horkheimer and the institute and what he saw as Lowenthal's attempt to deny the truth, lashed out at both of us as swindlers who refused to recognize Critical Theory for what it was, a duplicitous code word for Marxism and nothing more. Whereas Adorno had worried that I was looking for filth to discredit him, Scholem paradoxically had assumed the very opposite, that I was in cahoots with those who sought to cover the dirty secret of the Frankfurt School's real political agenda. "People like Lowenthal and Jay . . . " he had fulminated, turning us into a type reminiscent of others he had been fighting for years.

Even putting aside the unintended honor of being placed on the same plane as Lowenthal, a player in the history of the Frankfurt School rather than a mere chronicler, I have to admit to a certain perverse sense of gratitude for Scholem's outburst, as well as for the disclosure of Adorno's nasty remarks to Marcuse. For both have served to clarify the transferential dimension of my relation to their legacy by revealing its countertransferential double. Historians are sometimes accused of playing tricks on the dead; occasionally, it appears, the dead can play a few in return. It would, however, be foolish to turn this new knowledge into a warrant for a kind of God-that-failed reversal of my previous admiration, whose foundation was and remains dependent far more on ideas than personalities. Working through transference is, after all, supposed to promote a more sober reaction to real people, not a simple inversion of the valences, with demonization replacing idealization. Even when pedestals are kicked over, life-sized figures can sometimes remaining standing on their own two feet. But now the historian has the opportunity to look them a little steadier in the eye, rather than gaze up from below. I'm anxious to give it a try.

5

WHEN DID THE HOLOCAUST END?
Reflections on Historical Objectivity

We all know the harrowing pictures, the unwatchable films. On April 15th, 1945, Bergen-Belson is liberated by British soldiers, revealing the existence of some 58,000 prisoners, many of them human skeletons starved to the point of imminent death. In the next few weeks 30,000 will, in fact, perish from disease, abuse and the effects of malnutrition. Three days after the liberation, the British film producer Sidney Bernstein, representing the Ministry of Information, begins recording the scenes of horror: bodies bulldozed into mass graves, camp guards forced to drag corpses to their resting places, crematoria still smoldering with the ashes of the incinerated, and the gaunt, numbed faces of the half-dead, the Musselmen as they had come to be called, who somehow tenuously held on to a simulacrum of life. Elsewhere, there is more devil's work to be done. Gassings still take place at Mauthausen as late as April 28th, a week before the Americans liberate the camp. On May 8th, the day the Nazis surrender, the Red Army enters Theresienstadt in Bohemia, the last of the camps to be freed. Its grisly residues now documented on film, the unspeakable nightmare that became known as the Holocaust is finally over.

Or so it seems. For what does it mean to say something as difficult to comprehend and explain as the Holocaust, something as resistant to all our normal tools of narration and assimilation, is truly at an end? Was there ever a performative speech act that could declare it over in the way, say, that the signing of a peace treaty brings a war to a conclusion or the pounding of a gavel ends a legislative session? Although it is self-evident that all historical events or actions or periods have effects, sometimes immediate, sometimes delayed, that survive their putative end, there is something especially difficult about a neat division between cause and effect, event and repercussion in the case of the Holocaust. The linear temporality of before and after so vital to the surface level of historical chronicle is perhaps never as simple as it may seem, but in the case of so traumatic and ineffable a phenomenon as the Holocaust, it is even more difficult to sustain.

A great deal of effort has been expended trying to establish just when the Holocaust began, with a variety of accompanying explanations implied for its causation. But little attention, in fact, has been paid to its conclusion. Did it neatly end in 1945 with the liberation of the camps and the cessation of the mechanized killing? Or perhaps is it better to say with Yehuda Bauer that "although the Holocaust itself occurred during the world war, the *period* of the Holocaust stretches from the rise of the Nazi regime in 1933 to the dissolution of the displaced persons (DP) camps in Central Europe after the war. In these camps, the core of the survivors lived until 1948."[1] Bringing the story up to 1948 would allow such events to be included as the infamous pogrom in the Polish city of Kielce in July 1946, as well as taking into consideration the fate that befell many of the DP's who were forced to flee helter-skelter from one region of Europe to another before finally being allowed to emigrate to Palestine or North America. It also tacitly allows the creation of the State of Israel to serve as the act of closure that turns the page of Jewish history from despair to hope.

At the war's end, there were some 50,000 Jews on German or Austrian soil, the majority from Eastern Europe, who had somehow survived the extermination centers and forced marches. But many soon succumbed to disease and malnutrition. The survivors of the survivors, who became known by the Hebrew expression *she-erit hapletah* (the "surviving remnant," a term from the Bible) were swelled by those fleeing the still virulent anti-Semitism in liberated Poland and the Soviet Union. By 1947, more than a quarter of a million Jewish DP's were sheltered in the territory of the defeated enemy, most in the American occupation sector. Only after Israel was founded were about half of them able to leave for Palestine, some 80,000 or 90,000 for the United States, and virtually all the rest to Canada, Australia, and South America.

Should their experiences be included in any calculation of the end of the Holocaust? According to one of their historians, Michael Brenner, "in many respects the life in DP camps was based on the traumatic experiences of the war years spent in German concentration camps. The return to 'normal life' was extremely difficult after years of physical deprivation and psychological hardship."[2] What made the situation even more difficult to bear was the continued forced incarceration of the inmates, whose hopes of leaving for Palestine or North America were long delayed by political forces outside their control. Brenner again: " 'We were liberated, but we are not free,' was a line often found in the statements of Jewish DPs. Most of the DP camps had barbed wire around them, all had armed guards, and survivors were often forbidden to leave the camp even to search for surviving family members."[3] On a few occasions, the camps were entered by German policeman searching for black marketers; at times they met resistance, and in one case, at a camp near Stuttgart in March, 1946, they killed one of the camp inmates. Can we deny with any certainty that he too was one of the victims of the Holocaust? And if we cannot, do we then perhaps have to extend its terminal date to the closure of the final DP camp, Föhrenwald, which took place only in February, 1957?

Still more problematic are the ongoing implications of the profoundly traumatic nature of the Holocaust, which has perhaps been more responsible than any other historical phenomenon for putting that very concept on the map.[4] Trauma, as we are now so often told, involves the repression or denial of the painful event, which then is not "worked through" or resolved in a psychologically satisfactory way. The original event is so unassimilable to the person's prior sense of self that it is driven to the edge of awareness or even below its threshold. Whether willed or not, a lapse in memory occurs that prevents the horrific experience from being fully claimed as part of a meaningful life narrative. The result, at least for some, can be a delayed or deferred coming to terms with the past, a belatedness (or *Nachträglichkeit*) that manifests itself in both individual and collective terms.

Individually, it may be expressed in a flight into a new identity in which the pain of the past is driven from consciousness, an escape that in the case of the Holocaust survivors who emigrated to Palestine was intensified by their adoption of a new Zionist self-understanding. Even those who came to North America tended to try to put the past behind them, as had many Jews who emigrated from the pogroms of nineteenth-century Europe and quickly adopted an American identity. On a collective level, it might mean an entire culture's inability to come to terms with what the Germans came to call "the unmastered past," a locution that for a while at least could be applied to victims as well as perpetrators. With the rapid onset of the Cold War, moreover, new alliances necessitated avoiding dwelling on recent events, the responsibility for which would not be comfortable to establish without disrupting those very alliances. Only in the 1960s, and often displaced to countries like America, which were only indirectly involved, was it possible to remember the Holocaust, and then only with all of the multiple meanings and sometimes dubious motivations of which historians like Peter Novick have made us all so aware.[5]

But if it took a while for the belatedness to wear off and both individual survivors and different national cultures to recover from their amnesia, this does not mean that the traumatic impact of the Holocaust was not deeply felt and expressed in indirect ways in the interim. As Cathy Caruth has noted, what may be just as traumatic as the confrontation with death is the guilt involved at having survived it. As she describes it, referring to literary versions of trauma, "at the core of these stories . . . is thus a kind of double telling, the oscillation between a *crisis of death* and the correlative *crisis of life*: between the story of the unbearable nature of an event and the story of the unbearable nature of its survival."[6] What we have come to know as posttraumatic stress disorder, already evident in the so-called shell shock suffered by soldiers in the First World War, involves repetition without resolution of the initial psychological wound. It is produced, she conjectures, because the encounter with the initial brush with destruction was not directly experienced, but rather avoided. The trauma's return is thus "not the signal of the direct experience, but, rather, of the attempt to overcome the fact that it was *not* direct, to attempt to master what was never fully grasped in the first place. Not having truly known the threat of death in the past, the survivor is forced, continually to confront it over and over again."[7] What is incomprehensible for the survivor is not the threat to life but the inability to make sense of survival, which seemed inadequately explained by sheer dumb luck.

Although one may wonder about the claim that death camp survivors did not know the threat of death—perhaps what Caruth intends here is the simple tautology that sheer survival means that they were spared the direct experience of their mortality—the argument that melancholic repetition rather than healthy mourning characterized many survivors' lives after 1945 is compelling. As one survivor told an interviewer about his response to the liberation, "then I knew my troubles were *really* about to begin."[8] What is, moreover, important to note for our purposes is the potentially destructive effect of the repetition of the unworked-through traumatic experience. According once again to Caruth, "as modern neurobiologists point out, the repetition of the traumatic experience in the flashback can be retraumatizing, if not life-threatening; if not life-threatening, it is at least threatening to the chemical structure of the brain and can ultimately lead to deterioration. And this would also seem to explain the high suicide rate of survivors . . . of concentration camps, who commit suicide only *after* they have found themselves completely in safety."[9] Can, in other words, we deny that such self-inflicted deaths by survivors were also part of the Holocaust, which did not end with their apparent rescue?

What, moreover, of the trauma suffered by the perpetrators themselves or the not-so-innocent bystanders? I've already mentioned the catchphrase often used to describe Germany's difficulty in confronting its responsibility for the horror, "the unmastered past." Along with it went what the German psychologists Alexander and Margarete Mitscherlich famously called "the inability to mourn."[10] In the case of many Germans, the lost object that could not be properly mourned was not, however, the victims of the Holocaust, but rather their idealized image of the regime that had produced it. That is, until virtually the end of the Third Reich, Hitler and the Nazi Party were the objects of an adoration, a psychologically powerful investment, that could only be given up with great difficulty, if at all. For the perpetrators as well as the victims, the Holocaust did not really end in 1945. Even those who were passive bystanders rather than "willing executioners," to borrow Daniel Goldhagen's now famous phrase, could have difficulty in putting the past behind them.

Yehuda Bauer makes a similar point when he contests the frequent assumption that the Nazis dehumanized their victims:

> The common use of the term *dehumanization* would leave the perpetrators as the "human" and the victims as less than human. That, indeed, was the intended outcome, but in fact the Nazi treatment of those interned in camps and ghettos showed the opposite, because it was the Nazis who lost the characteristics of civilized human beings. When that minority of inmates who survived were liberated, they returned to their civilized ways of life; it is highly doubtful whether their torturers did, unless they repented, which apparently very few of them did. In other words, the Nazis remained dehumanized even after the nightmare ended; those of their victims who survived did not.[11]

Thus, not only surviving victims, but also their perpetrators could be so radically affected by the Holocaust that it never really ended for them. This is not, to be sure, to obscure the distinction between the two, between those who suffered and those responsible for their suffering, just to note that even the unpunished among the latter cannot be said to have escaped the ongoing effects of their own unclaimed experiences.

Added to these considerations is the powerful impact of a phenomenon that distinguishes the Holocaust from many other traumatic events in history: the deliberate attempt to keep the wound unhealed and the memory of its pain fully alive. Whatever one may think of the ulterior motives of this attempt or the dubious uses to which it has sometimes been put, it is incontrovertible that the international campaign to prevent the Holocaust from fading from active collective memory and slipping into mere historical pastness has successfully saved it from any final closure. The outcome of the famous Historian's Debate in Germany in the 1980s was not a victory for those who wanted to relativize and normalize the Holocaust. Even if there remains a lively discussion about the vexed relationship between history and memory, especially as the latter manifests itself in popular culture and public commemoration, it is clear that neither historians nor "memorians," to borrow Carol Gluck's felicitous coinage, feel comfortable with approaching the Holocaust with the disinterested distance that betokens an allegedly objective relationship to the past, a past that is clearly and safely behind us.

As Dominick LaCapra has noted in his recent collection, *Writing History, Writing Trauma*,

> Those traumatized by extreme events, as well as those empathizing with them, may resist working through because of what might almost be termed a fidelity to trauma, a feeling that one must somehow keep faith with it. Part of this feeling may be the melancholic sentiment that, in working through the past in a manner that enables survival or a reengagement in life, one is betraying those who were overwhelmed and consumed by the traumatic past.[12]

LaCapra goes on to wonder if the Holocaust may have functioned for some as a "founding trauma," which provides a kind of psychologically powerful source of a new group identity. This may explain its abiding power not only among Zionists but also those secular, nonobservant, "imaginary Jews" discussed by the French theorist Alain Finkelkraut in a widely remarked book of the same name.[13] Paradoxically, the same may be said in reverse for the so-called Holocaust revisionists (better put, deniers), whose tortured identities may well be dependent on their deep investment in denying its very existence. They too cannot let it simply rest in peace.

Yet another expression of the investment in keeping the Holocaust painfully alive rather than allowing it to pass into history is its elevation into a metaphor for something fundamental in the human condition. Sometimes this takes the form of making it into a cautionary example for the future, a warning that it can happen again, and therefore something that should be constantly in front of our eyes as a spur to vigilance against its repetition. At other times, it becomes warrant for a general pessimism about the limits of human perfection, a kind of latter-day version of the Lisbon Earthquake's rebuke to Panglossian optimism. Often it has seemed that post-structuralist thinkers in particular have been keen on transcendentalizing the melancholic, unworked-through nature of Holocaust memory into an emblem of all relations to a damaged past that cannot be repaired. In so doing, as LaCapra has argued, they turn historical into structural trauma and substitute a permanent sense of ontological absence for the concrete loss that was produced by Nazi actions during the Second World War.[14]

For all of these reasons, it has been extremely difficult to provide a conclusive finality to what has come to be called the Holocaust and whose ability to haunt our historical imaginations seems destined to continue well into the twenty-first century. How, I want now to ask, do the implications of this lack of closure bear on the vexed question of objectivity towards the past? There are, it seems to me, two salient ways in which it does. The first involves the question of the relationship between the historian's own experience and that of the figures in the past whose history he or she is writing. The second touches on the passage from discrete facts or events, what we might call the atomic particles of historical analysis, and the larger-scale concepts we inevitably use to organize, periodize, and narrativize them.

Among the most poignant imperatives for writing history, it is often argued, is the desire to recover the experiences of past generations, preventing their stories from falling into oblivion. Rather than examine structures or trends or events or discourses, historians should be concerned, so it is urged, to get back to the felt experiences, replete with meaning and value, of the actors who make the seemingly impersonal structures and events. When the figures involved are construed as victims of injustice, the desire to redeem their suffering by giving them voice can be even stronger. Certainly, in the case we are examining, there is a powerful desire to avoid allowing the Nazis the last word in turning their victims into faceless statistics in a campaign to rid the world of an abstract and generic racial category. This desire is often expressed in terms of remembering and honoring what the Warsaw ghetto rabbi Yitzhak Nissenboim called "sanctification of life," by which he meant those instances of meaningful Jewish existence that could somehow take place even amidst the most horrible of conditions.[15] It also manifests itself in the extraordinary efforts that have been made since the 1980s to record for posterity the reminiscences of survivors by organizations like the Fortunoff Video Archive for Holocaust Testimonies at Yale University and Stephen Spielberg's Survivors of the Shoah Visual History Foundation.

Precisely how one can recover past experience is, of course, a particularly vexed issue, especially when the techniques of "re-experiencing" or "re-enactment" advocated by theorists like Wilhelm Dilthey and

R. G. Collingwood are cast into doubt, as they now so often are.[16] Even in the best of circumstances, when we have comparatively dense records of the everyday lives and personal recollections of those who came before us, it is never easy to construct an account of their experiences that might be construed as objective. There is always a large measure of imaginative reconstruction involved, as well as the challenge of figuring out how to bridge the gap between past experience and its present counterpart, a gap that is inevitable if we take historical difference seriously as a check on the unwarranted extrapolation of present realities onto the past.

But in the case of the experience of those whose lives were directly involved with the Holocaust, both victims and perpetrators, these difficulties are further complicated by the way trauma itself has an impact on the very possibility of experience in the first place. That is, if we take seriously the argument made by Cathy Caruth and others that traumatic experience is "unclaimed," delayed, unassimilated, and therefore lacking in narrative closure, it is impossible to construe the task of the historian as reexperiencing or reenacting it, as if it had been entirely meaningful in the first place. That is, precisely because of the systematic and deliberate impoverishment of experience as a meaningful story for the original Holocaust victims, historians cannot assume their ability to recover it as if it had once been whole. No objective account of such shattered and disrupted experience, further disorganized for the survivors by the mechanisms of melancholic repetition and denial mentioned above, can ever really succeed. Sadly, the same might be said of the recorded testimonies forty years later by survivors themselves, which have inevitably been filtered by the intervening years of delayed mourning and inflected by the expectations of listeners who want dramatic narratives. This is not to say that their recollections are necessarily fabricated or false, just that they function like what Freud called the secondary elaboration in dreamwork, in which the incoherencies of primary process are transformed into more or less meaningful stories, parables with exemplary intentions. This transformation is, to be sure, a quality of post facto testimony in general, but in the case of the survivors of so traumatic an experience, it is surely intensified. What they demand therefore is hermeneutic sensitivity on the part of historians rather than blanket acceptance as historically objective accounts. Even a willingness to contradict memory may be warranted, if other surviving documents or accounts call it into question.[17]

An even greater interpretive sensitivity is necessary if we turn from the discrete reminiscences of the experiences of witnesses and survivors to the larger issue of how we narrativize, explain, and periodize the multiple happenings that we have come to subsume under the collective term of the Holocaust. The passage from the level of individual stories and experiences to that of more general patterns will be problematic even when the stakes are not so high. But the difficulty becomes more explicit when they are. It is perhaps not by chance that one of the most insightful ruminations on this issue was presented by a German refugee intellectual, who barely escaped Europe before the doors were closed. In 1969, a posthumously published book by Siegfried Kracauer appeared with the title *History: The Last Things Before the Last.*[18] In a chapter called "the structure of the historical universe," Kracauer tackles the problem of the relationship between micro and macrohistorical accounts. Challenging the assumption, which he identifies with Tolstoy and Sir Lewis Namier, that the smallest historical entities or facts are the ones closest to objective truth and are thus the building blocks of historical generalizations, Kracauer argues that there is a "law of levels" that makes the transition from micro to macro history discontinuous rather than smooth. Analogizing from the montage of establishing or long shots and close-ups in the movies, about which he had already written at some length, he claims that both are necessary for historical method, but that no matter how many discrete and individual facts or experiences or actions are amassed, they cannot be brought together through induction to produce an objective view of the past.[19] For the historical universe is itself heterogeneous rather than homogeneous, the product of a binocular vision that cannot be reconciled into a single image. Broader accounts may gain in intelligibility through their wider perspective, but they sacrifice the mastery of precise information. "According to the 'law of levels,'" Kracauer writes, "the contexts established at each level are valid for that level but do not apply to findings at other levels; which is to say there is no way of deriving the regularities of macrohistory . . . from the facts and interpretations provided by micro histories."[20] Thus the results of individual microhistorical accounts cannot be adduced to verify or disqualify the larger synthetic patterns or ideas or periods that macrohistorians necessarily concoct from afar. Not even the falsification procedures proposed by Karl Popper against the more ambitious verification methods of logical positivism will help us here. We cannot, in other words, hope to build an objective account of something as immense as the Holocaust by recalling and recording the discrete experiences of victims, perpetrators, and bystanders or establishing the veracity of discrete facts from reliable documents, and then generalizing from them. The difficulties we have already seen in trying to periodize it, fixing an indisputable moment of closure, are thus exacerbations of a more general problem that historians who deal on the macrolevel inevitably face.

This is not to say, however, that microhistorians are misguided in their desire to rescue the discrete, individual stories, actions and figures of the past from oblivion, just that their efforts will not work to buttress arguments for objective truth on the level of the phenomenon as a whole. There is, to be sure, one argument that Kracauer introduces—and here the source is clearly the work of his friend Walter Benjamin, although he neglects to credit him directly—which he says is explicitly theological, for the labors of the microhistorian: "according to it, the 'complete assemblage of the smallest facts' is required for the reason that nothing should go lost. It is as if the fact-oriented accounts breathed pity with the dead. This vindicates the figure of the *collector*."[21] Although never mentioning the Holocaust—a neglect typical of the 1960s, even among émigrés—the resonance of this remark is obvious. But the mode of relating to the past that it endorses is closer to that of the uncritical antiquarian than the selective historian, and its motivation, which Benjamin had identified with the religious idea of "apokatastasis," the ultimate redemption of all that seemed lost or forgotten, is a far cry from the sober notion of historical objectivity and disinterestedness.

A similar argument has recently been made by the Dutch philosopher of history, Frank Ankersmit, albeit without the saving gesture of the Benjaminian defense of collecting. In an essay entitled "Representation and the Representation of Experience," Ankersmit posits a strict distinction between epistemological questions, which deal with the veracity of discrete facts or experiences, and the large-scale representations that historians use to organize their narratives of that absent object we call the past. The reason that epistemological criteria of truth or falsehood do not apply to such a general representation is "logically, a historical representation is a *proposal*—that is, a proposal to see part of the past from a certain (metaphorical) point of view. Put differently, the historian's representation is a proposal for the *organization* of knowledge (i.e. the knowledge expressed by the singular true statements that constitute the representation) and therefore is not knowledge itself."[22]

Such sets of true statements are not arbitrary fictions, but it is impossible to judge them in the same terms as their individual components. Nor are they comparable to the lawlike generalizations that natural scientists use to subsume particulars. They work dialectically by denying and superseding other competing representations, but can never be finally confirmed as true to the past themselves. For this reason, Ankersmit argues, historical representations are intertextual, always in relation to alternative models, rather than freestanding and self-sufficient, relating only to the past in itself. Although there may be no progress towards some perfect truth about the past, historical representations can learn from the discussion that preceded them and thus produce in what Gadamer called a "*Wirkungsgeschichte,*" a history of effects or receptions history. If there is any comparable cultural phenomenon, Ankersmit avers, it is a work of art, which also organizes discrete sensations or perceptions into meaningful patterns, which do not correspond mimetically to a prior reality. As in the case we are now examining, in which the "end" of the Holocaust is impossible to establish with any epistemological certainty, a work of art must have a sense of an ending, but one that cannot be given by the material itself.

To avoid the charge that he is complicit with a wholesale postmodernist fictionalizing of the past, which would make it difficult to resist the outrages of Holocaust denial, Ankersmit introduces an original and suggestive notion of historical experience, which serves as a check on the arbitrary willfulness of the historian in the present. Such experience he compares to the shudder of recognition that sometimes overtakes us when we are in the presence of some relic of the past, which insists on its difference from our present context. "Many historians and poets since Herder and Goethe have recorded how, in a moment of supreme historical grace, they underwent a direct and immediate contact with the past. . . . Historical experience is 'an ebriety of the moment,' as Huizinga puts it; it is something the historian undergoes rather than constructs or conveys at will."[23] Such direct contact is, of course, a scandal to radically constructivist philosophies of history, indeed to any contemporary stress on the cultural mediation of all knowledge, and Ankersmit struggles to make it plausible. He ultimately compares it with the experience of the sublime, as understood by Kant, which gets us in touch—and this is the sense, rather than sight, that he wants to privilege—with what cannot be represented.[24] Because of such experiences, it is not current representation all the way down.

Like Kracauer, Ankersmit thus tries to leave us with more than just a constructivist relativism, although like the former's theological argument for redeeming everything that has happened, the latter's reliance on isolated moments of experiential "ebriety" before the overwhelming power of the past may not do much to instill confidence in those who still hold out hope for objective history. My own hunch is that nothing ever really will, because there are just too many ways in which the selective imperatives of history writing in the present cannot do justice to the inexhaustibility of a past that can never reveal itself in its fullness. In fact, it may well be that the very desire for that revelation bespeaks a deep wish for restoration of a wholeness that never really was and therefore cannot be recaptured. Writing from a psychoanalytic perspective, Angelika Rauch has recently speculated in a book entitled *The Hieroglyph of Tradition* that both historical and aesthetic representations are motivated by a hidden desire to return to the bliss of the mother's body, which has been lost through the fall into language. She thus valorizes a melancholic relationship with the past over one in which complete working through is a plausible goal. Her models are Benjamin and Novalis, for whom "it is precisely not the point to let go of the lost object with a healthy but temporary period of mourning, as Freud suggests. Instead, to be fully in touch with the past insofar as that is possible, is to be emotionally in contact with what has happened; it is to remember the importance of a lost origin within a perception of the present that is indebted to the past. Such remembrance, of course, involves feelings of *Sehnsucht*—nostalgia or tolerated sadness."[25] But melancholy is precisely not the same as nostalgia, she explains, because "it does not regress to an imaginary place libidinally invested as home or maternal ground If nostalgia signifies the pain of such longing for another place and another time, the distance and separation between self and other is nonetheless keenly observed. In contrast, melancholy actively transports this other into the present and relocates it in the symbolic status this object or place may have in the here and now."[26] Thus whereas nostalgia is beholden to the imaginary, melancholy can have a cognitive function by exhuming "the past's potential for a symbolic sense in the future and for the very concept of a future."[27]

Although it might appear as if Rauch is arguing for precisely that transcendentalizing of melancholy, that substitution of structural for historical trauma against which LaCapra warns, the point she makes is, I think, still compelling. She wants to mobilize the power of melancholic repetition by making us aware of the inevitable belatedness of all historical understanding, which can never claim past experience entirely as its own. We—and I'm deliberately employing the collective pronoun in the most universal way possible—are always thwarted in our desire to reexperience the past as it really was experienced at the time or in our hope to give voices to the forgotten masses. We cannot in other words know when the Holocaust ended—and here that failure rightly serves as an especially powerful instance of a more general point—because we can never really work it through and be fully healed of its effects. No matter how much we strive for objective truth, we can never know the past in a fully disinterested way, as if it were a natural object entirely external to ourselves. Nor can we really undo the injustices whose memory we want so desperately to keep alive. The ancient commandment to repair the world, the *tikkun olam* that takes the shards of creation and glues them together, may inspire religious yearnings, but is not a plausible project for those of us who have to live in the profane world of history instead.

If we return in conclusion to the images mentioned at the beginning of this chapter, the films taken by the British producer Sidney Bernstein, we can discern a modest expression of this inability. It turns out that the film he wanted to make of this material was never produced, partly because the Cold War reshuffling of alliances made it problematic to rub the faces of West Germans in their recent past.[28] In a documentary made for British television in 1985 called *A Painful Reminder*, Bernstein revealed that it was no less a figure than Alfred Hitchcock who had done the filming and editing. Apparently, the master of suspense and horror films had deliberately used a panning camera and long takes to include the Germans and the victims in the same shot and thus give the lie to the suspicion that the evidence was faked. He also employed montage to juxtapose heaps of hair, glasses, and false teeth of the victims with images of the beautiful landscape around the Bergen-Belsen camp.

Kracauer, it will be recalled, had compared cinematic long shots with macrohistorical ideas, because both produce effects very different from those created by close-ups and microhistorical detail. Hitchcock's pans were making a polemical point, one with which we might perhaps agree: that ordinary Germans were directly involved in the horrors of the camps, but it was clearly a cinematic device nonetheless that produced this effect. The montages of the physical traces of the victims, which worked metonymically to refer to those no longer able to be represented, were used ironically against the peaceful, bucolic countryside. Here the impression of reality was less direct and more inferential. But in both cases, what was involved was more than an objective recording on film of what was simply there to be seen. In both cases, it necessitated the eye of no less a cinematic master than Alfred Hitchcock to organize and give meaning to what was filmed. And no less significantly, it was only after a forty-year delay that his intervention was revealed. Belatedness, it seems, operates even when we are confronted with the apparently direct visual evidence of the Holocaust, the putatively objective evidence of the outcome and cessation of the horrible deeds that are embraced by this terrible term. Not even the visual recording of the end can be said to have been completed when it when it was supposed to have been. These are images that resist closure and mourning and normalization; they are testimony to the ways that we can never know the Holocaust as an objective reality, but will surely still feel its unsettling power long after the last survivor goes to her grave.

6

THE CONVERSION OF THE ROSE

On December 9, 1995, the British philosopher and sociologist Gillian Rose succumbed to the ovarian cancer that had ravaged her body for the previous two years. She was forty-eight and the author of a series of remarkable books ranging with sovereign authority over the entire terrain of modern philosophy and social theory. None, however, gained her the audience of her last effort, *Love's Work*, which wrested from her physical suffering a painfully eloquent autobiographical memoir. A unique exercise in proleptic self-mourning, it interlaced wrenching accounts of the deterioration of her body with personal reminiscences and philosophical meditations. Resolutely antisentimental, Rose somehow found an idiom to fuse the private and the public in a way that brilliantly avoided the confessional self-indulgences of contemporary culture. With only Althusser's tortured *L'avenir dure longtemps* to rival it, *Love's Work* can justly be called the most fascinating philosophical memoir of our age.

Gillian Rose's need to give her life retrospective meaning as her death approached did not, however, end with this book (or indeed with a sequel volume that she apparently left in manuscript form).[1] For only a few hours before her life slipped away, she was baptized into the Anglican Church by the Right Reverend Simon Barrington-Ward, the Bishop of Coventry. The consolation of philosophy had ultimately proven inadequate to her spiritual needs. Five days later, after she had been buried in consecrated ground, a long and admiring obituary in *The London Times* concluded with the ringing affirmation that "she died reconciled to her family, to God and to her own cruel fate."

Rose's religious conversion came as a thunderbolt to the public at large, as well as to many of her closest friends. For in the works she published in the early 1990s, most notably *The Broken Middle* (1992) and *Judaism and Modernity* (1993), it seemed as though she had returned to her Jewish roots. Under the tutelage of Julius Carlebach, her former colleague at Sussex and the scion of a long line of rabbis, she had adopted a Judaism that she called "cerebral and consciously learnt," permitting her to "develop a perspective on quandaries which would otherwise remain amorphous and alien."[2] The struggles with her own identity, which had been waged within the world of speculative philosophy in her earlier work, had led her to the religion of her forebears, not as "the sublime Other of modernity,"[3] but rather as expressive of the dilemmas of modern life at their most fundamental. Now in dialogue with Jewish scholars such as Paul Mendes-Flohr, Alan Udoff, and Norman Solomon, soaking up the atmosphere in Jerusalem, she told her readers that that she finally entered the "international world of Jewish philosophy."[4] In 1993, she was even invited to advise the Polish Commission on the Future of Auschwitz as a representative "Jewish intellectual," whose family had lost many members during the Holocaust.

With the knowledge of her deathbed conversion, it is, however, now possible to reread her last works as containing, at least between the lines, an anticipation of her shocking decision to leave that identity behind. In *Judaism and Modernity*, to take one salient example, she had asserted that "Philosophy and Judaism want to proclaim a *New Testament* which will dispose of the broken promises of modernity."[5] In particular, they yearn for the realization of an ethical community, which will somehow overcome the alienating "diremptions" of modern life, its "broken middle." But many of the most distinguished modern Jewish thinkers, Rose lamented, had failed to point the way to do so. Referring to Rosenzweig, Buber, and Levinas, she argued that "the separation in their work of the lesson of love or perficient commandment from the actualities of law or coercion suffuses their ethics with an originary violence that has been borrowed from the political modernity which they refuse to historicize."[6]

The need to historicize what seemed irreparably split—to overcome in particular the gap that she saw between law and love—was one of the main imperatives of Rose's philosophizing as a whole, which reflected her early fascination with Hegelian Marxism, most notably that of Theodor Adorno. Rose's dissertation and first book had, in fact, been dedicated to Adorno's "melancholy science."[7] Written at the height of the New Left and in the teeth of her supervisor Leszek Kolakowski's disdain for its subject, it urged Adorno's more insistently utopian version of the Frankfurt School's Critical Theory over that of Jürgen Habermas's less redemptive alternative, claiming that however "melancholy" Adorno's science may have been, it was never "resigned, quiescent or pessimistic."[8]

In her next major work, the remarkable *Hegel Contra Sociology* of 1981, Rose concluded that Adorno too had not been sufficiently grounded in the concrete realities of the historical world or heeded the ethical call to overcome its fractures. What at the end of *The Melancholy Science* she had praised as his "morality," a "praxis of thought not a recipe for social and political action,"[9] she now charged had "inherited all of the aporias which accompany method and moralism. . . . Adorno's sociology of illusion, like Lukács' sociology of reification, remains abstract."[10] Their acceptance of the typical Marxist distinction between Hegel's allegedly conservative system and his more radical dialectical method was, she argued, a "conservative, neo-Kantian one."[11]

Hegel Contra Sociology was, in fact, an uncompromising defense of Hegelian speculative philosophy against all variants of neo-Kantianism. Defending a dialectical transcendence of the antinomies of contemporary life against a transcendental naturalization of them as inherent in the human condition, she insisted on the necessity of "thinking the Absolute" as ultimately realized in the ethical life of a community against any attempt to separate facts from values, validity from norms. Audaciously damning all schools of sociological thought—Weberian, Durkheimian, Simmelian, and so forth—as well as such Western Marxists as Lukács, Habermas, and Althusser, Rose even found Marx wanting in his grasp of the failure to acknowledge the complete integration of the ethical and the actual. The Marxist insistence on changing a world that stubbornly resists that imperative, she concluded, reveals a residual Fichtean reliance on the subjective will rather than a realization that "reality is ethical."[12]

No less deficient in this regard were the targets of her next critique, the post-structuralists decried in *Dialectic of Nihilism*, published in 1984. Rejecting attempts, such as those of Heidegger, to return to a moment of equiprimordiality prior to the splits of modernity, she excoriated Deleuze, Derrida, and Foucault, all of whom somehow duplicate the old neo-Kantian antinomies, which themselves can be understood as regressions to stages of legal theory. Although they claim filiation from Nietzsche, Rose insisted that they lacked his appreciation of the fact that going "beyond good and evil involves the most strenuous immersion in historical labor and imbues our acts with a greater not a sparer density."[13] Whereas Deleuze's Bergsonian celebration of intensity and will comes down on the side of the antinomian "other" of abstract law, Derrida and Foucault end up by substituting their own versions of the transcendental law for those posited by such neo-Kantians as Hermann Cohen. "Derrida replaces the old imperialism of *Logos*, the old law table, by the imperialism of the *grapheme*, prepared as a new law table, but displaying the old Marburgian dream—as naturalized and as utopian as any which Derrida indicts—to be carried down into the valley and engraved in hearts of flesh."[14] Foucault's transcendental pole is not "writing," but first "discourse" and then "power." Although, as well known, he sought to get beyond the Kantian notion of man as a "transcendental/empirical doublet," he fell back, Rose contended, on a typical neo-Kantian dichotomy of a mathesis of origin (what he called an "archive") and its nihilistic opposite, which he dubbed "the body." Once again, only Hegel's speculative philosophy, which the post-structuralists crudely caricature as a totalitarian system or, in Bataille's phrase, a "restricted economy," can provide a nonnihilistic dialectic, which goes beyond rehearsing in displaced form the age-old aporias of legal thought.

Although Rose made no sustained attempt to relate the arguments about the law she developed in this often cryptic book to the religious themes that would preoccupy her in her subsequent works, at one point she did describe the translation of older debates into the new vocabularies of post-structuralism as "the moment at which the rationality of the critical philosophy based on the drama of the fictions of Roman law—persons, things, and obligations—is fantasized into an Orientalism which borrows the identity of wandering Dionysus or Persian Zoroaster, but which, in its celebration of writing, returns the concept of tradition to an Hebraic setting."[15] Clearly, wandering in the wilderness, preserving the "diremption"—one of her favorite words—between law and ethics, did not satisfy Rose's longing to return home.

In *The Broken Middle*, which focused on Kierkegaard's challenge to Hegel, Rose sought to do justice to what she called the "pathos of the concept," the repetition of ancient aporias and dualities, while still insisting on the "logos of the concept," which mends what has been fractured. Arguing against a postmodernism that merely situates itself on one side of a dualistic divide between rational metaphysics, stigmatized as "ontotheology," and its alleged "other," Rose urged a return to a "triune" middle ground in which universality, particularity, and singularity cross and contest each other in all their motley variety. Kierkegaard, in her reading, shared on a deep level Hegel's project, knowing that law and ethics ultimately need to be brought together. Arguing against Adorno's Marxist critique of Kierkegaard as a defender of a logic of sacrifice, a critique which she had embraced in *The Melancholy Science*, Rose praised the Danish thinker for bringing back Revelation into philosophy, for leaving, as had Hegel, "the ethical open and unresolved."[16] In *Judaism and Modernity*, she further rejected Buber's claim that *Fear and Trembling* implied a supersession of the ethical in the name of faith, contending instead that "*the knight of faith* inherits the world in all its mediation and law. . . . Kierkegaard refuses to imply that love and law, commandment and coercion, can be separated."[17]

In these works, the theme of love is, in fact, introduced in subtle and surprising ways. Resisting attempts to achieve a lost wholeness through premature fiat, Rose warned that "made anxious by inscrutable disjunctions, we invariably attempt to mend them . . . with *love*, forced or fantasized onto the state."[18] There is thus a complicated relationship between love and violence, which Kierkegaard understood. But rather than seeking to banish violence entirely in the name of a prelapsarian state of grace, it is necessary to include it too in the larger drama of redemption. For "without 'violence,' which is not sacrifice, but risk, language, labor, love—life—would not live."[19]

These and other themes too numerous to mention reverberate through Rose's remarkable oeuvre, which repays far more careful evaluation than this space allows. I want to return, however, to the implications of her deathbed conversion, which cannot help but cast a light back on her trajectory as a whole. Before doing so, two disclosures are in order. First, I should make clear that I was a personal friend, albeit not an especially close one, of Gillian Rose and had an abiding interest in her remarkable work, which traversed much of the same territory as my own. Our friendship began, oddly enough, with an indignant letter she wrote in January, 1974 to the British journal *New Society*, which had just published a generous review of my first book, *The Dialectical Imagination*. Her letter vigorously protested against what she took to be my relegation of the Frankfurt School to the realm of mere history of ideas, arguing that "we should not historicize before we've even tasted." It was clear that she was primed to provide a hearty portion of Critical Theory to an Anglo-American public unaccustomed to its bitter flavor, and was not happy with the preemption of that role.

By chance, I was spending that year at St. Antony's College, Oxford and was thus able to meet this fierce defender of the ideas I thought I was helping to recover rather than bury. Wayne Hudson, an Australian then writing his dissertation at Oxford on Ernst Bloch, was, if memory serves, the intermediary, or perhaps she introduced herself. In any case, it turned out that we had a lot to say to each other, all of it cordial, and over the years, I came to relish the chance to cross paths at conferences and see where her extraordinary intellectual odyssey was taking her. The last opportunity came in London in 1992 at a conference at Birkbeck College on the centenary of Walter Benjamin's birth. Characteristically unconventional, she went against the celebratory mood of the gathering by condemning Benjamin's reliance on the Jewish concept of memory or *Zakhor* for putting "eschatological repetition in the place of political judgment."[20] What she called his "aberrated" as opposed to "inaugurated mourning" lacked the capacity to forgive, to struggle towards reconciliation.

As always, Rose was adamantly certain about her own take on the world and willing to chastise anyone, no matter how respected an authority, who came to different conclusions. I was reminded, as I had been before, of Lord Melbourne's reaction to Macauley: "I wish I were as cocksure of anything as he is of everything." Rose's extraordinary self-confidence, fondness for gnomic pronunciamentos, and hedgehoglike ability to incorporate every possible position into her own worldview meant that productive dialogue with her was, in fact, difficult. Although she was by all accounts an inspirational, if tough mentor—ten doctoral students dutifully accompanied her when she moved from Sussex to Warwick—and had a number of devoted friends and intellectual soulmates, including the philosophers J. N. Bernstein and Howard Caygill, her influence seems to have been relatively modest. Among the legions of post-structuralist defenders, few, if any, chose to respond to her diatribe against their "nihilism." Habermasians have been equally indifferent to her accusations of neo-Kantianism. The burgeoning literature on Levinas, as far as I can tell, has not taken much note of her critique. And sociology, the discipline she so sweepingly condemned in her second book, seems to have blithely gone about its business without losing any sleep. Even the success of *Love's Work* has not yet led to a revival of interest in her more demanding philosophical writings, which have little of the raw emotional power of that extraordinary memoir.

This relative neglect seems to me regrettable, as Gillian Rose was an uncommonly intelligent, learned, and passionate thinker, who was able to reveal the deeper stakes involved in virtually every controversy she entered. Even if one comes away ultimately unconvinced by her conclusions, an encounter with so powerful and original a mind inevitably raises one's understanding of the issues involved. Although she had a sadly truncated career, she left enough behind to occupy us for many years to come.

In addition to disclosing my own personal intersection with Rose's life and work, I should also candidly admit an a priori bias against the gesture that ended them: her deathbed conversion to Anglicanism. Although a nonobservant Jew unperturbed by any disaffection from the tenets of Judaism, I cannot avoid an involuntary shudder at the news of a positive decision to convert to another religion. I am unable to throw off the troubling memory of nearly two thousand years of eager attempts to convert Jews to Christianity, either through persuasion or coercion, attempts that are intimately related to the sorry history of antisemitism. Although there are many explanations why in certain circumstances Jews willingly purchased this "entry ticket to European culture," as Heine famously called it, none fails to leave a bad taste in my mouth. I know this is unfair to the particularly of specific decisions, which may well reflect a spiritual quest whose subtle music I am too tone deaf to hear, but there it is.

With these clarifications behind me, let me now turn to the vexing issue of what Gillian Rose's own decision may mean for her legacy as a thinker. There is, to be sure, a risk in even raising such an issue. An outsider has, after all, scarcely any right to judge so intimate a choice, especially if it may have brought comfort and solace at the end of a life that ended in such pain. And so I hope that nothing I say will be construed as petty carping at a personal decision whose motivations can, alas, only now be a source of speculation. Nor am I interested in discrediting Gillian Rose's remarkable oeuvre by saying it somehow is reducible to this one final leap of faith. I am also loath to trot out shopworn categories like "Jewish self-hatred" to psychologize a decision that clearly had roots in lengthy and serious intellectual deliberation (even if it may be troubling that she had so little resistance to Hegel's demeaning characterization of Judaism as a legalistic religion incapable of mediating the finite and the infinite).[21]

Still, it would do an injustice to Gillian Rose to ignore entirely the implications of her conversion. The author of so frank and pitiless a memoir as *Love's Work*, who understood very well the intertwining of the private and the public, would surely have welcomed an unblinking response to this gesture. After all, Hegel's owl, as she well knew, flies at dusk, when the narrative reaches its end, and hindsight is a powerful tool of philosophical comprehension. Although perhaps an embarrassment for those who remember her primarily as a Marxist theoretician—it is striking that in neither Howard Caygill's obituary in *Radical Philosophy* nor Kate Soper's discussion of *Love's Work* in *The New Left Review* is the conversion even mentioned[22]—it cannot be brushed aside in any serious attempt to assess her legacy.

The initial point to be noted in connection with the conversion is that it was not the first time that Gillian Rose underwent such a radical shift of identity. When she was sixteen, as she reveals in her autobiographical memoir, she changed her patronym from "Stone," her father's name, to "Rose," her stepfather's. Calling it a "violent act of self-assertion," she described it as her "bat mitzvah, my confirmation as a daughter of the law."[23] The triumph was immediately followed, however, by a loss, as her father angrily disowned her, refusing to see her for five years. The great themes of her work—diremption, violence, law, love, loss, and mourning—are all already evident in this act of defiant reinvention. When not too long after, her mother and stepfather split up after apparently attempting suicide (or at least phoning to tell her they were going to), she relived the trauma of her parents' divorce and recognized that name changes alone do not guarantee the healing of diremptions. Her second identity change may thus have been an attempt to mend the rift created by the first, or at least find a richly symbolic simulacrum of that much desired healing.

This yearning for reparation and reconciliation helps explain the ultimate direction of her religious journey, for although she identified "Rose" with a daughter's obedience to the Jewish law, she soon came to see it as representing the grace that softens the hardness of the legal "Stone." Hegel's famous injunction "to recognize and know reason as the rose within the cross of the present and thus to enjoy this present,"[24] although unlikely to be known to even as precocious a sixteen year old as she, adds another layer of retrospective meaning to the name change. "Enjoying" her present, even before the cancer began its sinister work of demolition, must have required all the symbolic resources at her disposal, and if her new name happened to work in tandem with an affirmation of the immanent rationality she was so determined to find in the world, all the better.

Rose's decision to turn to Anglicanism, not just any version of Christianity, should also be seen as of a piece with her larger intellectual project (as well, I have been told, as an echo of a choice her mother had also made some years before). Conversion to a more universalist creed like Roman Catholicism might be understood as implying an embrace of an abstraction, hovering above the world, while accepting the evangelical imperative to be born again through faith in scriptural truth could be read as seeking a kind of ahistorical immediacy. The Church of England can be more easily understood as a particular, concrete historical instantiation of the divine intervention in the world. As the Tractarian Movement at Oxford in the 1830s had stressed, the Church, even after its break with Rome, should still be seen as an apostolic succession, a Divine Society that progressively realized revelation in its own institutional history. For a Hegelian hopeful of realizing reason over time in the ethical life of a community, Anglicanism would thus have an obvious appeal. For a believer in healing the diremption between public and private, a state church with little patience for the world-denying inwardness of other versions of Protestantism would also be especially attractive. For an adherent of the stern credo that love has work to do in the world, hard, unrelenting, often unrewarded work, a religion that resists the instant gratifications of mystical epiphanies would have its lure.

Rose's acceptance of a new religion was, moreover, prepared by her philosophical distrust of the insistence on human autonomy and self-assertion that characterized modern philosophy, perhaps nowhere as insistently as in the work of Kant. In *Love's Work*, she called this humanist faith an "unrevealed religion" and damned it as "the baroque excrescence of the Protestant ethic: hedonist, not ascetic, voluptuous, not austere, embellished, not plain, it devotes us to our own individual inner-worldly authority, but with the loss of the inner as well as the outer mediator. This is an ethic without ethics, a religion without salvation."[25] Its ultimate offspring, she claimed, is postmodern relativism, which anyone wise enough to "think the absolute" will find abhorrent. For Rose, ethics, which is lost when the middle is broken, "finds itself always within the imperative, the commandment, and hence already begun."[26] It cannot therefore come from self-assertion, but from elsewhere, from a revelation.

So in the end, it turns out that Gillian Rose, who for so many years presented herself as an advocate of negative dialectics and "revolutionary practice"—these are the final words of *Hegel Contra Sociology*—was really harboring a theologically inspired urge to be a yea-sayer, someone who could look at all the ugliness and horror of life and still see reconciliation, a comic rather than tragic emplotment of narratives, grand and small. What Howard Caygill said of *Love's Work* might well be said of Gillian Rose's oeuvre as a whole: it was "an exercise in affirmation, one which does not shy from the violence that comes with saying yes to life, even, or especially, in the face of untimely death."[27] Rose, in short, seems to have possessed what she claimed was missing in Walter Benjamin: "inaugurated mourning," the capacity to forgive, the strength to transcend melancholy, "the power of love, which may curse, but abides . . . a power to be able *to attend*, powerful or powerless."[28]

At a time when melancholic repetition and cynical reason seem to define the spirit of the age, at least among many fin-de-siècle intellectuals, Rose's stubborn and lonely crusade to "think the absolute" will seem self-evidently quixotic. Her faith in the redemptive power of love beyond mere personal relationships will fail to move those who agree with Hannah Arendt that "love, by its very nature, is unworldly, and it is for this reason rather than its rarity that it is not only apolitical but antipolitical, perhaps the most powerful of all antipolitical human forces."[29] Her insistence on restoring an ethical community beyond fissures will invite dismissal as a projection of her own desperate search for a means to heal the wounds of a life that was anything but harmonious. Her deathbed embrace of religion may appear an unwitting disclosure of the fideistic basis of all redemptive political positions, including the Hegelian Marxism she once so truculently championed. And perhaps most damaging of all, her yea-saying belief that "reality is ethical" may well invite the charge that she had embraced a theodicy in which partial evil could somehow be justified by a larger good.

But now when alterity, heterogeneity, nonidentity, difference, and otherness have become the tired buzzwords of our fractured culture, it is Rose who paradoxically represents a form of genuine strangeness, unassimilable to any school of thought, *à l'écart de tous les courants*. Even those of us who lack the energy or even desire to seek absolute answers and remain content to play among the shards of a middle that seems permanently broken can justly mourn the premature departure of a unique figure who lived the drama of the contemplative life with a rare passion. Whether or not she did die, as *The London Times* would have it, "reconciled to her family, to God, and to her own cruel fate," Gillian Rose exemplified the very human struggle to achieve those goals with luminous intensity.

7

PEN PALS WITH THE UNICORN KILLER

Letters from interested readers, provoked to respond by something you've written, are always welcome gifts. Especially when they come with no expectation of being printed themselves as a "letter to the editor"—lacking, that is, the ulterior motive of gaining a public platform for the writer's own views—they are about as gracious a testimony to the tacit bond that ties together writer and audience as one can imagine. So it was with no small amount of pleasure that I received a thoughtful, three-page missive dated May 23, 1997 in response to an earlier column in this space devoted to the deathbed conversion of the British philosopher Gillian Rose.[1] The letter was sent from "Le Moulin de Guitry" in Champagne-Mouton, France, and signed "Peace, Eugene Mallon."

About three weeks later, shortly after I had sent back a note expressing my gratitude for the time and effort spent in composing the letter, my eye was captured by the headline in the *San Francisco Chronicle*: "Philadelphia Murderer Caught in France." The fugitive in question turned out to be Ira Einhorn, described as "a hippie guru who gained a following among the rich and influential in the 1970s before he beat his girlfriend to death and stuffed the body into a steamer trunk," who had been on the run for sixteen years. "French police arrested Einhorn at the converted windmill rural Bordeaux region where he was believed to have lived since 1992," the article continued. And then in a sentence that made my blood run cold, it added: "He was using the name Eugene Mallon, borrowed from an Irish friend." My new pen pal, it turned out, had had more than time to kill.

Since the moment of his discovery, the saga of the Unicorn Killer, as he was already dubbed before he went on the lam, has become an international media dream story, with countless articles devoted to the colorful life of the charismatic counter-cultural hero, the gruesome death of Helen "Holly" Maddux of Tyler, Texas and Bryn Mawr, the desperate attempt by her family to track down the killer, and the tireless devotion of a prosecuting attorney to bring him to justice. The Fox television network even produced a two-night miniseries dramatically recreating the story with Tom Skerrit starring as the distraught and vengeful father of the victim.

If not quite at the level of the O. J. frenzy, the coverage of the "hippy guru" whose spurned love resulted in horrific violence has continued at a brisk pace.[2] For to complicate the plot still further, the French courts shockingly refused to extradite Einhorn in December, 1997 on the grounds that because he had been convicted in absentia in 1993—he had jumped the modest $40,000 bail successfully arranged by his influential lawyer Arlen Spector before the trial could begin—and would not be retried in Pennsylvania, he wasn't being treated according to the "higher standards" of French law, which insists that the accused must be allowed to present his defense. A more recent ruling in May that went against Einhorn seems to indicate the likelihood that he will be returned. But at this writing, negotiations to resolve this dispute are still at an impasse, with the Einhorn case turning into one of those increasingly frequent spats between us and the French, a darker version of the boycotting of McDonald's or a quota on American movies.

There is little that I can add to the story, except to share the contents of the letter that arrived some two years ago, on the eve of Einhorn's capture. For what seemed at first glance the harmless ruminations of a reader kind enough to respond to a simple column have now gained the subtextual resonance of a indirect apologia . . . or perhaps confession. What did "Eugene Mallon" reveal in his letter and what, if anything, can be learned about Ira Einhorn from it?

Without wasting polite preliminaries, the letter begins with a burst of the kind of overwrought rhetoric that must have galvanized his listeners back in the 1970s:

> How few, any (?) have the courage to live in the shattered whole that is the detritus of our world of remnants? How many repetitions do we need of Auschwitz, the Gulag, Pol Pot, Bosnia to realize our situation. How long will we go on paying heed to dead institutions or those rebelling against them in a counter theology of absence that is as vacant as the missing

> presence in all those locked buildings that pay lip service to a fading memory of experience or the hope of resurrection.
>
> So much of the philosophical quest or scholarly quest is based on deep unfaced needs to feel whole, saved, loved if you will; a failure to deal with the real sense of the time, that should (it doesn't) make us aware that we are animals with highly developed brains and a long dependent childhood. Our illusions about unity and wholeness, based on historical models that all of our weekly 168 hours are working overtime to destroy, are just that: illusions, and all of us would be so much better off if the impulses that lead to the illusions were quite clearly spelled out by those escaping the buzz words you mentioned in the last paragraph of your piece on Gillian Rose.

The "buzz words" in question were "alterity, heterogeneity, non-identity, difference and otherness." Einhorn seems here to be mocking their current fashionableness in poststructuralist discourse, but embracing the repudiation of holistic redemption that they express, a fantasy based on "the unfaced need to feel whole, saved, loved if you will." Implying that he has successfully faced that need and come out on the other side, no longer needing the illusions that still compel so many others to promote a nightmare politics of pseudoredemption, he then asks "Where are the American Furets?" But after praising the liberal French historian whose denunciations of communism and its antecedents in the French Revolution would seem to indicate a disillusionment with his radical past, he declares "Marx is still the best description we have of capitalism even in its present ever escalating global madness and a page of [Adorno's] PRISMS is worth all of Levinas and Derrida."

After delivering himself of these somber judgments about the state of the world and his preference for the Frankfurt School over post-structuralism, "Mallon" settles down to reveal a bit about himself:

> I am a veteran of the 60s in the USA, now living in France *Profond* that might as well be Los Angeles or New York as far as the emerging behavioral patterns: latch key children, both parents absent all the time, working two or three jobs; TV=life and exponentially increasing psychic breakdown. For me, life is relatively peaceful and calm as the population in the Charente is sparse and the old are living out a disappearing life that is still human. A luxury that I will treasure as long as it lasts, but among the young its (sic) speed and spend, no gardens, no home cooked meals and lots of TV. The teens will drive to Amsterdam, c.1000 miles, for the weekend, to turn on to the super dope now available there.

Like lots of other sixties radicals, Einhorn seems to have discovered that no one under thirty these days can be trusted. Although the "relatively peaceful and calm" life he would "treasure as long as it lasts,"was about to be shattered by his arrest, it seems it was already in danger of being swamped by the evils of modernity. What had he been doing in his refuge from the threat of the "exponentially psychic breakdown" he saw in France as well as in America?

"I have just spent five years doing a novel on the holocaust and read well over 750 books in the process, so what Gillian Rose did for whatever personal need makes me a little ill as I have lived through very thoroughly the church's long preparation for Hitler. Would you speak about T. S. Eliot in the same terms?"

Rose's conversion to Anglicanism rankled Einhorn, as it bespoke an escape from the need to confront the evils of the world head on rather than sugarcoat them. He went on:

> I respect her work, as I do yours, in particular, as your book was the first one, of many, that I have read on the Frankfurt School, but I wish you hadn't ended on an upbeat note as the only genuine strangeness worth paying attention to is the one that fully faces our horror, not without energy or desire, but with resolution and the courage to say "YES" in spite of, without the aid of a very dead religion like the Church of England. The contrast between her Nietzsche quote on page 44 [going "beyond good and evil involves the most strenuous immersion in historical labor and imbues our acts with a greater not a sparer density"] and a conversion tells the whole story.

Read in the retrospective light of "Eugene Mallon's" unmasking, these words are particularly resonant. The "genuine strangeness" these days is not Rose's unfashionable Hegelian search for the absolute, but rather for Einhorn the one that "fully faces our horror, not without energy or desire, but with the resolution and the courage to say 'YES' " without the comfort of religion. Without naming "our horror," Einhorn seems to have rationalized its affirmation as an act of Nietzschean yea-saying.

The letter ends with a plea to descend from the level of abstraction and turn instead to the concrete:

> We have all been lead (sic) deeply astray by the desire for some promised end and those most responsible, left leaning scholars and intellectuals, ought to be dealing with the creation of that almost overwhelming tendency in modern thought from a deeply personal angle or the mess will only get worse. The jargon (your last paragraph) is an escape that is clogging all thought. In the present election here, the only people saying anything at this local level was THE NATIONAL FRONT: what a sad situation. But no sadder I guess than TELOS plugging Carl Schmitt.[3]

And then a last plaintive question: "What do you read that keeps you alive?"

I don't recall how or even if I tried to answer that final question in the perfunctory thank-you note I sent. I want now to try again, indeed to respond much more seriously than before to the letter as a whole. It was, I think, Sartre who said somewhere that writers always imagine their readers to be like themselves. In this case, there is some empirical truth to the assumption. Einhorn, after all, is approximately my age, came from the same assimilated Jewish background, and was drawn to the same political milieu in the 1960s. Although less of a "veteran" in the sense of being a public activist on Einhorn's scale or possessing his gifts of charisma and organization, I find much of what he advocated familiar and even congenial, or at least did so in the context of those overheated times. His letter confirms the continuity of this complicity, evidenced by the offhand remark about *Telos* and Schmitt, which Einhorn correctly assumed expressed a shared disappointment.

What, of course, I cannot begin to fathom are the depths of a rage that could lead to violence of the kind Einhorn has been found guilty of committing. What I guess I want, therefore, is some help in understanding the tear in the fabric of a life narrative that on the surface seems so familiar. What I need is a signal that even so unimaginable a deed can be given some halting meaning, made in partly intelligible by a kind of unflinching depth hermeneutic that eschews glib rationalizations and no longer seeks oblivion by escaping into the French countryside. Or more modestly, I want some hope that people like Einhorn—people, that is, like me—can still struggle to seek that intelligibility, refusing with all their might to concede to radical evil the terrible power of utter ineffability. No dream, to be sure, of redemptive transparency, albeit not a nightmare of total opacity either. No way to atone for past horrors, not even a potential means to forestall their future repetition. But at least letters no longer sent with pseudonyms; only ones signed by those with the courage to know who they are and face what they have done.

So given a second chance, I would respond as follows:

Dear Ira Einhorn,

I know you are still in public denial and may well consider my assumption of your guilt a reason to tune me out, but somewhere inside you cannot help but be haunted by the truth. Your letter—written with no small irony while you were on the run—returns again and again to the need to avoid escaping from "our horrors" and urges us to face them with courage and resolution, even somehow affirming them without consolation. I'm sure these are sentiments easier to express than realize, and I can only imagine the depths of your struggle to make sense of the rage that led to your dreadful deed.

But if you really think that only personal explanations can help us understand the false need for a promised land, you need to set aside the years of deception and try to make some sense of what happened. Writing a novel about the Holocaust only displaces the question of evil and responsibility onto a distant plane. There are already enough attempts, fictional or otherwise, to address the now distant crimes of the Nazis; you need to ask harder questions about demons closer to home.

I know that such a suggestion may seem impertinent and presumptuous. But your letter reveals powers of feeling and intellect that suggest you are up to this task, if you can somehow summon the courage to embrace it. There is, in fact, a recent model that suggests itself, a model you doubtless know. While incarcerated in a mental institution for the murder of his wife, the French philosopher Louis Althusser produced a wrenching autobiography called *L'avenir dure longtemps*, published posthumously in 1992. Denied the chance to testify about his crime at the hearing that declared him incompetent, he sought another venue for his tortured thoughts on an act he could only remember with the deepest remorse. The result is a moving, troubling, ultimately unsuccessful attempt to make sense of the senseless; but it is a relentlessly honest effort to confront his personal horror. And it salvages a certain modicum of dignity out of his abasement.

Like you, Althusser was a leftist hero of the sixties, if more a theoretician than activist, but someone who had to abandon the false consolations of his abstractions when faced with the bewildering intimacy of his own violent rage. If you ask me what books keep me alive, it is perhaps one like *L'avenir dure longtemps* that ironically does the trick. By exposing the darkest and most inexplicable sides of the human condition, and yet doing so without apology or pretense, it touches a chord that a hundred predictably lachrymose novels about the Holocaust cannot. You have, I would venture to guess, such a book in you. You are right to think that it won't bring redemption or undo the terrible act that ruined so many lives; no cliched outcome of "closure" or "healing" or "working through" will follow. But it may bring you a bit closer to that "genuine strangeness" you have rightly identified with fully facing the horror "not without energy or desire, but with resolution and the courage to continue to say 'YES.'" For you cannot reach so cosmic a level of yea-saying unless you are first willing to make the simplest of affirmations: that which acknowledges the responsibility you bear for the death of another human being.

Peace,
Martin Jay

8

KWANGJU
From Massacre to Biennale

"First, you must visit the cemeteries," they insist; "only then will you understand." So you take the short trip on a chilly November afternoon in 1997 from the city center to the hill overlooking Kwangju in the Cholla province of South Korea, not knowing quite what to expect. When you arrive, they take you first to the old gravesite, which was hurriedly filled with the civilian victims of the massacre that took place on May 18, 1980.[1] The years have passed, but it is clear that the wound still festers. The makeshift graves have photographs, now slowly fading, of those who lost their lives when the military government of South Korea, backed by American support, slaughtered perhaps as many as 2,000 of its citizens that spring day. Some have small glass cases in which mementoes of the dead are preserved—a schoolboy's diary, a favorite book, a piece of clothing—which poignantly evoke the fragility of their interrupted lives. Fresh flowers are placed on many of them, banners and posters intermingle with the graves, promising that their sacrifice will not be forgotten. You are given a joss stick to light in their memory and when you fastidiously take a cigarette butt out of the bowl in which you place it, they gently tell you to put it back, for it too was meant as a tribute.

But what is perhaps most moving is the disclosure that the graves themselves are, in fact, now vacant. Under the traditional mounds of dirt that mark Korean burial sites and behind the small stones with names and dates are freshly emptied tombs. Earlier in the year, the government, trying to put as much distance as it can from the regime that fired on its people, had moved them to a new and more permanent cemetery a short distance away. It had planned to level the old burial ground, removing all vestiges of the popular commemoration of the dead, and create a more fitting place of public remembrance. But astonishingly, protests against the plan by those suspicious of the government's motives prevailed, and the old site still remains, uneasily juxtaposed to the new. It is as if those who remembered the massacre as the beginning of the slow and painful democratization of South Korea were not yet willing to call the movement a complete success, not yet comfortable with the act of official closure that the new cemetery betokens.

When they then take you to that remarkable site, the symbolic significance of the gesture becomes clearer. The government has created an enormous, theatrical space in which the actual victims are dwarfed by the monument to their memory. Walking up an imposing flight of wide stairs, you pass through a traditional, gaily colored, Korean gate like those gracing the temples that dot the landscape. Beyond it is a mammoth plaza, fit for political rallies, with a giant abstract sculpture rising hundreds of feet in the air. It looks perhaps like two hands cupping an egg; perhaps not. Beyond that, on a slight rise, are the newly reburied victims, but without the pictures or the glass cases with their effects. A small building off to the side of the plaza contains a number of photographs, but they are not connected with any immediacy to the graves themselves. In the immensity of this space, these look relatively small in number, far fewer than the casualties who are said to have died in the massacre. They seem an afterthought, tucked away beyond the great plaza. Often, you are told with some bitterness, people come to pass time at the cemetery, as if in a park, and never actually make it to the graves themselves.

Then your glance is caught by something that seems to disturb the controlled environment of the site: small pieces of paper with eyes drawn on them, which are pasted to the risers of the stairs. Near the graves there is another odd sight: a pool of blood red liquid in the ground, with no explanation of its meaning or origin. Then you are told that they are the residues of a recent festival of reunification that took place in the cemetery, in which Korean artists were allowed to present their work to the public. It is as if Arlington Cemetery in Washington, you muse, were selected as the location for a display of the most avant-garde installations of the day, a scenario that would make the veins on Jesse Helms' neck stand out even more prominently than usual.

What may seem incongruous to foreign eyes is, however, far less so in Korea, a country where unexpected juxtapositions seem almost the norm. On a previous trip in 1994, this truth came home to me when my wife and I were taken to the DMZ only a few miles north of Seoul by a professor of English and one of his graduate students. Settling down next to a highway for a picnic lunch prepared by the professor's absent spouse, we were within earshot of the North Korean propaganda loudspeakers blasting across the river. Watch towers and barbed wire were our backdrop. After a few minutes, our host wondered if we might answer a personal question. Could we please explain to him, he earnestly asked, the Western concept of romantic love? His marriage had been arranged, as had that of the twenty-something-year-old student, and he wanted to know how the other system worked. And so there at the site of the most virulent remnant of Cold War hatred, a political border whose transgression could easily lead to death, we did our best to explain the rewards and risks of the practice of allowing individuals to cross social, ethnic, and cultural borders and fall in love on their own.

With such a memory, the unexpected transformation of an officially sanctioned space of solemn commemoration into a site for artistic/political expression did not seem so peculiar. Even to the casual visitor, Korea is a country of radical disjunctions. Its modernization has been so rapid and uneven that traditional values and behavior have scarcely had time to be effaced. But resolved to leap ahead and gain a role on the world stage, the Koreans have sought to rush as rapidly as possible into the future. One side effect is the haste with which the new infrastructure of a modern country has been constructed, a haste whose dangerous potential was evident when a new bridge suddenly collapsed over the Han River in Seoul during our 1994 visit. Corruption and inferior building standards were blamed for the disaster.

Another consequence, which was the reason for my return three years later, is an evident determination to involve Korean culture more extensively in a global network of artists and intellectuals. In 1995, Kwangju was selected—with the added intention of commemorating the events of 1980—as the site of the first international Art Biennale ever to be held in Asia. Under the rubric "Beyond the Boundaries," it brought together artists and their works from around the world. Following the lead of such venerable exhibitions as the Venice Biennale and the German Dokumenta, it attracted more than a million and a half visitors. Its success was such that a second was staged two years later, which included an international conference organized by Chungmoo Choi, who teaches East Asian Cultures at UC, Irvine, to which I had been invited. The theme of both the 1997 exhibition and the conference was "Unmapping the Earth," which implied challenging the geopolitical/geocultural power relations that had relegated Korea, and a fortiori the capital city of isolated Cholla Province, to the margins. With the end of the Cold War and the rise of the Asian "tigers," the old division of nation-states into First, Second, and Third Worlds was no longer relevant. Traditional roles, it was clear, would thus have to be "repositioned," in the jargon of postcolonial studies used by the organizers. In fact, even the privileging of former European colonies in postcolonial discourse itself would need to be challenged by foregrounding the experience of Korea as a colony of Japanese imperialism and a bifurcated client of the Cold War adversaries.

"Unmapping" extended as well to the structure of the exhibition itself. Eschewing the traditional national exhibitions and competitive judging typical of other Biennales, the organizers, led by the festival's artistic director Lee Young-chul, subcontracted the curatorial tasks to figures from Asia, Europe, and America, Harald Zeemann, Kyong Park, Richard Koshalek, Sung Wan-kyung, and Bernard Marcadé, who imaginatively grouped the works they chose under five rubrics: speed, space, hybrid, power, becoming. These in turn were roughly correlated with more traditional Asian notions of water, fire, wood, metal, and earth to stimulate unexpected juxtapositions and creative cross-fertilizations.

Generously housed in a series of massive pavilions in a large park, the exhibition provided ample space for the complex installations, multimedia presentations, and conceptual provocations that constitute art at the end of the twentieth century. Such international stars as Cindy Sherman, Gilbert and George, Chris Marker, Yves Klein, Joseph Beuys, Bill Viola, John Cage, Louise Bourgeois, and Bruce Naumann were shown alongside artists who, at least to this observer, were still unknown (perhaps the most exciting discovery for me was the Swiss video artist Pipilotti Rist, whose "Sip My Ocean" in the Speed pavilion was a dreamlike gem). A separate building was also reserved for an "Aperto"—Italian seems to push aside English as the international language of these events only in their titles—of contemporary Korean art. Judging by the exuberance of the crowds, which appeared to manifest the same mixture of fascination and bewilderment that Western audiences display in front of today's cutting-edge art, I would hazard a guess that the deprovincializing intentions of the organizers were bearing some fruit. For at least a few months, in the once remote city of Kwangju in Cholla Province, South Korea, the global cultural world, or at least that associated with the artistic avant-garde, was "unmapped" enough so that center and margins were no longer as rigidly demarcated as before and the metropole and its provinces lost their absolute distinction.

Globalization, such a process is now routinely called, and we are becoming more and more familiar with its various effects. In cultural terms, local identities are unhinged and float freely in a sea of circulating signifiers available for anyone who wants to appropriate them. Diasporic displacements, nomadic wanderings, traveling theories, hybridized identities, and cyberspace deterritorializations are now the norm and anything autochthonous is suspected of reactionary nostalgia. The technological compression of time and space has abetted the geosynchronous virtualization of reality. Mass cultural forms of this process are pervasive in everything from culinary offerings and MTV videos to sportsgear and blockbuster movies, as we become more and more entangled in a worldwide web that extends well beyond our computer screens. What is sometimes called "glolocalization" has entailed the dissemination of locally produced cultural products to unexpected markets in far corners of the world.[2] Imbalances in power and profit are still, to be sure, massive, but the trend to turn us all into cultural consumers in a global shopping mall (a far more apt metaphor than McLuhan's village) is unmistakable.

Although the homogenizing and universalist aspirations of earlier variants of this trend are frequently decried—think of the condescension now ritually heaped on Edward Steichen's "Family of Man" photography collection—the postmodernist version, for all its ritualized celebration of difference and particularity, ironically may be producing a similar outcome. As demonstrated by the academy's "cultural studies" machine, with its omnivorous appetite and methodological imperialism, an unmapped landscape without borders can sanction anyone to invade and stake out a claim.[3] What perhaps makes the process seem more promising than it was in the days when the invaders were all going in one direction is that now it is no longer clear who is staking out claims on whose territory; in fact, the current fashion is to rejoice in the belief that the "empire strikes back," which suggests that cultural cross-fertilization is a multidirectional process driven by no hegemonic logic, not even triumphant Americanization. To this extent, the project of tearing up the old order's maps may be construed as an emancipatory move, even if it is not clear what will replace them.

What, however, may be more problematic are the effects of globalization understood in more than just cultural terms. Just how fraught the process may be became evident shortly after the Kwangju Biennale closed at the end of November 1997. For suddenly, its more economic and political aspects shunted aside their cultural counterpart. The fragility of the South Korean economic boom, the so-called miracle on the Han, was exposed, producing a humiliating dependency on the world financial community, expressed in the conditions imposed by the International Monetary Fund for the massive bail-out loan it provided. The essence of globalization, some would argue, has always been its economic aspects: the amalgamation of transnational corporations with no local identity, the unimpeded flow of capital across national borders looking for increased profit margins, the informational revolution that creates ever more tightly intertwined financial markets, the decentralization of production increasing the migration of labor to jobs or of jobs to labor where it is cheapest, the ineffectiveness of national tariff barriers, the vulnerability of currencies to manipulation from abroad, the urgency of regional responses to ecological crises, and so on.[4] How to respond to the challenges and dangers of these trends has produced a flood of expert advice, often contradictory,[5] which amateurs such as myself can only approach with fear and trembling.

In fact, the average citizen's understanding of economic globalization may even be dimmer than was the case when more local or national issues are presented to him or her. What makes this outcome particularly ironic is the fact that in addition to its cultural and economic faces, globalization has also taken a decidedly political turn, which was also evident in South Korea immediately after the Kwangju Biennale. For on December 18th, the former dissident leader Kim Dae Jung was elected President of South Korea, in what was widely acclaimed as a triumph for democracy and human rights. The military regimes that had so long used the Cold War to justify their internal repression were now decidedly a thing of the past.

Kim's fate and that of Kwangju and the Cholla region has always been intimately tied together. He, in fact, had been blamed for the massacre of 1980 by the military government of General Chun Doo Hwan and was narrowly spared execution when a deal was struck with the Reagan administration to allow him to go into exile in America.[6] He bravely returned in 1985, only to be put under house arrest for the next two years. Kim's stunning electoral victory, inviting comparison with that of Nelson Mandela in South Africa, might be understood as suggesting that the political implications of globalization were the spread of democratic values and institutions, a fulfillment of Francis Fukuyama's famous prediction of a decade ago. Talk of an authoritarian "Asian road to modernity," based on the paternalist Confucianism that seemed a short while before to be the wave of the future, was suddenly no longer much to be heard.

On this reading, the electoral victory of Kim Dae Jung, followed by a number of magnanimous gestures to his enemies and a reaching out to North Korea, can be seen as part of a worldwide tendency toward some sort of popular government, which began to pick up speed with the fall of communism in Europe, the end of Apartheid, and the decline of military regimes in Latin America. Whether or not such a trend can be understood as a function of American domination of the New World Order or as something that has happened despite it is a question less important than the results, which many have taken as cause for genuine hope as we stumble into the next millennium. The nightmare politics that ravaged much of the earth during the not-short-enough twentieth century may now finally be at an end.

But rather than concluding on too optimistic a note about the political implications of globalization, it may be useful to return to the two cemeteries in Kwangju and recall where in fact the bodies are really buried. Kim Dae Jung is certainly to be identified with the people's memorial rather than that of the previous regime of Kim Young Sam, whose grandiosity, even with the softening effects of artistic interventions, bespeaks the power of the state, not the people. My guides through the two sites were all his fervent supporters and no doubt cheered by his triumph. But it may not be possible for one leader, or even a political movement, however well intentioned, to realize genuine democracy in an era of rapid and increased globalization. For the intrinsic logics of democracy and that of globalization, if we can agree that they possess such a thing, are deeply at odds.

Without launching into an extensive discussion of what constitutes genuine democracy, now perhaps more than ever the subject of vigorous debate,[7] suffice it to say that it normally implies an active citizenry able to deliberate about issues and participate in their resolution. Whether based on the direct model of the ancient polis or the more representative alternative necessitated by large-scale modern states, democracy has entailed a notion of popular sovereignty and collective responsibility. Either in terms of a substantive consensus or a procedural mechanism for producing compromises among factions that agree to suspend their disagreements, democracy has depended on a faith in the ability of common people to make informed judgments, both about their self-interest and what is perceived as the general good. Although always a regulative ideal that has been thwarted to one degree or another in reality, democracy has flourished only when a space for discussion and a mechanism for discursive will-formation has been possible, what Habermas has made famous as the "public sphere."

The precise boundaries of that public sphere have, of course, from the very first been at issue. Habermas's own formulation of a specifically bourgeois version of it came immediately under attack from those who insisted on proletarian or subaltern public spheres as well.

But the pressure has always been to expand it, to include the excluded. In the context of globalization in which information technologies permit unprecedented access and there is scarcely any limit on who can join the fray, the problem ironically may well be the opposite. That is, the rapid increase in participants in the discussion, or at least potential participants, means that it may be hard to hear any arguments over the din of so many voices, let alone have the ordered, rational discussion that democratic decision-making requires. The production and distribution of goods may benefit from economics of scale in which bigger is better (although this too is contestable), but meaningful democratic procedures break down when the numbers get too large. Rousseau's famous preference for small city states was ignored by his *soi-disant* followers who tried to realize his notion of a social contract in a country the size of eighteenth-century France. Even though his utopian notion of a univocal general will has been abandoned by most subsequent theorists of democracy, who prefer pluralist compromise to coerced consensus, his insight into the link between smallness and democracy has not.

Federalism and decentralization may, of course, be weapons in the struggle to keep the scale down. But when the challenges are those presented by a global economy that has long since left behind the boundaries of the nation-state, it is clear that local solutions may not really speak to mega-problems. No less disturbing is the realization that even if the procedures for registering informed opinion were operative and a virtual public sphere were made possible (Ross Perot's national referenda on an international scale), there is no mechanism through which decisions might be registered, let alone carried out. Globalization is a process in which the concept of sovereignty is outmoded, not merely because popular will is hard to express, but also because there is no actual sovereign who, in Carl Schmitt's celebrated definition, has the ultimate power to decide in a "state of emergency." The buck in the whirl of globalization doesn't stop anywhere; it just keeps on going. The system is increasingly interconnected and its fragmented parts totalized, but it has no apparent center. The metaphor of the rhizome, introduced by Deleuze and Guatteri a generation ago, has come into its own: there is a web, but there is no spider at the controls. Democracy cannot work unless chatter leads to action, but it is not at all clear how meaningful political action can occur in a globalized world in which things happen so fast that there seems time only for belated and defensive reactions.

To their credit, the organizers of the Kwangju Biennale were sensitive to this very issue. In the handsome catalogue that accompanied the exhibition, they included several essays that raised what one of their authors, the Slovenian philosopher/psychoanalyst Slavoj Žižek, called "the crucial question: *how are we to reinvent the political space in today's conditions of multinational globalization?*"[8] Žižek himself did not, however, really try to answer the question and other essays, such as John Rajchman's, only gesture to alternative possibilities. "Perhaps," he writes, "we need an image of 'the political' different from that of the 'enlightened republic' or of 'social transformation' which the nation-state form has managed to absorb. It might be put in this way: a politics of what cannot yet be 'represented' politically, of positing new questions *to* politics that are not yet *of* it; an art of thinking 'at the borders' of what counts as political, of introducing the other times and mapping other geographies into the simplicity of given determinations—a politics that complicates who we are, and may become."[9]

The vagueness of such formulations may be easy to lament, but it is much harder to come up with serious alternatives. The victims of the Kwangju massacre of 1980 were martyrs in a cause that cannot be belittled: resistance to an authoritarian and brutal military regime. They have achieved a posthumous vindication with the victory of Kim Dae Jung. But ironically, the democratization for which they died is still very much to be realized, at least to the extent that popular decision-making is increasingly impotent in a globalized world outside of anyone's control. The tombs of the people's gravesite have indeed been robbed and the simulacrum of an official cemetery put in their place. Although it may be possible to appropriate that space for the occasional artistic festival, when the installations are dismantled and the videos put back in their cassettes, the contradiction between globalization and genuine democratization remains glaringly unresolved. An unmapped world, alas, may be too protean and chaotic to produce the cleared space, like that of the ancient agora, where the institutional foundations of democracy can flourish.

9

MUST JUSTICE BE BLIND?
The Challenge of Images to the Law

Allegorical images of Justice, historians of iconography tell us,[1] did not always cover the eyes of the goddess, Justitia. In its earliest Roman incarnations, preserved on the coins of Tiberius' reign, the woman with the sword in one hand, representing the power of the state, and the scales in the other, derived from the weighing of souls in the Egyptian Book of the Dead,[2] was depicted as clear-sightedly considering the merits of the cases before her (figure 9.1). Medieval images of justice based on figures of Christ, St. Michael, or secular rulers likewise provided them with the ability to make their judgments on the basis of visual evidence (figure 9.2).

But suddenly at the end of the fifteenth century, a blindfold began to be placed over the Goddess's eyes, producing what has rightly been called "the most enigmatic of the attributes of Justice."[3] Perhaps the earliest image showing the change is a 1494 wood engraving of a Fool covering the eyes of Justice, illustrating Sebastian Brant's *Narrenschiff* (*Ship of Fools*), which was rapidly reproduced in translations throughout Europe (figure 9.3). Initially, as this engraving suggests, the blindfold implies that Justice has been robbed of her ability to get things straight, unable to wield her sword effectively or see what is balanced on her scales. Other medieval and Renaissance allegories of occluded vision, such as those of Death, Ambition, Cupidity, Ignorance, or Anger, were, in fact, uniformly negative. The figure of the nude child Cupid, as Erwin Panofsky pointed out many years ago, was depicted

Fig. 9.1a–9.1c Roman coins dedicated to Justice and Impartiality. Justitia's sword is not yet in place in these images, which show her with a staff instead. *Upper left,* dupondius of Tiberius, 22–23 A.D.; *upper right,* dupondius of Vespasian, 77–78 A.D.; *bottom,* areus of Marcus Aurelius, 168 A.D. Bibliothèque Nationale, Paris.

blindfolded not merely because love clouds judgment, but also because "he was on the wrong side of the moral world."[4]

By 1530, however, this satirical implication seems to have lost its power and the blindfold was transformed instead into a positive emblem of impartiality and equality before the law. Perhaps because of traditions transmitted by Plutarch and Diodore of Sicily from ancient Egypt that had depicted judges as blind or handless, the blindfold, like the scales, came to imply neutrality rather than helplessness. According to the French scholar Robert Jacob, the explanation may also have something to do with the reversal of fortunes experienced by the symbol of the Synagogue in medieval Christian iconography.[5] Traditionally shown as blindfolded—as well as with a broken lance—to symbolize her resistance to the illumination of divine light, the Synagogue was negatively contrasted with the open-eyed Church as in the famous early fourteenth-century statue on the south gate of Strasbourg Cathedral (figure 9.4).

What had been a sign of inferiority was, however, dramatically reversed when the iconophobic Reformation took seriously the Hebrew interdiction of images, the second of the Commandments Moses brought down from Mount Sinai. Now it was once again a virtue to resist what Augustine had famously called the "lust of the eyes." A blindfolded justice could thus avoid the seductions of images and achieve the necessary dispassionate distance to render verdicts impartially, an

Fig. 9.2 "The Eruption of Justice in Imaginary Causes: The Trial of Satan and the Queen Ratio," from *The Book of the King Modus and of the Queen Ratio,* fifteenth century. Library of the Arsenal, ms. 3080, fol. 103, xv. Bibliothèque Nationale, Paris.

Fig. 9.3 "The Fool Ties the Eyes of Justice," from Sebastian Brant, *La nef des folz du monde* (Lyon, 1497), figure 3. Bibliothèque Nationale, Paris.

argument advanced as early as the jurist Andrea Alciati's influential compendium of emblems, the *Emblemata* of 1531.[6] According to Christian-Nils Robert, this impartiality was required by the new urban, secular, bourgeois culture of the early modern period, which left behind the personalism of private, feudal justice. It was not by chance that many statues or fountains of blindfolded Justitia were placed in town squares in Northern Europe next to newly erected civic buildings, in which a nascent public sphere was in the process of emerging.[7] Even in Catholic countries like France, where churches remained flooded with images, secular edifices began to grow more austere.

Fig. 9.4 *The Synagogue*, sculpture on Strasbourg Cathedral, thirteenth century. Musée de Strasbourg.

The law was now to be presented entirely in language and justice dispensed only through language, necessitating discussion and persuasion, rather than appearing in images, which might overwhelm through dazzlement. Along with the iconoclastic purification of courtrooms of their artworks and lawbooks of their illustrations, at least in countries influenced by Reformation iconophobia, went the frequent robing of judges in sober black and white and the replacement of colorful seals by simple signatures on legal documents.[8] No longer would signs from heaven, like those informing medieval ordeals, be sufficient; now the words of men giving testimony about what they knew or had witnessed and then arguing about what rule might be violated would in most instances suffice. Although it is true that law was to be increasingly codified and preserved in written form, which has been interpreted by some as reflecting the modern privileging of sight because of its frequent use of visual metaphors,[9] the nonhieroglyphic script of Western languages meant that visual revelations of the truth, illuminations of divine will, were no longer relevant to the decision-making process. Along with the invisible "hidden God" of the Jansenists, who increasingly left the world to its own devices, went a justice that applied general rules and norms rather than looked for indications of divine dispensation. As with the later prohibition of laws referring to specific people with proper names condemned without due process, famously banned in the American Constitution as "bills of attainder," so too the interdiction on images was designed to thwart favoritism or personal vengeance. With the blindfolding of Justitia, we are well along the road to the modern cult of the abstract norm in juridical positivism.

If that road is paved with the prohibition of concrete images, we have to ask, however, whether or not building it had hidden costs, which we may still be paying today. In what follows, it is precisely this question that will occupy us. One place to begin an answer would be the observation in Max Horkheimer and Theodor Adorno's celebrated accusation in *Dialectic of Enlightenment* that the modern notion of justice was still beholden to a mythic assumption: the fetish of equivalence, the desire for perfect commensurability, the domination of the exchange principle:

> For mythic and enlightened justice, guilt and atonement, happiness and unhappiness were sides of an equation. Justice is subsumed in law. . . . The blindfold over Justitia's eyes does not only mean there should be no assault on justice, but that justice does not originate in freedom.[10]

Unexpectedly, in the light of the Frankfurt School's often-remarked embrace of the Jewish taboo on idolatrous images as a mark of resistance to a prematurely positive utopian thought, Horkheimer and Adorno here register a protest against the complete banishment of images. The preservation of the ability to see they cryptically associate with freedom, a freedom that is threatened when justice is reduced to law. What, it has to be asked, is this freedom which the blindfolding of Justitia denies? How does the reduction of justice to law threaten its very existence?

One explanation is suggested by the famous argument developed by Lessing in his classical treaty on aesthetics, *Laocoön*, in favor of the Greek regulation of images, an argument drawing the critical attention of W. J. T. Mitchell in his influential study of images, texts and ideologies, *Iconology*.[11] According to Lessing, images should be kept under legal control because of their capacity to depict monsters, those indecorous amalgams of the human and divine or the human and the bestial that are a scandal to the alleged order of nature. Mitchell interprets Lessing's iconophobia as symptomatic of an anxiety over proper sex roles and adulterous fantasies, but it might be just as plausible to see it as a fear of boundary transgression in general, especially the boundaries that define and circumscribe our bodies. Lessing's visual monsters are an affront to the law because they depart from the assumption that the boundaried categories we use to order the world are ones under which all its particulars can be subsumed. The image of a hybridized creature, at once man and beast, divine and human, male and female, confounds our reliance on conceptual subsumption by refusing to be an exemplar of a general rule.

The freedom of which Horkheimer and Adorno speak is thus the ability of the particular, the unique, the incommensurable, the improper to escape from the dominating power of the exchange principle that is manifested in universalizing concepts and in the reduction of justice to the law of equivalents. The eye, by far the most discriminating of the senses in its ability to register minute differences, must therefore be closed to produce this reduction. Justitia's vision is veiled so that she is able to maintain the fiction that each judgment before her can be understood as nothing more than a "case" of something more general, equivalent to other like cases, and subsumable under a general principle that need only be applied without regard for individual uniqueness. That general principle is understood to hover somewhere above specific cases, recalling the origin of the word justice in the Latin *iubeo* (to command). This is a version of justice, as Vassilis Lambropoulos has recently pointed out, that can be understood as "the right command, the command that rightfully deserves obedience. What is right is what is decreed as straight, the line of the ruler and the regime directing from above, the regal control, the reign of the supreme direction. . . . 'Justice' comes from above, from the realm of certainty."[12] It is thus unlike the Greek notion of *Dike*, which in certain of its acceptations involved a dynamic, polemical balance between contraries, an agonistic ethos based on proportion and analogy that could not be subsumed under a single *nomos* or law.[13]

It will doubtless have occurred to many of you that achieving this effect of regal control required not merely a blindfold, but also one placed over the eyes of a specifically female deity. Granted, as Christian-Nils Robert has argued,[14] Justitia may be a somewhat androgynous figure, at least to the extent that she wields a powerful symbol of coercive authority, a sword fit for swift decapitations. Traditional religious iconography had, in fact, permitted its use only infrequently to women, the most notable instance being Judith, the slayer of Holofernes, in the Hebrew Bible. The stern and vaguely menacing statues of Justitia in front of the Palaces of Justice in early modern Europe were certainly a far cry from the maternal images of the forgiving, mediating Madonna that populated so many medieval churches. Nor were they reminiscent of so many sainted, suffering female martyrs, whose assigned role was that of passive victim bearing witness to their faith, even if one might detect a certain symmetry between the blindfolded criminal condemned to die and the image of blindfolded executioner.[15] As a result, Justitia may plausibly be interpreted as a symbol of the very temporal power, firmly in male hands, that sought to displace the spiritual power that had accrued to the cult of Mary in the late Middle Ages. Neoclassical images with martial overtones were, after all, the source of this allegory, not religious ones.

And yet, it must be acknowledged that blindfolded Justitia, with all of her warlike attributes, was still primarily a female figure, as had been the Egyptian Maat (not only the Goddess of justice, but also of truth and order) and the Greek Dike, who was the daughter of Zeus. Male images of divine justice, such as that of God at the Last Judgment or Saint Michael, had not been prevented from exercising the power of vision. Solomon famously could see how the two contesting mothers felt about the dividing of the child they both claimed as their own. What was the implication of preventing a female judge from seeing? What power might still be lurking beneath her blindfold, which, after all, does not permanently rob the Goddess of her sight?

What that power may be is suggested by the traditional reading of another image from a slightly later era, Jan Vermeer's "Woman Weighing Pearls" of 1662–1663 (figure 9.5). Depicted in front of a picture of the Last Judgment, thought to be by Cornelisz Enhelbreecht, the woman with the delicate scales in her hands appears to be looking soberly and carefully at the individual pearls in each tray, as if she were contemplatively pondering their particular value. Or at least so the traditional interpretation of the canvas has assumed. Whether or not she is actually doing so is a question to which I will return shortly. But whatever the target of her gaze, there is no trace of judgmental harshness or vindictiveness in her visage; indeed these seem to be traits that the blissfully serene Vermeer was simply incapable of depicting. As

Fig. 9.5 Jan Vermeer, *Woman Holding a Balance,* 1664. National Gallery of Art (Widener Collection), Washington, D.C.

with the souls whose salvation is judged in the scene behind her, each pearl, that precious object mirroring the world around it that is so often at the symbolic center of Vermeer's paintings, seems worth careful, deliberate scrutiny. The setting, moreover, is a typical Vermeer interior, a private, intimate, humble realm, far from the public space of the early modern statues of Justitia.

The Goddess's gender as mediated by this comparison with Vermeer's painting is relevant here if we recall the contrast between male and female variants of moral reasoning posited by feminists like Carol Gilligan and Seyla Benhabib against moral theorists like Lawrence Kohlberg and John Rawls.[16] Whereas male judgment often tends to be abstractly universalist, decontextualized, and formalistic, its female counterpart, they tell us, is more frequently sensitive to individual detail, narrative uniqueness, and specific contexts. Instead of acknowledging only an imagined "generalized other," it focuses instead on the actual "concrete other" before it. The blindfolding of Justitia is thus not a thwarting of the gaze per se, but of the specifically female gaze, or at least of those qualities that have been associated with it in our culture.[17] It is thus ultimately in the service of the disembodiment, disembeddedness, and decontextualization that a legalistic justice based on the reductive equivalence of the exchange principle requires.

The complete victory of what has recently been dubbed "algorithmic justice"[18] because it involves following binding rules decreed from above is, to be sure, substantially modified in a legal system such as the Anglo-American, in which concrete precedent is often as important as statute as the basis for judgment. Here Kant's well-known contrast between reflective and determinant judgments, the former applied to aesthetic issues, the latter to cognitive and moral ones, might be invoked to justify the paradigmatic value of prior specific examples over abstract rules that are universally binding. But there is still in the law of precedent the presupposition of at least analogical commensurability from case to case. Even reflective judgments, after all, draw on the presumption of a "sensus communis," a shared sentiment that goes beyond the arbitrary whim of idiosyncratic taste. If not by subsumption, then by analogy, what is different is somehow compelled to become similar through resemblance. In addition, the common law of precedent can be said to collapse the temporal difference between past and present in its search for a replicable standard of measurement.

Although images can, of course, themselves be the object of such judgments, their initial, brute impact on the beholder's sense of sight may well be prior to any evaluation, reflective or determinant, of their meaning. Even Kant's a priori categories do not, after all, include a necessary mechanism of cultural, symbolic commensuration. If Horkheimer and Adorno are right, mute visuality retains traces of a mode of interaction between humans and the world that is prior to conceptual subsumption or the rule of common sense, a mode they call mimetic. This is not the place to launch a full-fledged analysis of the vexed concept of mimesis in their work, an analysis I have tentatively attempted to make elsewhere.[19] Suffice it to say that they understood mimesis to involve a nondominating relationship between subjects and objects in which the world was not "subjected" to categorical determination or even intersubjective consensus. Mimesis meant a more passive affinity between perceiver and perceived rather than a hierarchical control by one over the other. Affinity, it should immediately be noted, does not mean identity or equivalence, as the mimesis between subject and object maintains a certain, irreducible difference between them. Insofar as images and their referents, representations and originals, perceptions and objects, may be similar, but not ontologically identical, they resist the full power of the exchange principle. Thus the image need not be of an imaginary monster, transgressing natural boundaries, to do its work of resistance; it need merely evoke the primal power of mimetic affinity, which acknowledges differences even as it seeks similarities, against the counterpower of conceptual subsumption, which seeks to suppress the remainder left behind in the act of subsuming.

What ultimately distinguishes mimetic from conceptual behavior, according to this argument, is the absence of violence in the former, the symbolic violence, that is, of categorical subsumption, which finds an echo in the potential for literal force heard in the phrase to "enforce the law." Justitia, it should be remembered, is never depicted without her unsheathed sword.[20] As Jacques Derrida has recently pointed out in his meditation on Walter Benjamin's famous essay "Critique of Violence," there may well be a moment of originary violence or brute force in the foundation of even the most legitimate of laws: "Applicability, 'enforceability,' is not an exterior or secondary possibility that may or may not be added as a supplement to law," he writes. "It is the force essentially implied in the very concept of *justice as law*."[21] "Here we can detect an echo of the argument from Horkheimer and Adorno's *Dialectic of Enlightenment*: that a justice reduced to a law of equivalence based on the subsumption of individual cases under a general rule, the "algorithmic justice" produced by commands from above, involves violence and restricts freedom. A justice that would evade the binding force of the algorithm would follow the logic of the gratuitous gift, bestowed without an expectation of reciprocity, rather than that of the debt paid to even out a score, that primitive act of vengeance that Nietzsche famously saw at the root of modern notions of exchange.[22] It would be incalculable, impossible to capture in definitions, irreducibly aporetic, perhaps even dangerously mad. Always either a memory of what may have been or a hope for a future that can perhaps be, but never actually is, it haunts the project of fully realized justice in the present, a justice based on blinding one's eyes to the absolute alterity of each of its alleged cases, a justice reduced to nothing but the positive, formal, abstract law. As such, it is the basis not only of religious notions of divine justice, but also of every defense of a revolutionary "political justice" that can claim the right to suspend the laws prevailing in a system that can itself be deemed unjust.[23]

But both dialectical and deconstructionist modes of thinking, as we know, resist simple binary oppositions, and so too this overly abstract dichotomy must itself be shaken. Allegedly nonviolent, gratuitous justice based on respect for absolute particularity and the benign mimesis of nature cannot be placed entirely on the other side of a divide from the putatively sinister, coercive force of law as command from above. In "Critique of Violence," Benjamin had in fact juxtaposed a divine violence, which destroys laws and transgresses boundaries, to a mythical one that makes and conserves them.[24] Although he cryptically described the former as "lethal without spilling blood,"[25] the troubling implication was that a justice beyond the law of formal equivalence, the life-affirming justice of absolute qualitative singularity based on the logic of the gift, was not itself somehow beyond coercion. For without any rules or criteria at all, what was to prevent a *soi-disant* divine justice from descending into nothing more than the principle "might makes right?" As Derrida himself uneasily concludes, "in one form or another, the undecidable is on each side, and is the violent condition of knowledge or action."[26]

Similarly, Horkheimer and Adorno were never willing to pit mimetic affinity against conceptual reflection as if they were simple opposites, one inherently superior to the other, one the singular locus of freedom, the other of mere repression. Discussing the residue of mimetic behavior that can be found in the work of art in his *Aesthetic Theory*, Adorno wrote,

> The desideratum of visuality seeks to preserve the mimetic moment of art. What this view does not realize is that mimesis only goes on living through its antithesis, which is rational control by art works over all that is heterogeneous to them. If this is ignored, visuality becomes a fetish.[27]

In art, he argued, it was important to avoid the either/or of sensuality vs. spirituality, which simply repeats the alienation characteristic of modern life. Instead, the paradoxical mixture of the two must be preserved, for

> What lurks behind the false synthesis called aesthetic vision is a rigid polarity between spirit and sensuality which is inadequate. At the center of the aesthetic of vision is the false, thing-like notion that in the aesthetic artifact tensions have been synthesized into a state of rest, whereas in fact those tensions are essential to the work.[28]

If we return to our point of departure, the blindfolding of Justitia, we can now understand that it was perhaps not entirely without some reason that vision was denied even to a female gaze in the name of impartiality and the banishment of monsters. Like the other "fools" in medieval tales, who often speak a higher truth, the fool who blindfolds the Goddess on Sebastian Brant's ship may have known what he was doing after all. For like the false synthesis of the aesthetic artifact, a practice of judgment based solely on the power of an immediate visual apprehension of irreducible singularity risks succumbing to the illusory potential that always accompanies sensual perception, however acute.

There is also another powerful justification for the allegorical image of the blindfold. Because her eyes are covered, Justitia must walk cautiously into the future, not rushing headlong to judgment.[29] Vermeer's open-eyed, female weigher of pearls can be shown without a blindfold because her judgment is allegorically linked to that of the Last Judgment in the canvas depicted behind her. But a secular judgment that is anything but the last, a justice of mere mortals, cannot pretend to possess so clear-sighted a sense of whose soul merits salvation and whose does not. It must acknowledge that imperfect general laws and the concrete judgments of those who apply them somehow always fall short of an absolute and final justice, and yet that both are necessary means in the endless struggle to realize that unrealizable goal.

It must furthermore accept the fact that even the most comprehensive notion of justice contains within it a pluralism of distinct logics that may sometimes be in conflict.[30] Procedural notions of justice within an established order, those that subordinate it to positive law, are likely to be in tension with compensatory, distributive, restitutive, and retributive alternatives that may well point beyond that order. A justice that remembers and tries to redress the wrongs of the past and one that hopes to create a truly just society in the future can easily be at odds with formal procedures in the present, as any observer of the heated debate over affirmative action in the United States can well attest. Rather than a single overarching criterion, there may be several that cannot be perfectly reconciled, but this does not mean that it is better to throw out general considerations altogether and judge decisionistically.

Unexpectedly, this point is suggested in visual terms by the same Vermeer painting discussed earlier as an example of a benign woman's gaze at concrete particulars. For recent scientific analysis of the pigments on the canvas has revealed that the scales do not, in fact, contain pearls, as has traditionally been thought, but are empty instead.[31] What shines is apparently only the light reflecting off the trays. Rather than directed at individual cases, the woman's contemplative gaze, we now can appreciate, falls on the apparatus itself, as if she were weighing its merits as an impartial mechanism of fairness, albeit one then used to judge the worth of each pearl.

A justice, in other words, that tries to see only concrete, contingent, incommensurable particularity and judge without *any* abstract prescriptive criteria whatsoever—such as that recently defended, for example, by Jean-François Lyotard in *Just Gaming*[32]—may paradoxically be as blind is one that pretends to be entirely algorithmic. What is needed, as Adorno points out in the case of aesthetic judgment, is a creative tension between the two, a justice that can temper the rigor of conceptual subsumption, or more precisely, several such subsumptions, with a sensitivity to individual particularity. The unresolvable paradox of the relationship between law and justice, as the Slovenian philosopher Jelica Šumić-Riha has recently argued, may, in fact, require a certain measure of blindness. "We know," she writes,

> that law as such is not and cannot be just. However, if we accept that and behave according to this knowledge, we will have lost not only justice, but also law. Law is namely conceived as an instance that appeals to justice which means that a law that does not refer to justice is simply not a law. It is therefore in some way necessary to blind ourselves to this knowledge. In Derrida's terms: even if justice cannot be reduced to rule-governed activity we must respect rules. We must respect them because in the very undecidability of justice on the one hand and the groundlessness of law on the other lies the danger that the right to do justice can be usurped by bad legislators.[33]

Perhaps it is best, therefore, to imagine the Goddess Justitia neither as fully sighted nor as blindfolded, but rather as she was once visually depicted at the threshold of the modern world, in a mid-sixteenth century frontispiece to J. De Damhoudere's *Praxis rerum civilium*: Justitia, that is, as a goddess with not one face, but two. The first has eyes that are wide open, able to discern difference, alterity, and non-identity, looking in the direction of the hand that wields her sword, while the second, facing the other hand with the calculating scales of rule-governed impartiality, has eyes that are veiled (figure 9.6). For only the image of a two-faced deity, a hybrid, monstrous creature which we can in fact see, an allegory that resists subsumption under a general concept, only such an image can do, as it were, justice to the negative, even perhaps aporetic, dialectic that entangles law and justice itself.

Fig. 9.6 Justice with two faces, one veiled, the other with eyes open, frontispiece of J. de Damhoudere, *Praxis rerum civilium* . . . (Anvers, 1567). Bibliothèque Nationale, Paris.

10

DIVING INTO THE WRECK
Aesthetic Spectatorship at the Turn of the Millennium

The most successful movie in the history of the cinema, measured at least by international box office receipts and Oscar awards, is, of course, James Cameron's 1997 epic romance *Titanic.* Part of its magic—indeed for those of us resistant to the adolescent soap opera at its core, *all* of its magic—derived from the opening sequences in which actual footage of the recent exploration of the wreck of the *Titanic,* discovered in 1985 by Robert Ballard and Jean-Louis Michel, was used to frame the flashback recreation of the events that produced it. Here the thrill of penetrating the secrets of the deep and rummaging around in the barnacle-encrusted remains of the greatest ship ever built reaches almost voyeuristic heights. A giddy feeling of transgression accompanies the submarine camera's invasion of the noble wreck on the ocean floor, still the watery tomb of so many of its victims.

Accompanying that sentiment, and indeed reinforced by the class dynamics of the romance invented by the filmmaker, is an inevitable sense of rough justice produced by the humbling of those arrogant enough to defy nature, figured by an immovable iceberg, and proclaim the ship they crashed into it "unsinkable." This is not merely the wreck of a machine, we are immediately instructed to feel, but also that of the hubris of those who built and sailed it. As with all of the earlier allegorizations of the *Titanic* story, we are given a cautionary tale of the dangers of overweening Faustian technology. What, of course, complicates this moral is the use of the most advanced contemporary technological feats, robotic submarine cameras and the computer simulation of the wreck itself, in the making of the film. Postmodern virtual technology trumps the clunky machines of the modern technological era.

Such a complex reaction, we learn from reading Hans Blumenberg's remarkable essay *Shipwreck with Spectator: Paradigm for a Metaphor for Existence*, is not, however, a recent response to shipwrecks of the magnitude of the *Titanic*.[1] For the ancient Greeks, living at a time when any attempt to leave dry land was a dangerous and risky enterprise, all such wrecks bore witness to the costs of challenging the given order of things. "There is a frivolous, if not blasphemous moment inherent in all human seafaring," Blumenberg notes, "on a par with an offense against the invulnerability of the earth, the law of *terra inviolata*, which seemed to forbid cutting through isthmuses or building artificial harbors—in other words, radical alterations of the relationship between land and sea."[2] Whereas only mythical figures like Icarus sought to defy the comparable taboo against leaving the earth for the air and paid for their pride by falling to their deaths, many actual men were tempted enough by a sea voyage to allow the Greeks to make the shipwreck a metaphor for the perils of existence itself, or at least for those bold and impious souls who tempted their fate.

But what of the spectator who watches the spectacle from afar? What of the witness who sees the foolhardy sailors go under from the safe haven of dry land? Is the moral lesson he learns the only effect that it has on him? Is his only response mortification and humility? Or does he derive a secret pleasure from knowing that he is the survivor and not the victim? Does he perhaps even feel a certain *Schadenfreude* at the sight of transgression rewarded by catastrophe? There have been, in fact, several possible responses to these questions. Perhaps the earliest was voiced by the Roman poet and philosopher Lucretius, who did not enjoy the suffering he witnessed, but gained contentment from the security of his own position, that of the philosopher, sage, or theorist, who can view nature from the heights of his superior wisdom. Another reaction Blumenberg identifies with Montaigne, who justified the pleasure of the spectator, which he admitted is malicious enjoyment, "by his successful self-preservation. By virtue of his capacity for this distance, he stands unimperiled on the solid ground of the shore. He survives through one of his useless qualities: the ability to be a spectator." Rather than producing the real happiness of the classical sage, however, "its comfort is something like the cunning of nature, in that it sets a premium on taking as little risk as possible with one's life and rewards distance with enjoyment."[3] Still a third response was expressed by Enlightenment thinkers like Voltaire, who know that to gain something, something must be risked, and therefore that progress entails a willingness to leave safe harbors behind. Shipwrecks, of course, continue to happen, but now they only excite the morbid curiosity of spectators who lack the ennobling self-reflection attributed to them by Lucretius or even the prudent self-satisfaction assigned by Montaigne.

There was, Blumenberg points out, a significant displacement in the use of the metaphor in the 1770s by the Neapolitan Abbé Ferdinando Galiani, who moved it from the ethical to the aesthetic sphere by comparing viewing a shipwreck to the spectatorship of an audience in a theater. Human curiosity, he argued against Voltaire, is different from that of animals because of our ability to view horrors without being afraid. Indeed, the precondition of curiosity is precisely a sense of personal safety comparable to that enjoyed while viewing a play. In a theatrical experience, spectators know that the events are artificial and therefore are spared the sense of genuine anxiety produced by a real disaster. Aesthetic enjoyment, as other Enlightenment thinkers from at least the time of Shaftesbury made clear, is intimately tied up with disinterested contemplation. Even the awe, terror, and vertigo that we feel when confronted with what has come to be called the sublime are endurable because they are contained in an aesthetic frame. In the later variation on this position developed by Schopenhauer, it is precisely the ability to suspend interest and the will that provides respite from the unremitting turmoil of life. Not only does the spectator gain the ability to view without passion sublime scenes of horror and catastrophe, but she also achieves, if only fleetingly, a disinterested relationship to her own self and its petty interests.

A less coldhearted reading of aesthetic spectatorship is evident in the ruminations of a thinker who is not included in Blumenberg's discussion in *Shipwreck with Spectator*, although treated extensively elsewhere in his work, Immanuel Kant. In his famous response to the French Revolution in *The Contest of the Faculties*, Kant argued that despite the violence and turmoil of the events themselves, which he explicitly did not recommend for emulation in other countries, from the perspective of the disinterested spectator, they could be judged as playing a valuable role in the progress of the species. The precise metaphor of the shipwreck was not, to be sure, used by Kant, which explains Blumenberg's exclusion of him from his account, but the implication is very similar: from the contemplative point of view of the spectator, a point of view in which aesthetic and political judgment are conflated, it is possible to look dispassionately on a violent and even calamitous event and find in it something to applaud. The key is to judge from the point of view of an imagined future subject of history, who is able to look back on the process with an understanding denied to the present. Blessed with the gift of narrative, he is able to situate apparent random chaos in a longer meaningful story. Indeed, as Hannah Arendt pointed out in her posthumously published *Lectures on Kant's Political Philosophy*, Kant thought that by assuming the general viewpoint of the "world spectator" whose taste, imagination, and hope could transfigure events like shipwrecks or revolutions into ciphers of human improvement, one might transcend the despair aroused by a less elevated perspective.[4] Only then might the partial and incomplete vantage points of the actual actors be overcome and a more totalizing viewpoint be achieved, one which could provide a kind of historical theodicy for the suffering of those in the wreck itself.

Against all of these ethical and aesthetic metaphorizations of the shipwreck metaphor, which depend on the rigid distinction between the spectator and the disaster he or she witnesses, Blumenberg also discerns an important subordinate current, which was first evident in Pascal and emerged full-blown in Nietzsche. Here the main claim is that the security of the safe haven, the belief that one can be a spectator on dry land, is nothing but a fraudulent illusion. Existence in this use of the metaphor is identified precisely with always already being embarked on the sea voyage that is life. In Blumenberg's gloss, "the skeptic's abstention, which Montaigne had expressed through remaining in the harbor, is in Pascal's view not an option. The metaphorics of embarkation includes the suggestion that living means already being on the high seas, where there is no outcome other than being saved or going down, and no possibility of abstention."[5] Pascal's Christian version of this trope, which underpinned his famous argument for the need to wager without secure knowledge on God's existence, was turned by Nietzsche into a kind of "heroic nihilism," in which no dry land really exists. The pretense of modern science, like that of dogmatic religion, to provide such a terra firma cannot, according to Nietzsche, be upheld.

The result, as Nietzsche's great friend Jacob Burckhardt was to understand, is that the disinterested observer position—in historical scholarship as well as natural science—is an inherently impossible goal. "We would like to know the waves on which we sail across the ocean," the Swiss historian writes, "but we ourselves are these waves."[6] Kant's judge cannot avoid being caught up in the tumultuous events he wants to view from afar; disinterested aesthetic contemplation or post facto totalization is not given to humans who must be actors, whether they want to or not. We are, in other words, like the wretched survivors on Géricault's *Raft of the Medusa*, forever waving in vain towards a ship on the horizon that never comes back to pick us up (or, like the actual ship on which the painting was based, comes too late to save most victims). To put the same point in a somewhat different vocabulary, that of contemporary philosophy, we live in a world without ontological or axiological foundations; there is no firm ground beneath our feet. It is, we might say, swirling water "all the way down," and, like poor doomed Leonardo di Caprio at the end of *Titanic*, all we have are random planks on which to cling desperately for temporary support as we are buffeted by the icy waves. In fact, even modern scientists like Emil Du Bois-Reymond came to understand, according to Blumenberg, that all we can do is build new ships out of the planks left behind by previous wrecks, which may be better than grasping at mere straws, but is not sufficient to put us on dry land.

These two alternative readings of the shipwreck metaphor are not only metaphors for existence in general—*Paradigma einer Daseinsmetaphysik* is the subtitle of Blumenberg's book—but also can be taken to represent two opposing modes of aesthetic experience more narrowly construed. It is in this latter, more modest guise that they will attract our attention in this essay. In what follows, I want to explore the modes of aesthetic spectatorship that dominate much of contemporary culture. The first position, that of the disinterested spectator able to view and judge the wreck from the safe distance of dry land, retains a certain power for those who still maintain the possibility of a contemplative or reflexively detached relationship to the objects of aesthetic experience. Whether in the guise of Duchampian visual indifference, New Critical formalist ironism, or Brechtian epic drama, just to suggest a heterogeneous sampling of this position, its proponents share a sense that a frame still separates us from the object. Although we can thematize the frame, even, as in the case of the Brechtian alienation effect, turn it into a source of critical enlightenment about the illusions of traditional theatricality, what endures is a sense that we can still avoid being drawn entirely into the picture. In the manner of Lucretius, Montaigne, Voltaire, and Galiani, we can still hold on to the distinction between spectator and shipwreck. Even for those approaches suspicious of the Enlightenment fetish of disinterestedness—the Brechtian alienation effect, for example, is designed to show us how interested we should be in what we are watching—critical distance and the ability to distinguish between what is on one side of the frame and what is on the other are still highly valued. Even those who understand the frame in essentially nonaesthetic terms, as a product of art as a social institution, do not seek to dissolve it entirely as mere historical artifact.

There has, however, been an intermittently powerful resistance to this position, now increasingly getting the upper hand, which prefers the aesthetic equivalent of the Pascalian/Nietzschean alternative. That is, it distrusts the distinction between spectators and shipwrecks, striving instead to give us the experience of being embarked on the tumultuous seas, whether we like it or not. An exemplary instance of this position can be found in the famous poem of 1972 by Adrienne Rich, whose title I have borrowed for this essay. In the first line of "Diving into the Wreck," Rich's narrator tells us that she has first read the book of myths before getting her equipment on to jump into the water; she has first encountered whatever it is that is her goal through a textual mediation, an aesthetic cum metaphysical frame. But she must descend into the water-logged wreck itself to find what she seeks:

I came to explore the wreck.
The words are purposes.
The words are maps.
I came to see the damage that was done
and the treasures that prevail.
I stroke the beam of my lamp
slowly along the flank
of something more permanent
than fish or weed

the thing I came for:
the wreck and not the story of the wreck
the thing itself and not the myth"[7]

No longer a distant spectator of a shipwreck or one who knows it only through the legends that have crept up around it, the narrator becomes an androgynous mermaid/merman in a black rubber suit, who dives into the hold and becomes one with the victims:

I am she: I am he

whose drowned face sleeps with open eyes . . .

. . . .

we are the half-destroyed instruments
that once held to a course
the water-eaten log
the fouled compass

We are, I am, you are
by cowardice or courage
the one who find our way

back to this scene
carrying a knife, a camera
a book of myths
in which
our names do not appear.[8]

"Diving into the Wreck" has often been understood as a feminist manifesto, the obsolete myths to be discarded being those of patriarchy—books where women's names are not written—and the wreckage that of traditional gender relations.[9] But Rich's hunger for more direct experience, her desire to mingle with the victims and lose her privileged identity as a survivor, even to become one with the never animate "half-destroyed instruments" of the ship, can also be understood to express a widely shared impatience with the safety of spectatorial distance. It betrays a yearning to conflate historical returns to previous wrecks with the vertiginous experience of being in an actual one here and now.

Various manifestations of this desire can be discerned across the divide that separates high from low culture, the avant-garde from popular entertainment. To take examples from the latter first, the late nineteenth century saw the rapid dwindling of interest in such mass cultural devices as the panorama or the diorama, which had enjoyed enormous success in the preceding hundred years.[10] These all involved stationary or slowly turning subjects, who could marvel at the visual illusions created by the magic of the scenes in front of or surrounding them. Despite the extraordinary efforts made to create effects of reality, what inevitably was missing was any sense of the corporeal integration of the viewer into the action. Indeed, in panoramas, the lack of action was precisely what produced their supreme tranquility, as even battle scenes of great violence were frozen in a moment of eternalized time.

Near the end of the nineteenth century, however, new, more kinesthetic amusements arose to collapse the gap between viewer and viewed, indeed to dethrone the contemplative eye as the predominant sensual mediation with the world. As visitors to the great world exhibitions began to grow bored with panoramas or traditional static pavilions showing the quaint customs of the exotic other, they demanded more stimulating, carnivalesque distractions, ones designed to shock and dazzle. "Distractions," let it be noted, not instructional or reflective tableaux. In such inventions as the roller coaster and loop-the-loop, a land-based version of being tossed by the stormy seas was concocted to produce a new sensation of excitement and danger. In fact, in the Paris exhibition of 1900, something called the "mareorama" was designed to give the actual sensation of seasickness.[11] These "incredible scream machines," to borrow the title of Robert Cantrell's history of their advent, broke down the barrier between spectator and at least the feeling of being in or on the verge of a wreck.[12] No moral lessons were being learned, no metaphors of existence were being mobilized, no theodicy of historical improvement was invoked; all that counted was the thrill and terror of the vertiginous experience itself, the delicious shock of what tellingly came to be called "kicks."

Not only did the visuality of contemplative spectatorship give way to the more tactile and kinaesthetic charge produced by disorienting motion, so too did the very distinction between subject and object. As the cultural critic Lieven de Cauter has argued, vertigo machines, unlike such predominantly visual counterparts as the outmoded panorama, entailed a conflation of self and apparatus. Their purpose was what he calls "synergetic pleasure," literally "joy-rides" caused by the projection of lust onto the machine in which the hurtling body was precariously cradled.[13] Fixed gender roles, other commentators have claimed, were temporarily disrupted by amusements that threw men and women together in a frenzied disequilibrium.[14] Later devices from speedboats and snowmobiles to skateboards and bungee-jumping reinforced the transition from a scopic regime of pleasure relying on visual representation to a kinaesthetic regime based on rapturous stimulation and participatory immediacy.

Often, as Jeffrey Schnapp has noted in a recent essay entitled "Crash (Speed as Engine of Individuation)," the boundary between amusements like the roller coaster and new modes of functional transportation with increased velocity, such as the railroad and motor car, began to break down.[15] In fact, it was already beginning to erode, he argues, as early as the eighteenth century, with the dissemination of passenger-carrying mail-coaches. Although the invention of such devices could be used to transport people more rapidly like passive commodities, they also could serve as nonutilitarian mechanisms of titillation, whose thrills went hand in hand with the risks they entailed to life and limb. What Schnapp calls the intoxicating "sublime of speed" experienced by a "kinematic subject" ultimately found its fulfillment not in safe journeys, but in "spectacular accidents—fires, revolutions, hallucinatory landscapes, crashes, news events, panics—unruly events that, no matter how remote, remain so menacingly close that they can be measured on a scale of intensity but not delight. Aesthetic play has been recast as dangerous play. . . ."[16]

Perhaps the most widespread example of a new popular entertainment producing effects of vertiginous disorientation can be found in what is often seen as a quintessentially visual medium, the cinema. It was Sergei Eisenstein who employed the term "attractions" to describe "the sensual and psychological impact" of a nonrepresentational, non-realistic theater, whose impact he sought to duplicate through the use of montage in his films of the 1920s. The film historian Tom Gunning has extrapolated from this usage to coin the phrase "cinema of attractions" to describe early, prenarrative movies before 1907, movies whose sensational appeal went beyond the mere illusionistic effect of coolly reproducing what was later called the film's "diegetic" reality.[17] Rather than merely showing something in a dispassionate way or spinning out a narrative tale, these films actively attracted viewers as in a vaudeville show, producing a sensation of immediacy and involvement that narrowed the gap between spectator and spectacle. Instead of disciplining the viewer to sit quietly and contemplate the scene from a safe distance, a skill that historians have traced to eighteenth- and nineteenth-century concert hall and theater audiences,[18] they produced a viscerally excited, sometimes libidinally aroused, sometimes violently terrorized body that was more than a passive eye. Although surviving in such avant-garde films as *Chien Andalou*, this outcome was no longer as highly prized by what became known as "classical Hollywood cinema" launched by D. W. Griffith, which depended instead on a more dispassionate spectator able to master the story line that passed before his or her eyes and identify psychologically with the characters in that story.

Other commentators, however, have remarked on the vigorous return of the cinema of attractions to mainstream films in recent years. Linda Williams has suggestively read Hitchcock's *Psycho*, released in 1960, as the crucial transitional film. Rather than an attempt to exploit and expose the voyeuristic male gaze, as has traditionally been claimed, it is better understood, she argues, as an exercise in destabilizing gender identities through a masochistic involvement with the erotic violence depicted on the screen. "It is the moment," she writes, "when the experience of going to the movies began to be constituted as providing a certain generally transgressive sexualized thrill of promiscuous abandonment to indeterminate, 'other' identities."[19] By the 1970s, with blockbuster thrillers like *Jaws*, *Star Wars*, and *Raiders of the Lost Ark*, Hollywood was turning out films that relied on special effects and sensorial overload to duplicate the visceral impact of the early cinema of attractions. As another film historian, Thomas Schatz has argued, these box office monsters were more like amusement park rides than contemplative exercises in dispassionate viewing pleasure; in fact, at Universal Studies and Disneyland in Los Angeles, some of them were actually transformed into literal rides.[20] Significantly, as Williams has remarked, the biggest grossing film of all time—prior, that is, to *Titanic*—was itself the story of a theme park filled with prehistoric dinosaurs, which ends with violence, death, and the spectacular crash of its overweening owner's pretentious dreams: *Jurassic Park*.[21]

If students of popular culture have been able to discern many examples of spectators eagerly diving into the wreck or at least into its simulation, it is no more difficult to find comparable examples in what usually passes for its elite or avant-garde counterpart. The nineteenth-century separation between unruly mass cultural participation and constrained high cultural distantiation traced by historians like Lawrence Levine has increasingly come undone. In fact, such a reversal is often taken to be one of the marks of the postmodernist era. But, it can easily be discerned in such earlier avant-garde movements as Surrealism and Futurism. As I have tried to demonstrate at length elsewhere, there was a strong countercurrent in modernism that criticized the hegemony of timeless, visual form and the disinterested spectator, seeking instead a more visceral and proximate involvement in the formless mush of base materiality.[22] With Georges Bataille's now celebrated defense of the *informe*, Surrealism sought to dissolve the solidity of the Cartesian or Kantian subject, undo the primacy of ocularcentric spectatorship, and reunite us with the abjected "lower" dimensions of our psychic and cultural life.[23] In the terms of a Burckhardt, they wanted to bring us back to the precarious condition of being the waves themselves or at least tossed on the foam, and not a distant observer safely hovering above their surging tumult.

Even more explicitly, the Futurists were determined to thrust the spectator into the violent wreckage of modern life. An actual automobile accident in 1908, Jeffrey Schnapp shows in the essay mentioned earlier, preceded F. T. Marinetti's famous manifesto of the following year. "Recasting trauma as ecstasy, accident as adventure, death drive as joy ride," the Futurist leader, writes Schnapp, saw violent shocks as "engines of bliss: as orgasm, rapturous play, release from the constraints of analytical reason, regression to states of infantile narcissism or pre-Oedipal boundarylessness."[24] Significantly, as Gunning has noted, Marinetti was also an enthusiast of the theater and cinema of attractions, which he hoped would put an end to the "'static', 'stupid voyeur' of traditional theater."[25] As in the case of Dada and Surrealist devotees of film and its avant-garde potential, he was ultimately disappointed by the rise of classical narrative cinema, which domesticated its radical potential.

In fact, the Futurists were often impatient with the limited effect of avant-garde artistic techniques and new entertainment technologies. Singing the praises of car crashes soon led Marinetti, as we know, to extol that most radical wreckage of civilization called war, in which men and machines are intertwined and their mutual destruction a foregone conclusion. "Synergetic pleasure" in the vertigo machines of amusement parks could easily mutate into the sado-masochistic pain of the battlefield, at least as imagined by Futurists anxious to worship velocity for its own sake and praise the cleansing power of destruction. The sinister embrace of fascism was not far behind.

Even if the literalization of the trauma was resisted, as it was by many disquieted by the Futurists' political follies, the "power of horror," to cite the title of Julia Kristeva's well-known book, continued to fascinate many modernists.[26] Her prime example, of course, is Céline, whose apocalyptic, carnivalesque, scatological fantasies are expressed in a language, at once brutal and lyrical, that bursts the bounds of narrative coherence and symbolic sublimation. The result is a literary version, we might say, of the cinema of attractions' subversion of the story line of classical cinema, which, in addition, parallels the horror film's assault on the visual regime of contemplative pleasure.[27] Refusing to view the wreck from afar and draw moral lessons from it, the apocalyptic visionary invoked by Céline is the opposite of the philosophical spectator with his notion of *aletheia*, or the truth of being. Instead, according to Kristeva, his is "a vision that resists any representation, if the latter is a desire to coincide with the presumed identity of what is to be represented. The vision of the ab-ject is, by definition, the sign of an impossible ob-ject, a boundary and a limit."[28]

Presentation rather than representation, transgressive desublimation rather than symbolic sublimation, incorporating the abject rather than facing the extruded object, identifying with destruction rather than contemplating creation: all of these are evidenced in a wide variety of recent modes in contemporary art. From Raphael Montanez Ortiz's "Destructivism: A Manifesto" of 1960 and the "Destruction in Art Symposium" organized in London in 1961 by Gustav Metzer, the father of "auto-destructive art," to exhibitions of so-called abject art at the MIT Visual Arts Center and Whitney Museum in the 1990s, artists and the institutions that display their work have sought to dive into the wreck, strewn with body parts and human waste, and leave behind the safe haven of dry land.[29] J. G. Ballard's novel *Crash* of 1973, turned into a cult film classic by David Cronenberg twenty-three years later, explored the explicit sexual thrill accompanying near-fatal car crashes, many of them recreations of actual violent deaths by celebrities like

James Dean and Jane Mansfield. Artists like these gleefully dive, we might better say, as much into the dreck as the wreck.

Even less scatologically inclined voices like that of the environmental installation artist Walter de Maria have urged us to recognize "the importance of natural disasters" and wondered what would happen "if all the people who go to museums could just feel an earthquake."[30] The assumption that just such a beneficial disaster has already happened, at least metaphorically, is the premise underlying such outspoken critiques of traditional art institutions as Douglas Crimp's *On the Museum's Ruins*, which reprises the efforts of artists like Hans Haacke, Daniel Buren, and Marcel Broodthaers to disrupt the smooth workings of the artworld machine. What Hal Foster has recently called "traumatic realism," evidenced in such works as Andy Warhol's serial repetition of images of car crashes and ambulances, manifests an impatience with a purely conceptual art or the pan-textualization of reality.[31] Instead, it seeks more immediate encounters with the painful, savage, undomesticated "real," in Lacan's sense of the term, prior to its symbolic encoding or sublimated transfiguration. Damian Hirst's animal corpses in formaldehyde, Ron Mueck's reduced verson of his dead father's naked body, Marc Quinn's cast of a man's head sculpted from his frozen blood are the centerpieces of the Saatchi Collection's show tellingly entitled "Sensation," which was mounted in the Royal Academy in London in 1997 and the Brooklyn Museum in the fall of 1999.[32]

A similar impulse has also animated much of the performance art of our time, in which the body—violated, tortured, mutilated, deformed, soaked in blood or covered with excrement, penetrated by technology, pushed beyond its limits—becomes itself the wreck. Like living realizations of Francis Bacon's gut-wrenching images of fragmented, tormented flesh vulnerable to the lacerations of the world around it, such art seeks to draw the observer into the experience of pain and suffering undergone by the performer. The ne plus ultra of this trend—at least so far—manifests itself in the "work" of the French artist Orlan, who has subjected herself to repeated facial surgery and inflicted the images—and some of the removed flesh—on her public.

In short, there is ample evidence from both high and low culture, or rather the unstable flux that has replaced that simple hierarchy, of a widespread impatience with spectatorial distance and a desire to dive into the wreck. The apocalyptic tone that was destined to accompany our transition through the millennial divide has not been confined to religious fanatics or luddite technophobes, but infuses as well much of our contemporary culture in which even harmless quiz shows are called *Jeopardy*. Disinterested, contemplative spectatorship, drawing moral lessons from the disasters suffered by others, is less in fashion than a desire to experience the wreckage firsthand, swimming with Nietzsche and Pascal in a roiling sea on planks that provide no haven from the storm. We have come, it often seems, to identify with the dying man of Stevie Smith's poem who acknowledges with his last breath that

> I was much too far out all my life
> And not waving but drowning.[33]

Or rather we identify both with him and the narrator of the poem, whose voice intermingles with the dead man—there is no punctuation to differentiate the two—but who remains alive to tell the tale. For there is in all of the fascination with wrecks and disasters, for all of the impatience with spectatorial safe havens, a certain ambiguity about where we actually are located. That is, the turn from disinterested contemplation to synergetic pleasure, from an art of cool, analytical detachment to one of titillating or traumatic engagement, has rarely, if ever, been complete. The scream machines of our amusement parks, like the cinema of attraction based on their effects, produce, after all, not literal, but virtual experiences firmly based on the knowledge that it is ultimately all in fun. No one really gets hurt in the simulated shipwreck of the roller coaster or the vertiginous swoon of a bungee-jump, no one fails to survive a viewing of *The Texas Chain Saw Massacre* or *Titanic.* Indeed, the very profitability of such entertainments is based on the capacity to generate desire for a repeat experiences of the thrills they elicit, producing a kind of obsessive acting out rather than working through of the simulated trauma. Although there have been limit-cases of real danger faced by drivers of fast cars or parachutists whose chutes may fail to deploy, the vast majority of those who dive into the wreck can be confident knowing that they will emerge again having suffered little, if any harm.

The apparent ruining of museums are likewise often contrived events within the comforting confines of the white boxes in which they are staged, or at least survive as documented records and duplicated images that are then available for subsequent exhibition on the still-standing walls of the institutions they sought to raze. Even the intransigently antispectacular Situationists led by Guy Debord, after all, found their transgressive acts transformed into artistic "works" shown to well-behaved audiences at the Centre Pompidou and the Institutes of Contemporary Art in London and Boston only a few years after they were carried out.[34]

As a result, there is an aura of bad faith, or at least unconscious disavowal, surrounding much of the allegedly nonspectatorial art and entertainment that claims to liberate us from our boringly safe havens. It was, after all, Lacan's point that we can never get in touch with "the real" without the mediation of the imaginary and the symbolic, no matter how hard we try. The contradictions produced by that attempt have, in fact, not gone unnoticed. Abject art displayed in museums like the Whitney has, for example, been roundly condemned for its wanting to transgress the institutions of art and yet be recognized and valorized by them. Reifying the unrecuperable process of abjection into abject objects that appear in the framed aesthetic space of a gallery implicitly betrays whatever transgressive potential there might be in actual desublimation. As Hal Foster has put it, "Can the abject be represented at all? If it is opposed to culture, can it be exposed *in* culture? If it is unconscious, can it be made conscious and remain abject? In other words, can there be a *conscientious abjection*, or is this all there can be?"[35] Likewise, the cinema of attractions and its recent resurrection in Hollywood blockbusters has been interpreted by Linda Williams as providing a new way to produce the disciplined bodies that Foucault claimed were characteristic of modern regimes of normalization. Now, however, docility is no longer produced by subjecting the self to a kind of corporeal dressage through the suppression of vital emotions, but by eliciting and manipulating them in a certain way. The very performative engagement of the audience, screaming all at once and on cue, is part of the process of discipline via distraction.

Simulacral shipwrecks and virtual dives give us a frisson of horror, but when we compare them to the nonillusory traumas of actual disasters, there is clearly something lacking. Indeed, even when we measure them against certain metaphoric uses of the shipwreck trope, they seem wanting. The difference, I want to argue in conclusion, is powerfully illustrated in the wrenching use of the figure in a plaintive letter Walter Benjamin sent to Gershom Scholem from Berlin in 1931, almost a full decade before he ended his life fleeing fascism on the French-Spanish border. "I have reached an extreme," he wrote, "Someone shipwrecked, who climbs the crumbling mast of his boat's wreckage." And then he added with desperate hope: "But he has the chance from there to signal for his rescue."[36] Benjamin's signals were, as we know, not heard, at least not in his lifetime, and the debris to which he desperately clung provided no escape from the waters that rose to claim him. Benjamin was in a real wreck, hopelessly tossed to and fro on the waves that Pascal and Nietzsche said were the precarious human condition itself. His dive was no distraction, his merging with the machine no amusement park joyride producing harmless kicks. We are perhaps lucky we are spared his fate; no, we are certainly lucky we are spared it. But reflecting on it as spectators from afar, removed from it by time and space, is a useful reminder that an aesthetics of virtual immersion in the simulated wreckage of pseudodisasters may well prove to be an anaesthetics when it comes to reacting to the traumas outside of the aesthetic frame. If aesthetic judgment can in some way be a model for political judgment, as has been argued by commentators like Arendt and Lyotard,[37] the analogy will work only if we resist the urge to lose ourselves in the vertiginous pleasures of virtual desublimation and restore some dignity to the much-maligned contemplative eye. This is not the cold eye of scientific observation, to be sure, but the eye able to judge and weigh the merits of specific events and objects, the eye that ultimately provides the material for a process of discursive communication about the wrecks that have occurred in the past and the ones in the future that might perhaps be forestalled. Only if aesthetic spectatorship declines the invitation to conflate itself entirely with the entertainment industry's cinema of attraction can it provide a possible alternative mode of relating to a world that threatens to dissolve the distinction between reality and simulacra entirely and make every experience vicarious, derivative, and ultimately hollow.

11

ASTRONOMICAL HINDSIGHT

The Speed of Light and Virtual Reality

In September 1676, the Danish astronomer Ole Roemer (1644–1710) presented the recently created French Academy of Sciences with an audacious prediction. Successfully fulfilled two months later, it profoundly transformed not only the study of the heavens, but also the self-understanding of the humans who gazed at them in wonder.[1] Roemer had been working at the observatory of Uraniborg set up by his illustrious predecessor Tycho Brahe on the island of Hveen in the Baltic. His goal was the discovery of a precise astronomical clock for nautical navigation, but the unintended consequences of his efforts were far more momentous. On the basis of his observations, he predicted that the eclipse of the innermost of Jupiter's moons, Io, expected on November 9th at 5:25 and 45 seconds, would take place ten minutes later than had been calculated based on earlier sightings of the same phenomenon. He further reasoned that a similar delay would take place with the passage of the moon from behind Jupiter's shadow—what astronomers call its emersion as opposed to its immersion—on November 16th. These ten minutes delays, he claimed, were due to the time it would take for the light from the eclipse to reach the earth, a longer interval than in the previous recorded cases because the earth was now at the far side of its orbit around the sun from Jupiter and thus significantly farther away from the giant planet than during certain earlier eclipses. Light, in other words, could now be shown to have a velocity of its own and not pass instantaneously from its source to its recipient, or in the vocabulary of the day, its speed could be confirmed as finite and not infinite.

Roemer's precise calculations of light's finite velocity were in need of some correction and fleshing out. He reckoned the time it would take to cross the diameter of the earth's orbit at twenty-two minutes instead of the somewhat more than sixteen minutes measured by later astronomers. And it was not until a year or so later that Christian Huygens actually divided the supposed diameter of the earth's orbit by the time it took for light to travel across it to arrive at an actual, if still imperfect, velocity of light or *c* (from the Latin *celeritas*).[2] Nor was the entire scientific community fully and conclusively convinced by Roemer's claims until the experiments of the English astronomer James Bradley in 1728 concerning what he called "the aberration of light," which involved measuring discrepancies in the parallax relations of certain stars.[3]

But with Roemer, there was for the first time hard empirical evidence to settle a debate that had exercised scientists and philosophers ever since the Greeks. Those theorists from Aristotle to Kepler, Cassini and Descartes, who had held to the notion of the instantaneous propagation of light, were refuted.[4] Others, such as Avicenna, Alhazen, and Roger Bacon, who had speculated that it took some amount of time, were shown to have had the right hunch, even though they had had no verifiable evidence to back it up. Earlier attempts to provide such evidence by following Galileo's suggestion to open and shut lanterns at a distance of ten miles—an experiment actually tried by the Florentine Academy in 1667—had failed because of the shortness of earthly distances and the slow reaction times of the humans operating the lanterns.[5]

With the work of Roemer and Bradley on extraterrestrial objects, that evidence now existed and soon won over the astronomical community with consequences that were ultimately of vast importance for the future exploration of the universe. Although less widely heralded, they were, as Hans Blumenberg puts it in *The Genesis of the Copernican World*, "just as momentous . . . for the change in our consciousness of the world as the Copernican reform had been."[6] It was now certain that despite their apparent size to the naked eye stars were distant suns more or less comparable to the one that shone so brightly in our daytime sky, a conclusion hypothesized but not proven before Roemer.[7] It soon also became possible to begin conceiving of the previously inconceivable distances between stars, which were progressively revealed by the dramatic improvement of the telescope through the use of immense mirrors by William Heschel around 1800, and which continue to expand with the recent discoveries of the Hubble space telescope. And it soon became possible to realize that not only were stars and galaxies many light-years away, but that, as William Huggins announced in 1868, some were receding from us at an astonishing rate of speed (or, as the Doppler-Fizeau effect based on spectroscopic technology showed later in the century, some were zooming towards us as well). The speed of light also provided a limit concept for physics, as no faster propagation of anything else in the universe has ever been found. In addition, the experiments of James Clark Maxwell in the late nineteenth century on electromagnetic waves showed that light travelled at a constant rate in a vacuum, which could not be accelerated or slowed down, although it did change if the medium were altered, say to glass.

These and many other consequences too technical for a soft-headed humanist to present in detail followed from the discovery of the fact that light can travel 186,000 miles or 300,000 kilometers a second and six trillion miles or 9.5 trillion kilometers a year. Although the twentieth century had new surprises in store when Einstein's Special Theory of Relativity argued that the speed of light was the one exception to the rule that velocities were relative to the movement of the viewer and viewed, and the gravitational force of black holes was shown to effect its propagation,[8] Roemer's discovery had repercussions that we are still feeling today.

The one in particular that I want to explore concerns not the vast distances of interstellar space nor the amazingly fast, but still finite and noninstantaneous, speed that light waves or photons—particles of electromagnetic energy—travel through it. I want instead to speculate on the implications of Roemer's discovery for the relation between time and the image. For it was quickly recognized—at least as early as 1702 in a lecture by the astronomer William Whiston[9]—that not only was it now possible to see things that were very far away, but it was also possible to see them as they had existed an extraordinarily long time ago.

In this sense, the effect of the telescope was radically different from that of the other great ocular prosthesis of the early modern period, the microscope, which had no such temporal implication.[10] Only the former could be called a genuine time machine, or in the words of a recent commentator, "a probe that can take deep soundings of time, back to the most ancient cosmos."[11] By 1800, it was recognized that looking at the light from distant stars was gazing at something that had left its source before the very existence of the human race, indeed likely before the existence of the earth and perhaps even the solar system. By the late twentieth century, some astronomers were talking about seeing almost as far back as the birth of the universe itself.[12]

What can be called astronomical hindsight thus presented the viewer of the heavens with a remarkable conundrum. Sight is, after all, often understood to be the most synchronous and atemporal of the senses, capable of giving us a snapshot image of a world frozen in time, a trait that earned it the disdain of philosophers like Bergson who valued temporal duration instead.[13] As Hans Jonas typically puts it, "sight is *par excellence* the sense of the simultaneous or the coordinated, and thereby of the extensive. A view comprehends many things juxtaposed, as co-existent parts of one field of vision. It does so in an instant: as in a flash one glance, an opening of the eyes, discloses a world of co-present qualities spread out in space, ranged in depth, continuing into indefinite distance . . ."[14] Régis Debray adds that "a painting, an engraving, a photograph evade the linear succession of language through the co-presence of their parts. They are apprehended *en bloc* by the intuition, in an instantaneous perceptive synthesis—the *totum simul* of vision. A visual image arrests the flow of time like a syncope, contracts the string of moments."[15] Although recent research has emphasized the scanning movement of the eye and its restless saccadic jumps and stressed the mobile glance over the Medusan gaze,[16] in comparison with other senses, vision still seems for many tied to the Parmenidean or Platonic valorization of static, eternal Being over dynamic, ephemeral Becoming.

Or alternatively, vision is sometimes understood as the sense that gives us the best possible glimpse into the immediate future as we look out on the landscape that we are about to traverse, thus providing "foresight" about what may well come next. "Man's ability to plan," writes the anthropologist Edward T. Hall, "has been made possible because the eye takes in a larger sweep."[17] Hans Jonas adds, "knowledge at a distance is tantamount to foreknowledge. The uncommitted reach into space is gain of time for adaptive behavior. I know in good time what I have to reckon with."[18] Those who assume the exalted function of seer or visionary often claim the ability to foretell what they foresee in the distant future as well.

But in the case of stargazing, what we see instead of the present or proximate future is the past, often an immeasurably deep past whose ontological status is unlike anything else that we experience in mundane existence. We literally see what *is* not, or rather *is* no longer. And yet we are not seeing a mere later reproduction or simulacrum of what once was, but rather the real thing delayed—sometimes enormously delayed—in time. We can have, however, absolutely no way of knowing whether or not that real thing still exists or has long since disappeared. The gap between appearance and essence, subjective experience and objective stimulus, phenomenon and noumenon yawns as wide as it can be. Instead of the infamous "metaphysics of presence" that deconstruction tells us is based on the logocentric, phonocentric, and ocularcentric prejudices of Western thought, we get an explicitly visual instantiation of the ghostly trace of the past in the present, but one that is neither an hallucination nor a technologically induced illusion.

There is, moreover, no possible way to apply the other senses, especially the touch that so often functions to verify or confirm the existence of the past objects we see, as Bishop Berkeley claimed we must to determine spatial location.[19] In stargazing, the sense of sight is isolated from and privileged above the general human sensorium as perhaps in no other realm of experience. The oft-remarked link between abstracted theory and visual distance is given added weight by the impossibility of testing astronomical theories through nonvisual means. Parallels between sight and touch, drawn for example by Descartes in his *Optics*, where he compared sight to the instantaneous transmission of an object through a blind man's stick, break down;[20] how can you even imagine "touching" something that existed light years in the past and may no longer be there today?[21]

The cultural implications of the discovery of the speed of light were no less profound than the scientific ones, although they may have taken longer to register. The famous blow dealt to man's narcissistic assumption of his pivotal place in the universe by the Copernican replacement of a geocentric by a heliocentric cosmos was intensified as it was realized that celestial objects had existed well before we were around to behold them. As Blumenberg notes, "man could no longer be the designated witness of the wonders of the creation if the time required for light to reach him from unknown stars and star systems was longer than the entire duration of the world."[22] The already appreciated fact that the stars are that part of nature least amenable to human construction, domination, or intervention because of the distances involved was given added weight by the stunning realization that not only space but time would have to be conquered for humans to make a difference.

One corollary effect of this realization was the increased erosion of the belief, except among the most gullible, in the opposite assumption: that the stars could somehow causally intervene in human behavior. How, after all, could astrological causation operate, if it were impossible to coordinate the time of a sublunar event, such as one's birth, with the temporal events in interstellar space? How could a plausible horoscope be written that took into account the radically divergent, multiple temporalities of stars whose light came from vastly different distances from the earth? Here too the link between the human present and the images of light in the night sky was rendered deeply problematic by astronomical hindsight, which reveals that constellations are not just spatial relationships, but temporal ones as well. The result, if Maurice Blanchot is right, may have extended beyond the superstitious belief in astrological correlations. Playing on the etymology of the word, he introduces the notion of "disaster"—literally, ill-starred—to designate "being separated from the star . . . the decline which characterizes disorientation when the link with fortune from on high is cut."[23] Disaster can thus be called "*withdrawal outside the sidereal abode . . . refusal of nature's sacredness.*"[24]

The implications of that withdrawal were complicated still further by a later stage in the development of astronomy, the use of photography to record the faint light from distant stars that the human eye could not itself easily register. Here the opposite of the snapshot potential in the new technology, its medusan capacity to freeze flowing time in an instant, was realized as long exposures made it possible to preserve on the photographic plate the dim evidence of past light that could not be seen instantaneously, indeed could not be seen by the naked eye at all. Once again, it is Blumenberg who has most suggestively explored its implications:

> Astronomical photography raises to a higher power the simultaneity of the nonsimultaneous; it now completes the Copernican differentiation of appearance and reality by pursuing the logic of the finite speed of light, also, to its conclusion: the technical analysis and display of the heavens, as a section through time, which no longer has anything to do with the equation of intuition and presence. The product of the chemical darkening of a plate by a source of even the faintest light is, in a certain respect, no longer an auxiliary means, but has become the object itself, of which there is no other evidence but just this.[25]

But now paradoxically, with the advances in astronomical photography the privileging of sight was itself subtly called into question, and not only because of a new appreciation of the vastness of the invisible parts of reality.[26] For no sense, not even unaided human sight, could verify or falsify what the technological preservation of the light from past events had recorded. Appearance through technological mediation is the only reality we can know, even if we theorize that something lies—or rather, at some time in the distant past, lay—behind it. With astronomical hindsight the long-standing reliance on visually based intuition—from the Latin "intueri," to look at or regard, an association still present in the German *Anschauung*—to discern essences is fundamentally challenged. Only conceptually mediated knowledge based on the acknowledgement of sight's inability to present the truth of its objects through intuition follows from Roemer's discovery when it is combined with photographic enhancement; only a knowledge that is filtered through sign systems that are not directly perceptual is thus the lesson to be learned from the astronomical hindsight of the telescope.[27] Not surprisingly, when the Romantics sought to restore the power of intuition against the alleged fallacies of analytical reasoning, they also longed for the return of what Novalis called the "old sky" of celestial presence through a revival of "moral astronomy."[28] But theirs was a losing effort, as the symbolic resonance of the pre-Copernican sky was irretrievably shattered. Blanchot's "disaster" could not be undone.

Moreover, what has been recognized as the indexical nature of all photographic signification—in Peirce's well-known sense of an index as a physical trace of a past event, as opposed to an arbitrary symbol or a mimetic icon—is doubled by the fact that the index left behind on the photographic plate is itself a trace of an event that has happened in the far distant past. Whereas a normal index is once removed from its cause, which may have left nonvisual residues as well—I can feel the medium, say snow or mud, in which the fox's tracks are left as well as see it, and perhaps even smell its faint odor—a photographic image of stellar events is twice removed from them and without any other corroborative trace.

A melancholic link between photography in general and death—its status as a kind of "thanatography"—has been recognized by a number of observers, most notably Susan Sontag, Roland Barthes, and René Dubois.[29] The referent of an image functions as a memento mori, they claim, because of its inevitable pastness, a reminder that one day we too will no longer be here. Such a connection can only become more explicit when the image is of stellar light from an unimaginably deep past. Barthes, in fact, explicitly notes the link by citing Sontag's claim that "the photograph of the missing being . . . will touch me like the delayed rays of a star."[30] Photographs of stars may not be as poignantly mournful as those of our parents when they were young, as in Barthes's celebrated example of the Winter Garden shot of his mother at the age of five, but they intensify the sense of temporal disjunction that every photograph must convey. Blanchot's "disaster" is perhaps nowhere as palpable as when we hold in our hands, in the present, a photographic image of a far distant past that we know no longer exists.

This was a lesson, as Eduardo Cadava has recently shown,[31] that was learned with special thoroughness by Walter Benjamin, whose suggestive ruminations on mimetic similarity and auratic distance often invoked the example of astronomical constellations. In a world no longer able to believe in sympathetic magic and astrological correspondences, the heavens had become a vast cemetery of dead light. Benjamin believed, in Cadava's words, that "like the photograph that presents what is no longer there, starlight names the trace of a celestial body that has long since vanished. The star is always a kind of ruin. That its light is never identical to itself, is never revealed as such, means that it is always inhabited by a certain distance or darkness."[32] Although Benjamin may have hoped against hope for a messianic redemption that would restore meaning to a forlorn world, he registered with special intensity the mournful implications of the cosmic *Trauerspiel*.

But even if the emotion that ensues is not so morose, we must inevitably be struck by the conundrum of a visual presence that cannot be complete and self-contained. Taking seriously that lesson allows us to emend a bit Jonathan Crary's influential argument about the transformation of the protocols and techniques of observation in the nineteenth century.[33] Crary's claim is that only with advances in the physiological understanding of the eye, which involved such phenomena as afterimages (the fusion of discrete images into a simulacrum of duration) and stereoscopic vision (the transformation of two nearly identical flat images into the experience of seeing three dimensions), was the time-honored model of disembodied, atemporal sight based on the camera obscura effectively challenged. "The virtual instantaneity of optical transmission (whether intromission or extramission)," Crary writes,

> was an unquestioned foundation of classical optics and theories of perception from Aristotle to Locke. And the simultaneity of the camera obscura image with its exterior object was never questioned. But as observation is increasingly tied to the body in the early nineteenth century, temporality and vision become inseparable. The shifting processes of one's own subjectivity experienced in time become synonymous with an act of seeing, dissolving the Cartesian ideal of an observer completely focused on an object.[34]

Crary's premise that the dominant paradigm of vision based on the camera obscura—what can be called "Cartesian perspectivalism"[35]—privileged the disembodied, monocular eye has been recently challenged for underplaying the extent to which the body was already present in certain seventeenth-century optical theories.[36] Nonetheless, his central point that nineteenth-century physiology gave a much firmer empirical basis to the recorporealization and thus temporalization of sight than ever before seems to me still intact. Or at least it does from the point of view of the *subject* of vision, the viewer whose eye became firmly situated in a living, moving body rather than hovering above it in an ideal realm of pure opticality.

But what appreciating the importance of Roemer's discovery of the speed of light helps us to understand is that a similar temporalization had already occurred on the level of the *object* of vision, at least when it concerned astronomical hindsight. That is, the camera obscura model of synchronic presence could not be easily applied when the light coming through its little hole was from a distant star. Here "after-images," we might say, are not produced by lingering sensations on the retina creating a simulacrum of movement, but rather by the delays in the light from the object itself.

It must, of course, be conceded that this lesson took a considerable amount of time before it was widely appreciated; we might even say that it was appropriately not an instantaneous transmission. Crary's physiological technologists of observation thus still deserve the primary credit for the abandonment of the camera obscura model of atemporal presence. It may not, in fact, have been until Nietzsche, according to Blumenberg, that the deduction was drawn

> from the fact of the finite speed of light, and the nonsimultaneity of appearing objects with the observer's present, which follows from that, the consequence of the indifference of the present. Presence cannot enable us to apprehend the necessity of what is given in it, because it is only an accidental section through reality. The irregularity of appearances in space turn out to be a projection of the fateful delays into the plane of what is just now visible; it is a paradigm of the distortion of reality by time, not only, and not most painfully, in nature but also in history.[37]

"The indifference of the present" as a consequence of the speed of light was perhaps also tacitly implied by one of the most celebrated evocations of the telescope in modern thought, Freud's comparison in *The Interpretation of Dreams* of psychical locality in the unconscious with an optical apparatus. Such a compound instrument, he noted, produces images "at ideal points, regions in which no tangible component of the apparatus is situated."[38] The relevance to our argument about astronomical hindsight comes from Freud's further claim that we could just as easily conceptualize the relation between the lenses in that apparatus in temporal as in spatial terms. In so doing, we can then understand that the image produced at the ideal point is not fully present, but is rather the place of a memory trace, an unlocalizable compound that connects past with present.

Freud's metaphor has attracted considerable attention, at least since Jacques Derrida foregrounded its implications in his 1966 essay "Freud and the Scene of Writing."[39] To reduce a complicated argument to its most fundamental lineaments, Derrida suggested that Freud's "optical machine" metaphor would be transformed in his later work into a graphic one based on a "mystical writing pad" on which the traces of previous inscriptions could be discerned in the wax beneath a transparent sheet of celluloid. The writing pad produced a kind of spatialized time which denied the possibility of any full symbolic presence. It instantiated instead the temporal spacing of difference without reconciliation.

Writing in response to Derrida, Timothy J. Reiss has argued in *The Discourse of Modernism* that it is unnecessary to posit a transition from a perceptual to a linguistic or graphological model of the unconscious, from the telescope to the mystical writing pad, to arrive at the logic of the trace with its internally split temporality.[40] For already in the workings of the apparatus producing an intangible image at once present and a memory trace of the past can we see the mediation of intuitive perceptual immediacy by a discursive sign system. The telescope, *pace* Derrida, is already a kind of writing machine in which the trace of the past continues to haunt the apparently self-contained present. This point, it seems to me, becomes even stronger, if we separate out, as Freud did not, the telescope from other imaging apparatuses, such as the microscope and the camera, and emphasize its role in producing what we have been calling "astronomical hindsight." For here the temporal spacing produced by the delay between the emission and reception of starlight is even more pronounced. The images collected by the mirrors of the reflecting telescope and then preserved on photographic plates are like memory traces without any single temporal location.

How do these ruminations on the temporally delayed implications of the discovery of the speed of light help us to understand the second theme suggested by our title, the meaning of the new technologies of virtual reality, or more ambitiously, the purely simulacral world of which they are sometimes taken to be emblematic? Can we simply extrapolate from the lessons of interstellar space to the implications of cyberspace? Haven't we, in fact, argued that the telescope, for all its disruption of notions of visual presence and immediacy, nonetheless resists reduction to an apparatus of pure simulacral construction, a model of total visual semiosis without an original object behind it? In contrast, isn't virtual reality normally understood as precisely such a reduction, producing a hyperreality that has no referential origin? And isn't that hyperreality often assumed to be rooted in the accelerated temporality, even simultaneity, of a cyberspace in which distances no longer matter?[41]

For an answer to these questions let us turn to the figure who has done more than any other to explore and—at least for some commentators—legitimate the postmodern world of simulacral self-referentiality, the French theorist Jean Baudrillard.[42] In one of his key texts, *Fatal Strategies* of 1983, Baudrillard introduces precisely the speed of light as a metaphor to explain what he describes as the progressive attenuation of meaning in the contemporary world. "Somewhere a gravitational effect causes the light of event(s), the light that transports meaning beyond the event itself, the carrier of messages, to slow down to a halt;" he writes, "like the light of politics and history that we now so weakly perceive, or the light of celestial bodies we now only receive as faint simulacra."[43] Until recently, he continues, the sense of reality in normal terrestrial experience has been based on the very high velocity of light producing a sense of contemporaneity, in which object and its perception are coordinated. But now everyday life is beginning to resemble the experience of stargazing, in which information paradoxically seems to travel much slower from a source that grows dimmer and less certain. Echoing the rhetoric of disaster we have already encountered in Blanchot, he exhorts us to face the consequences of this transformation: "We must be able to grasp the catastrophe that awaits us in the slowing of light: the slower light becomes, the less it escapes its source; thus things and events tend not to release their meaning, tend to slow down their emanation, to harness that which was previously refracted in order to absorb it in a black hole."[44]

Although the gravitational pull of black holes suggests absolutely no meaning escapes from objects, Baudrillard backs away a bit from this conclusion, and talks instead of the possibility that we live in a world of slow-motion images that take a long time to reach us. "We would thus need to generalize the example of the light that reaches from stars long since extinct—their images taking light-years to reach us. If light were infinitely slower, a host of things, closer to home, would already have been subject to the fate of these stars: we would see them, they would be there, yet already no longer there. Would this not also be the case for a reality in which the image of a thing still appears, but is no longer there?"[45]

Baudrillard's grasp of twentieth-century physics may be faulty, as he misses the implication of Einstein's Special Theory of Relativity, which has since been experimentally confirmed. Light itself, the theory argues, is an absolute constant that cannot be accelerated or decelerated, although paradoxically space and time can be understood as relative. Because light, unlike other waves such as sound, is able to travel in a total vacuum unaffected by the medium through which it moves—such as the "ether" whose existence modern physics has disproved—and the speed and directional movement of its observer do not effect its velocity, it is strictly speaking wrong to speak of the "slowing down" of light. Distances become smaller and time longer for moving bodies as they approach the speed of light, but that speed remains the same. The gravitation of black holes only deflects light, it does not effect its velocity. As Sidney Perkowitz puts it, "the universe is made so that light always travels its own distance of zero, while to us its clock is stopped and its speed is absolutely fixed. These sober conclusions read as if they come out of some fevered fantasy. Light, indeed, is different from anything else we know."[46]

But for all its imprecision, Baudrillard's metaphoric invocation of the effects of Roemer's discovery that light is not instantaneous in terms of the time it takes for images to travel is not without its instructive implications. For it unexpectedly undermines the equation of virtual reality entirely with a nonreferential system of signs totally indifferent to any prior reality that might have caused or motivated them, an equation that admittedly is operative at other moments in his work.[47] That is, by comparing the world of virtual reality with the delayed light from distant stars, Baudrillard alerts us to the attenuated indexical trace of an objective real that haunts the apparently self-referential world of pure simulacra. Like the memory traces in Freud's optical apparatus version of the unconscious, such images are not made entirely out of whole cloth existing only in an atemporal cyberspace, but are parasitic on the prior experiences that make them meaningful to us today. The temporality of virtuality is thus not pure simultaneity or contemporaneity, but the disjointed time that disrupts any illusion of self-presence.

As N. Katherine Hayles has pointed out in a recent discussion of "Virtual Bodies and Flickering Signifiers," "the new technologies of virtual reality illustrate the kind of phenomena that foreground pattern and randomness and make presence and absence seem irrelevant. . . . Questions about presence and absence do not yield much leverage in this situation, for the puppet [on a computer screen duplicating the movements of the user] both is and is not present, just as the user both is and is not inside the screen."[48] Moreover, the new information technologies produce signifiers that do not float entirely free, but rather "flicker," disrupting the absolute alternative between presence and absence. They are thus ultimately dependent on the material embodiment that they seem to have left behind, especially those that interact with the human sensorium and its environment. They are, we might say, reminiscent of those other flickerings of information that come to us from the twinkling of the stars, even if Hayles herself does not make the connection.

Another way in which the apparent self-sufficiency of the virtual universe may be disrupted, Mark Poster has added, is through the transformational interaction of subjects who construct the world they enter when they put on the glove and headset.[49] The result is thus more than the passive acceptance of a world of pure simulation; it plunges us from the present into the future. As such, it accords with the definition of virtuality per se—derived from the Latin *virtus*, the word for "force" or "power"—provided by the French media theorist Pierre Lèvy in his recent *Qu'est-ce que le virtuel?*, where it is opposed not to the real or the material, but to the actual.[50] Virtuality here means something like an Aristotelian final cause, a potentiality that "displaces the center of gravity of the object considered,"[51] which is neither a pure presence nor a simulacral phantasm.

The alternative way in which the alleged self-sufficiency of virtual reality is called into question suggested by the analysis of this essay—and the two are not mutually exclusive—is through the memory traces of the reality that haunts virtual reality from the start, inadvertently betrayed by Baudrillard's metaphor of sidereal light that reaches us after a long delay. Here, as in the case of Crary's argument about the importance of ocular physiology in dismantling the camera obscura paradigm, the story of subjective construction must be balanced by an acknowledgment of the disturbing effects that come from the object. Or more precisely, when the lessons of astronomical hindsight are applied broadly, we are in an uncanny world of what Derrida has dubbed "hauntological" rather than "ontological" reality,[52] a world in which temporal delay and the indexical trace of the past prevents the present—virtual or not—from assuming the mantle of synchronic self-sufficiency.

Whether or not the result is a melancholic memento mori, as has been claimed in the case of photography, or a "disaster" in Blanchot's sense of being ousted from a realm of sacred meaning, is, however, uncertain. For might it be just as plausible to experience a feeling of wonder at the survival of the seemingly dead past? And might that wonder at the virtual residues of the long dead stars be connected to the virtuality that, according to Poster and Lèvy, opens us as well to a potential future. For after all, is not the light reflecting off us, radiating our images to any eyes open to receive them, somehow destined, even if in increasingly diffused form, to travel forever, making our present the past of innumerable futures still to come?

12

RETURNING THE GAZE

The American Response to the French Critique of Ocularcentrism

Let me ask you to accept on faith what I lack time to demonstrate now, but have tried to spell out in a recent book entitled *Downcast Eyes*:[1] that a wide variety of French thinkers and artists in this century have been conducting, often with little or no explicit acknowledgment of each other's work, a ruthless critique of the domination of vision in Western culture. Their challenge to what can be called the ocularcentrism of that tradition has taken many different forms, ranging from Bergson's analysis of the spatialization of time to Bataille's celebration of the blinding sun and the acephalic body, from Sartre's depiction of the sadomasochism of "the look" to Lacan's disparagement of the ego produced by the "mirror stage," from Foucault's strictures against panoptic surveillance to Debord's critique of the society of the spectacle, from Barthes' linkage of photography and death to Metz's excoriation of the scopic regime of the cinema, and from Irigaray's outrage at the privileging of the visual in patriarchy to Levinas's claim that ethics is thwarted by a visually grounded ontology. Even an early defender of the figural as opposed to the discursive like Lyotard could finally identify the postmodernism that he came to champion with the sublime foreclosure of the visual.

Although there are many nuances in the work of these and other figures of comparable importance who might be added to the list, the cumulative effect of their interrogation of the eye has been a radical challenge to the conventional wisdom that sight is the noblest of the senses. Instead, its hegemonic status in Western culture has been blamed for everything from an inadequate philosophy and idolatrous religion to a pernicious politics and impoverished aesthetics. Often some other sense, usually touch or hearing, or the essentially non-visual realm of language, has been offered as an antidote to sight's domination. Although at times, attempts have been made to rescue a less problematic version of visual experience, most of the thinkers whose ideas I traced in *Downcast Eyes* would agree with Lacan when he wrote: "The eye may be prophylactic, but it cannot be beneficent—it is maleficent. In the Bible and even in the New Testament, there is no good eye, but there are evil eyes all over the place."[2]

In the recent American appropriation of French thought, the critique of ocularcentrism has, I want to argue, struck a particularly respondent chord. Paradoxically, what has been called the new "pictorial turn" or "visual turn"[3] in cultural studies has been fueled in large measure by the reception of ideas from the antiocularcentric discourse developed most notably in France. As a result, it has often been accompanied by a hostility or at least wariness towards its subject matter, which seems very different from that generally celebratory mood accompanying the previous "linguistic turn."

There have, to be sure, been influences from elsewhere, for example Heidegger's trenchant analysis of the "age of the world picture" and Gadamer's defense of the hermeneutic ear over the scientific eye. Domestic traditions have played their part as well, as shown by the importance of John Dewey's pragmatist critique of the "spectator theory of knowledge," recently revived by Richard Rorty in his widely read *Philosophy and the Mirror of Nature*.[4] American psychologists of visual experience like J. J. Gibson also produced important work that had a potent impact beyond their narrow discipline.[5] And the media theories of Marshall McLuhan and Walter J. Ong, which caused an intense, if short-lived, flurry of excitement in the late 1950s and early 1960s, must also be acknowledged as preparing the ground.[6]

But it was not really until the wave of translations and interpretations of post-1968 French theory washed over the American intellectual scene that a sustained, nuanced, and still by no means exhausted discussion of the dangers of privileging the eye—or at least certain dominant regimes of visuality—gained center stage. Even when the original political momentum of the reception was largely spent, many of its elements remained potent in the debates over postmodernism—and its counterenlightenment dangers—that began in earnest in the early 1980s. Journals like *October*, *Camera Obscura*, *Visual Anthropology Review*, and

Screen—the last although British, having a wide following in America—helped plant the French-inspired suspicion of the visual at the very center of contemporary cultural debate. As a result, to borrow the title of a recent collection, modernity and the hegemony of vision have come to seem inextricably, and for some, ominously, intertwined.[7]

In fact, the variety and range of the American reception of the French critique of that hegemony has been so great that easy generalizations about its contours and tensions are hard to provide. Rather than attempt, therefore, what might be called an Icarian or synoptic overview of the entire field, let me focus on a few salient landmarks within the discourse surrounding the visual arts in the hope of illuminating some of the effects of the recontextualization of the anti-ocularcentric polemic on our side of the Atlantic. In particular, I want to examine developments in recent art history and criticism, which are themselves now in danger of being absorbed into a larger and more amorphous realm of inquiry called visual studies in part because of the importation of ideas about ocularcentrism from France.

As has been widely remarked, the center of gravity of modernism in the visual arts shifted from Paris to New York in the years after 1945, when abstract expressionism emerged as the dominant school at the cutting-edge of artistic innovation. Whether or not, as Serge Guilbaut has provocatively contended, this shift was tantamount to a theft based on the calculated Cold War strategy of purging art of any political implications, it certainly meant purifying the visual of any apparently extraneous interference, such as a narrative, didactic, or anecdotal function, and imbuing it instead with a claim to universal value in itself.[8] Although anxieties about the commodification or functionalization of the visual object can be detected as early as the nineteenth century, when the invention of replicable photographs seemed to threaten aesthetic autonomy,[9] it was only in postwar modernism that the strategy of resisting such incursions by essentializing the opticality of the medium came its own.

Here the influential criticism of Clement Greenberg, himself a recently disillusioned Trotskyist rapidly shedding his political past, was pivotal in elevating what he called the "purity" of the optical to the defining characteristic of modern art.[10] For Greenberg, genuine avant-garde art should have no truck with the commodified kitsch of mass art, nor should it register the resistant materiality of its supporting media. Pure visuality meant the presence of atemporal, essential form, the old Platonic dream now paradoxically realized—or at least ever more closely manifested—in the world of visual appearance on the flat surface of a canvas. Greenberg's was thus a modernism reminiscent of the strictly self-referential formalism of earlier critics like Roger Fry and Clive Bell, but now for the first time successfully elevated to a position of cultural hegemony.[11] His standards could be applied not only to define genuine art, but also to decide qualitatively between its good and bad exemplars.[12]

Along with this argument for visual purity went a banishment of movements like Surrealism, which Greenberg called a "reactionary tendency" because it attempted to "restore 'outside' subject matter,"[13] such as the unconscious. Others like Dada were also not worth taking seriously because of their radical antiformalism and hostility to the differentiated institution of art in general and painting in particular. Only pure opticality detached from any external inference—whether political, economic, psychological, or even the materiality of media and the artist's own body—met the highest standard of aesthetic achievement for Greenberg and those he influenced. The defense of photography as high art made by important critics like the Museum of Modern Art's John Szarkowski in the 1960s, to take one prominent example, followed virtually the same line of argument.[14] So too did the critique of debased theatricality in art, its degeneration into spectacles for an audience instead of absolute self-contained presentness, vigorously made by Michael Fried in his celebrated essay "Art and Objecthood" of 1967.[15] Although later Fried vigorously tried to put some distance between his argument and that of Greenberg, which he claimed had been too ahistorically essentialist and based on a privileging of pure opticality he had not himself embraced,[16] he was widely considered his ally at the time.

The Greenbergian consensus began, however, to unravel in the late 1960s and early 1970s with the introduction of new art movements difficult to accommodate in his terms, notably Pop Art, Minimalism, and Conceptualism, a growing politicization of the art world, which found his Cold War liberal universalism jejune, and most important for our purposes, a new openness to theory from abroad, especially from France.[17] Although it would be an unwarranted exaggeration to attribute developments in American art primarily to the influence of that theory, it would also be wrong to see the theory as nothing but a post facto justification for changes that were happening on the purely practical level. For, as Daniel Herwitz has recently emphasized, virtually from the beginning avant-garde art was developed in intense dialogue with the theories that explained and legitimated it.[18] The result was often, to borrow the title of Joseph Kosuth's 1969 conceptualist manifesto, the production of "art after philosophy."[19]

Put schematically, the new movements of the late 1960s and early 1970s shifted the ground away from the postwar consensus in the following ways. Mocking his belief in standards of artistic quality, Pop Art undermined Greenberg's rigid distinction between high and low, provocatively blurring the difference between commodity and disinterested aesthetic experience. Minimalism—like the performance art and happenings that also came into their own during this period—restored the temporal and corporeal dimensions of aesthetic experience, in defiance of Greenberg's stress on atemporal visual presence and Fried's excoriation of theatricality.[20] Conceptualism increasingly substituted dematerialized ideas or at least language about art for visual presence, impure discursivity for pure opticality. All of these movements, moreover, in one way or another reflected the art world's growing politicization, which encouraged a skeptical reflexivity about the institutions of art—museums, galleries, the art market, and so forth—and their relation to larger social forces in place of an internal reflexivity about aesthetic form or the characteristics of the medium itself.

The theories—in most cases French—that were marshaled to explicate and legitimate all of these changes can be usefully divided into three categories, which helps us see the overdetermined nature of the onslaught against the idea of high modernist pure opticality: (1) those that stress the importance of language as opposed to perception, (2) those that emphasize the forgotten role of the (often sexualized) body, and (3) those that stress the political implications of certain visual practices. In reality, of course, many of the arguments in each of these categories were combined by different thinkers in a variety of ways, whose intricacies cannot be adequately reproduced in a survey as brief as this one.

With the American reception of what became known as Structuralism in the late 1960s, identified primarily with Saussure, Lévi-Strauss, and the early Barthes, came a powerful imperative to conceptualize all cultural production in terms of language and textuality. That is, everything could be treated as a sign system based on arbitrary, diacritical signifiers, whose ability to convey significance could be uncoupled from their referential, mimetic function. In visual terms, it thus now seemed possible to "read" rather than simply look at pictures, movies, architecture, photographs, and sculpture. As the British artist and critic Victor Burgin put it in 1976, "the ideological resistance, in the name of the 'purity' of the *Image*, to the consideration of linguistic matter within and across the photograph is no more or less well founded than that which met the coming of sound in the cinema."[21]

A salient example of the new openness to language from a critic whose other work we will encounter again shortly can be found in Rosalind Krauss's 1978 essay "Sculpture in the Expanded Field."[22] Krauss provocatively identified certain modern and even more post-modernist works as negativities rather than positivities, defined by their relationship to what they were not, that is, landscape or architecture. By then reversing these negative terms and relating them in a quaternary field of multiple contradictions, Krauss was able to situate contemporary sculpture in a discursive rather than purely visual context. "The logic of the space of postmodernist practice," she concluded, "is no longer organized around the definition of a given medium on the grounds of its material, or, for that matter, the perception of the material. It is organized instead through the universe of terms that are felt to be in opposition within a cultural situation."[23]

When more so-called poststructuralist versions of language, especially those identified with deconstruction, became available to American critics, the neatness of such diagrams became less compelling,[24] but the textual interference with pure opticality was, if anything, strengthened. Thus, for example, W. J. T. Mitchell in his widely admired *Iconology: Image, Text, Ideology* of 1986 would write that

> Derrida's answer to the question, "What is an image?" would undoubtedly be "Nothing but another kind of writing, a kind of graphic sign that dissembles itself as a direct transcript of that which it represents, or of the way things look, or of what they essentially are." This sort of suspicion of the image seems only appropriate in a time when the very view from one's window, much less the scenes played out in everyday life and in the various media of representation, seem to require constant interpretative vigilance.[25]

Although at times, the textual threatened to replace the optical entirely in the reception of structuralist and even post-structuralist modes of thought, more often the result was their mutual problematization. Here a new appreciation for the experiments in verbal and visual punning conducted by the Surrealists emerged, as evidenced by the enthusiastic reception of Foucault's essay on Magritte, *This Is Not a Pipe*, when it was translated in 1983.[26] Combined with the powerful impact of his strictures against panopticism and the medical gaze, Foucault's homage to Magritte's "non-affirmative painting" provided new ammunition in the campaign to disrupt pure opticality through the introduction of discursivity. Comparable lessons were drawn from Lyotard's *Discours, Figure*, still not fully translated, but an evident influence on such widely read works as *Vision and Painting: The Logic of the Gaze* of 1983 by the art historian Norman Bryson, which also drew on Derrida, Barthes, and Lacan.[27]

Bryson's influential book, which was one of several by him in the 1980s showing an evident debt to French thinkers like Lyotard and Lacan,[28] also lamented the suppression of corporeality in the dominant tradition of viewing in the West from the Renaissance through modernism. In what Bryson called the "Founding Perception" of that tradition, "the gaze of the painter arrests the flux of phenomena, contemplates the visual field from a vantage-point outside the mobility of duration, in an eternal moment of disclosed presence; while in the moment of viewing, the viewing subject unites his gaze with the Founding Perception, in a perfect recreation of that first epiphany."[29] In both cases, what is lost is the deictic location of the glancing eye—or more correctly, both eyes—in the body, a body moving temporally through a concrete spatial location rather than somehow suspended above it in an eternal present. Merleau-Ponty's celebrated critique of disincarnated God's eye views and defense of preobjective experience also could be adduced to support a temporalized rather than static notion of formal abstraction, as Krauss was to argue when she introduced Richard Serra's work to a Parisian audience in 1983.[30]

What is also suppressed in the elevation of opticality to an ideal realm above the temporal body, Bryson, following Lyotard rather than Merleau-Ponty, added, is the power of the desire coursing through the experience of sight.[31] Ocular desire, ever since at least the time of Augustine, has troubled those who want to privilege sight as the noblest of the senses, for it seems to undermine the disinterestedness of pure contemplation. In the French antiocularcentric discourse, it is precisely the inevitability of such impure desiring that undermines the claims of the eye to be dispassionate, cold, and above the fray.

Often this has meant exploring the complicated links between the fetishism of the image and specifically male desire, an exploration carried out in the French feminist critique of visuality most explicit in the work of Irigaray. Not only has this critique had its echoes in Anglo-American film criticism, beginning with Laura Mulvey's now classic essay of 1975 on the male gaze,[32] but it has also played a role in the turn against Greenberg's reading of modernism. Witness again Victor Burgin, who argued in 1984 that "structurally, fetishism is a matter of separation, segregation, isolation; it's a matter of petrification, ossification, glaciation; it's a matter of idealization, mystification, adoration. Greenbergian modernism was an apotheosis of fetishism in the visual arts in the modern period."[33]

So too an awareness of the body as a site of suffering as well as pleasure, of abjection in Julia Kristeva's sense as well as beautiful form, helped call into question the hegemony of the dispassionate eye. As the artist Mary Kelly noted in 1981, "The art of the 'real body' does not pertain to the truth of a visible form, but refers back to its essential content: the irreducible, irrefutable experience of *pain*."[34] Kelly's sensitivity to bodily pain clearly reflected her feminist concerns, especially her resistance to the objectification of women's bodies. A more general theoretical recovery of the desiring body and the suffering body, both of the artist and the beholder, in the post-Greenbergian climate can, however, be most clearly traced to a new appreciation of two French figures from the traditions of Dada Surrealism who had been scorned by the exponents of abstract expressionism, Marcel Duchamp and Georges Bataille.[35]

The extraordinary American reception of Duchamp, himself a long-time resident in the United States, has been the object of considerable scholarly interest, culminating—at least for the moment—in Amelia Jones's ambitious feminist study, *Postmodernism and the Engendering of Marcel Duchamp*, Jerrold Seigel's bold attempt to unite life and work in *The Private Worlds of Marcel Duchamp*, Dalia Judavitz's imaginative *Unpacking Duchamp*, and the recent issue of *October* devoted to "The Duchamp Effect."[36] Although the explosive impact of his *Nude Descending a Staircase* at the legendary New York Armory show of 1913 was not entirely forgotten, it was Duchamp's later, very different work that gained center stage in the 1960s. No history of the origins of many movements of the period, including the neo-Dada of Jasper Johns and Robert Rauschenberg, the Conceptualism of Joseph Kosuth, the Minimalism of Robert Morris, and the Pop Art of Andy Warhol, can ignore his importance. In more general terms, Duchamp's readymades, aggressively "indifferent" to their intrinsic aesthetic value, have been recognized as a powerful challenge to the differentiated institution of art, the traditional privileging of cultivated aesthetic taste, the modernist distinction between high and low, and even the fetish of originality in Western art as a whole. His self-parodic foregrounding of the artist's constructed persona has been praised for effacing the boundary between artwork and performance art, and sometimes blamed for allowing their complete transformation into marketable commodities (e.g. the Warhol phenomenon). And his campy disruption of his own gender identity—Duchamp photographed in drag or signing his works as Rrose Sélavy, among other pseudonyms—has been credited with inspiring the postmodernist assault on modernist assumptions about male creativity, exemplified by the macho posturing of many of the abstract expressionists and their supporters, as well as the modernist figuring of mass culture in misogynist terms as an inferior realm of "feminine" entertainment.[37]

But it is perhaps Duchamp's celebrated disdain for what he called "retinal art," the art of pure opticality and visual appearance, that has most earned him a place in the pantheon of current American critics of ocularcentrism. Here both his apparent withdrawal from the art scene to play chess in the 1920s (his last oil painting was *Tu m'* done in 1918) and the surprising discovery after his death in 1968 that he was all the while preparing the shocking installation or "sculpture-construction" known as *Étant donnés* (*Being Given*) now at the Philadelphia Museum of Art, have combined to make him the leading critic of the voyeuristic assumptions of conventional painting, perspectival realist as well as abstract and two-dimensional. Indeed, he has been enlisted as a weapon in the battle against the society of the spectacle as a whole, even if Debord and Situationists themselves had thought his attempt merely to abolish art, rather than both abolish and realize it, was flawed.[38]

Duchamp also presented a challenge to the Greenbergian defense of pure opticality by directing attention away from the essence of specific arts, visual or otherwise, to the general, sensually abstracted category of "art" as such. As Thierry de Duve has recently pointed out, Duchamp foregrounded what Foucault was to call the "enuciative" capacity of language, its ability to make performative statements rather than merely describe what already exists.[39] Although he performatively designated visually accessible objects as art—some of the readymades can, in fact, be looked at and appreciated in formal terms—it was the act of designating that was crucial, as evidenced by his indifference to the found or fabricated quality of the objects themselves. This generalization of the act of aesthetic fiat with no attention to the differences among the arts was a key instance of what Michael Fried had damned as "theatricality" in "Art and Objecthood."[40]

What made Duchamp so powerful a resource for those who wanted to challenge the Greenbergian paradigm was not only his subversion of received notions of aesthetic value, not only, that is, his intellectual stimulus to conceptualism, but also his restoration of the desiring body in much of his work. Duchamp's erotic preoccupations, evident for example, in the undulating optical discs he dubbed "rotoreliefs" or the "Large Glass" (also called *The Bride Stripped Bare by Her Bachelors, Even*), initially invited reductive psychological explanations. But more recently, they have been the stimulus to a very different set of questions, which deal with the interference produced by the intervention of repetitive and unfulfilled desire into the space of the seemingly plenitudinous visual object. Lyotard's 1977 *Les Transformateurs Duchamp* had already addressed some of the same issues, but in America, it was Rosalind Krauss and her collaborators at the journal *October* who most insistently explored their implications.[41]

Krauss's role in the dissemination and elaboration of post-Greenbergian ideas has been central, so much so that Amelia Jones could turn her into "a sort of institutional author-function whose influence on this level has been vast."[42] Although a considerably more personal reading of Krauss's animus towards Greenberg, who had been her teacher in the 1960s, is invited by the bitter evocation of his baleful presence in her recent book *The Optical Unconscious*, it is clear that one of the reasons for their falling out concerns a radical difference in their appreciation of Duchamp.[43] As Krauss recalled, "what Clem detests in Duchamp's art is its pressure towards desublimation. 'Leveling' he calls it. The attempt to erase distinctions between art and non-art, between the absolute gratuitousness of form and the commodity. The strategy, in short, of the readymade."[44]

As early as 1977 and her *Passages in Modern Sculpture*, Krauss was already finding much to admire in Duchamp's challenge to a welter of traditional assumptions about art as sublimation, including those that informed the Greenbergian defense of high modernism. She approvingly acknowledged his debt to the writer Raymond Roussel's demolition of the idea that works of art expressed a creator's interiority by acting as "a transparent pane—a window through which the psychological spaces of viewer and creator are open onto each other."[45] Duchamp's radical antipsychologism, his denial that works reveal the artist's soul or even his intentions, Krauss compared to the antisubjectivism of both the Minimalist artists of the 1970s and the "new novelists" of the same era: "it is no accident that the work of [Robert] Morris and [Richard] Serra was being made at the time when novelists in France were declaring: 'I do not write. I am written.' "[46] In all these cases, the art object was situated in a discursive field rather than understood as a self-sufficient visual presence. For Krauss, the trajectory of contemporary sculpture from Rodin to Robert Smithson increasingly brought to the fore precisely the theatricality and temporality—the "passages" mentioned in her title—that Greenbergian purists like Fried had tried so hard to banish.

The temporality introduced by Duchamp, Krauss later claimed,[47] was that of a blinking eye rather than the fixating stare of the modernist artist/beholder. Anticipating Derrida's famous deconstruction of Husserl's reliance on the instantaneity of the *Augenblick*,

Duchamp's work showed that even a blink has duration. And when the blink is repeated, it reveals what Krauss called, in still another essay on this theme, the "im/pulse to see," which expressed the rhythms of erotic desire and its frustration. Now her reading of Duchamp admitted a psychological dimension, but one that revealed a divided, partly formless rather than unified and expressive subject. It was the unstoppable beat repetitively coursing through that disunified subject, she charged, that "modernism had solemnly legislated out of the visual domain, asserting a separation of the senses that will always mean that the temporal can never disrupt the visual from within, but only assault it from a position that is necessarily outside, external, eccentric."[48]

Moreover, the moment when the eye was closed could be understood as providing a screen on which the nonplenitudinous, heterogeneous signs of what Derrida called *écriture* could be projected. Here the figurality of which Lyotard had written in *Discours, Figure* was crossed by discursivity, but both were internal to vision rather than one within and the other without. In still another way, Krauss contended, the purity of visual experience was undermined by the blink of the eye. Like the interruption experienced by the voyeur suddenly caught looking through a keyhole, so trenchantly described in Sartre's *Being and Nothingness*, the body intervened to subvert the illusion of pure, disincarnated sight. Instead, a chiasmic intertwining of viewer and viewed, of the subject and object of the gaze, ensued, which mobilized specular processes of projection and identification.

A similar sensitivity to the ways in which temporality and the body disrupted the ideology of visual presence was evident in Krauss's celebration of Surrealist photography, so long maligned as impure gimmickry by advocates of modernist formalism.[49] Here she employed Derrida's notion of spacing to explain the ways in which internal deferral and doubling subvert seemingly unified individual prints.[50] The result, she argued, was a visual heterogeneity that presents what is seen as always already discursively coded, as in fact, a kind of disseminating *écriture* in the complicated sense of that word introduced by deconstruction.

Even non-Surrealist photography could be understood to deny the visual plenitude, the formal self-sufficiency, assumed by the high modernist defense of the medium. Here the comparison Duchamp once made between his readymades and snaphots was telling, Krauss argued, because it suggested that the photographs also needed some textual supplementation to become fully meaningful. That is, snapshots were empty signifiers, wrested from any narrative coherence and produced by the indexical trace, the brute physical residue, of the objects they reproduced. As a consequence, they needed captions to make them meaningful.

Whether like *écriture* and thus internally coded in heterogeneous ways or like uncoded indices and thus in need of a supplementary text to give them meaning, photographs could be understood to challenge the ideology of pure visual presence promulgated by Greenberg and his followers. In much of the art of the 1970s, including that which seemed an extension of abstract expressionism, Krauss detected the impact of the photograph in precisely this fashion: "its visual and formal effect," she wrote of one example, "was that of captioning: of bowing to the implied necessity to add a surfeit of written information to the depleted power of the painted sign."[51]

It was not, however, until the introduction of even more explicitly antiocularcentric, antisublimating arguments from Bataille in her work of the 1980s that Krauss was able to demonstrate how depleted that power actually was.[52] Krauss first evoked the author of the scandalous pornographic novel *Histoire de l'oeil* in her 1983 essay "No More Play," published in a Museum of Modern Art collection on *Primitivism in 20th Century Art* and reprinted in her enormously influential collection *The Originality of the Avant-Garde and Other Modernist Myths.*[53] Bataille's violent fantasies of enucleation and the metaphoric displacement of the eye by other objects like the sun, eggs, and testicles work, Krauss recognized, to deprivilege vision in general and formal clarity in particular. His introduction of the word *informe* in the Surrealist journal *Documents* in the 1930s indicated a challenge to the formalist bias of high modernism, indeed to any notion of vertical hierarchy as opposed to horizontal leveling. The word denoted, according to Krauss, "what alteration produces, the reduction of meaning or value, not by contradiction—which would be dialectical—but by putrefaction: the puncturing of the limits around the term, the reduction to the sameness of the cadaver—which is transgressive."[54] Here the body as base, unformed materiality, a materiality always susceptible to corruption, mutilation, and decay, was pitted against the elevated, sublimated, timeless body of formal perfection in traditional Western art. Here a "hard" primitivism of transgression and expenditure replaced the "soft" primitivism of aestheticized visual form. Here was undone the alleged superiority of the spiritualizing, formalizing head over the materializing, grotesque body, an acephalic body whose tangled innards mimic the obscurity of the labyrinth.

Perhaps the high-water mark of Krauss's adoption of the antiocularcentric rhetoric emanating from France came in the 1986 issue of *October* dedicated to Bataille, to which she contributed an essay with the straightforward title "Antivision."[55] Bemoaning what she called the "modernist fetishization of sight,"[56] whose effects she disappointedly detected in Bataille's late book on Manet, Krauss celebrated his earlier embrace of the values of darkness, blindness and dazzlement in the obscurity of the caves at Lascaux or the labyrinth of the Minotaur. Her essay ended by eagerly anticipating the effects of rereading modernism in antivisual terms, such as "*informe, acéphale, basess,* automutilation and blindness:"

> It is not clear what an alternative view of the history of recent art—one operated through Bataille's disruption of the prerogatives of a visual system—would yield. It is my assumption that in gesturing toward another set of data, in suggesting another group of reasons, another description of the goals of representation, another ground for the very activity of art, its yield will be tremendous.[57]

Ultimately, the simple binary implications of pro- and antivision seem to have proven too restrictive for Krauss, whose most recent book borrowed Walter Benjamin's notion of the "optical unconscious" and gave it a Lacanian spin to suggest a split *within* vision itself.[58] Although in some of her earlier work she had adopted ideas about the fractured nature of the visual field developed by Lacan in his *Four Fundamental Concepts of Psycho-analysis*, Krauss now was also able to draw on the research of Jonathan Crary, whose *Techniques of the Observer*, published in 1990, demonstrated the importance of the nineteenth-century recovery of physiological optics, the workings of the actual two eyes in the human body, in overturning the dominant model of vision based on the disembodied workings of a camera obscura.[59]

Crary's own debts to Krauss in return and the French critique of ocularcentrism are evident in this remarkable study, but he went beyond her in teasing out the explicitly political implications of his material.[60] Situating the modernist rejection of perspectivalist realism in an earlier and more widespread shift in the status of observation, which he dates as early as the 1820s, Crary argued that it was less of a liberation than has been supposed. The new protocols of the observer seemed to allow the body to come back, but actually only permitted the two eyes to return, while still keeping the other senses, especially touch, at bay. "This autonomization of sight, occurring in many different domains," Crary concludes, "was a historical condition for the rebuilding of an observer fitted for the tasks of 'spectacular' consumption."[61]

Unlike earlier Greenbergian celebrants of modernist visuality, who saw in its emancipation from previous perspectival regimes a genuine liberation, Crary had absorbed enough of the French distrust of all scopic regimes to recognize the insidious implications of high modernist optical purity. Among the many French theoreticians he cites, including Deleuze, Lyotard, Lacan, Bataille, and Baudrillard, two in particular stand out for their impact on the political significance Crary wrests from his story: Foucault and Debord. As mentioned above, the allegedly sinister political implications of ocularcentrism were often an important source of the American interest in its subversion, complementing the fascination with language and the body. *Techniques of the Observer* deliberately combines Foucault's celebrated critique of surveillance in the carceral society of panopticism with Debord's attack on the Spectacle, a combination that neither French theorist would have been likely to find felicitous.

For Crary, however, both regimes of visual power have worked in tandem to rationalize vision in the service of the status quo:

> almost simultaneous with this final dissolution of a transcendent foundation for vision emerges a plurality of means to recode the activity of the eye, to regiment it, to heighten its productivity and to prevent its distraction. Thus the imperatives of capitalist modernization, while demolishing the field of classical vision, generated techniques for imposing visual attentiveness, rationalizing sensation, and managing perception. They were disciplinary techniques that required a notion of visual experience as instrumental, modifiable, and essentially abstract, and that never allowed a real world to acquire solidity or permanence.[62]

Once again, the modernist visual regime, which a generation ago during the postwar era, seemed emblematic of emancipation from extraneous constraints, is damned as itself a subtle form of discipline and regimentation, somehow complicitous with the imperatives of capitalist rationalization. Although the alternative strategy of evoking the desublimating effects of the Lyotard's sublime or Bataille's *informe* has itself recently been questioned by another member of the *October* circle, Hal Foster, in his new book on Surrealism and the uncanny, *Compulsive Beauty*,[63] it is clear that for anyone who has absorbed the last twenty or so years of French theory in American, there can be no turning back.

Not surprisingly, the most vociferous champions of high modernism in 1990s America, at least in the visual arts, often turn out to be outspokenly conservative figures like Hilton Kramer and Roger Kimball, whose distaste for French theory goes along with their hatred of anything that questions literary canons or subverts the distinction between high and low culture, thus threatening the traditional value hierarchies they so doggedly defend. Although Paris has not yet stolen back the idea of modern art from New York, or rather recovered its place as the dominant locus of contemporary artistic creation, the infiltration of French theory, in particular its critique of ocularcentrism, has been a powerful weapon in the dismantling of the critical consensus that made the theft seem worth the effort in the first place. What French artists may not have been able to bring about, French theory seems to have ultimately accomplished: the dissolution of the triumphalist reading of modern art as the realization of aesthetic truth in the context of political freedom. We now see things differently on our side of the Atlantic, if indeed we feel able to see anything very clearly at all.

13

LAFAYETTE'S CHILDREN

The American Reception of French Liberalism

In 1994, Princeton University Press launched with considerable fanfare an auspicious series of translations called "New French Thought," edited by Thomas Pavel, Professor of French at the University of California, Santa Cruz, and Mark Villa of the Political Science and French Studies Departments at New York University (both recently transplanted to the University of Chicago). Pavel, the author of an earlier critique of structuralist and post-structuralist thought, and Lilla, best known until then for his book on Vico as an antimodernist, were not coy about their agenda.[1] Their aim was to introduce "the younger generation of philosophers, historians, and social commentators who represent the new liberal, humanistic bent of French intellectual life."[2] In so doing, they hoped to break the stranglehold in the English-speaking world of what had come to be called "French Theory" in the quarter century after the events of 1968. Tacitly allied with the historian Tony Judt and the political philosophers Charles Larmore and Stephen Holmes, Pavel and Lilla boldly set out to compel the *Zeit* to find a new *Geist* (or rather the *temps* a new *esprit*), permitting us to recover from what they see as the dire effects of too much ill-digested Barthes, Blanchot, Bataille, Lévi-Strauss, Lyotard, Debord, Foucault, Althusser, Lacan, Kristeva, Irigaray, Derrida, Deleuze, Bourdieu, Levinas, Nancy, and Lacoue-Labarthe. For there has been, they hasten to inform us, an alternative and healthier tradition of "continental philosophy" and post-1968 politics emanating from France that should now command our serious attention.

In addition to the initial volume in the series edited by Lilla, which is a kind of coming-attractions trailer for the theorists they want to promote, eight other books have appeared so far, with more doubtless on the horizon.[3] Each is prefaced by an introduction written by an eminent North American scholar.[4] Along with a number of independent translations of some of their most prominent authors and works by like-minded historians, such as François Furet, who have revised the conventional wisdom about the French past, in particular the centrality of the Revolution and its unfinished business, they combine to form an identifiable, albeit not always completely consistent, intellectual formation, which signals a new and more salubrious chapter in the American reception of European thought. Or at least so their promoters clearly hope.

At a time when signs of exhaustion with the master thinkers they want to topple are not, in fact, hard to find, it is certainly worth examining the alternative Pavel, Lilla, and their allies have proposed as a refreshing intellectual stimulus and prudent political guide. Although in an essay of this scope it would be impossible to canvass the entire terrain of contemporary French humanist and liberal theory and evaluate its achievement in its own right, it may be a more manageable task to survey the selective American presentation and reception of those ideas and thinkers chosen to represent the whole. In what follows, I want therefore to concentrate solely on the texts and figures who have been selected to generate the *nouvelle vague* of intellectual fashion coming from Paris.[5] How "new" is New French Thought, I want to ask; in fact, how "French" is it? And most important of all, what does it have to teach us?

The term intellectual fashion is itself not chosen casually, as the second book in the series is Gilles Lipovetsky's provocative *The Empire of Fashion: Dressing Modern Democracy*, a work that celebrates the virtues of consumer capitalism driven by the insatiable demand for the new. Marking the realization of a hedonist utopia, the culture of fashion, according to Lipovetsky's sunny reversal of the pessimistic assessment of leftist and rightist culture critics alike, is a mark of individualist democracy rather than its betrayal. May '68, in his reading, must, in fact, be understood more in terms of a craving for immediate personal gratification than as a serious attempt at revolutionary transformation. We are now benefiting from the triumph of surface over depth, the abundance of possible ways to define ourselves through our consumption patterns, and a frankly narcissistic individualism.

Whether or not this analysis is persuasive, it has the virtue of betraying one of the underlying assumptions of the campaign to promote "new French thought": the belief that intellectual trends must themselves be treated as fashions in the marketplace of ideas and little sympathy need be extended to those who insist on wearing yesterday's clothes. Or as Lilla puts it, we must resist the tendency to hold on to " 'Continental thought' of a particular period and tendency . . . preserved as if in amber, venerated and defended with a passionate dogmatism of which only Americans are capable."[6] Nowhere is this more evident than in the frequent proclamations found throughout these texts that Marxism is no longer as modish in France as it was a generation ago, a conclusion that would be hard to gainsay, but which is then taken to mean that it need no longer be taken seriously in any way, which may be not quite as self-evident. A similar argument functions to diminish the importance of Freud, whose waning popularity will, of course, not be news to North Americans either.

Another expression of the marketing impulse, which to be sure is not an invention of this particular movement, is the deliberate mobilization of catchphrases to characterize the forces on either side of the frontlines. Like a prosecuting attorney trying to make a case against an alleged criminal, they display little hermeneutic charity in their typifications of their opponents' positions. Borrowing the terminology of Fritz Stern, who used it with regard to German proto-fascism, Lilla decries the long hegemony of "French illiberalism," while Holmes entitles one of his books *The Anatomy of Antiliberalism*.[7] The antithesis between "responsible" and "irresponsible" politics is introduced by Tony Judt in his moralistic attempts to defend figures like Leon Blum, Albert Camus, and Raymond Aron against the *marxisant* intelligentsia of the postwar era and their mutant offspring, the left Heideggerians of the post-1968 generation.[8] The charged rhetoric of "humanism" and "anti-humanism" is also frequently marshaled, albeit in reaction to the sweeping critique of humanist universalism first made by many post-structuralist thinkers. Luc Ferry and Alain Renaut, for example, could legitimately subtitle their critique of *French Philosophy of the Sixties* "An Essay on Anti-Humanism."[9] Modernism, broadly speaking, is also defended against its alleged postmodern successor, and the Enlightenment is favored against the Counter-Enlightenment, a preference visually instantiated in the jackets for the *New French Philosophy* series with their serene images of neoclassical architecture from the eighteenth century. Concomitantly, the knee-jerk anti-Americanism of much previous French thought, which cut across the political spectrum,[10] is challenged by the claim, as old as Alexis de Tocqueville, that the American experiment in combining liberalism and democracy has much to teach the Old Continent (and by extension those on the new one who take their cues from abroad).[11]

Although it would be fair to say that this explicit campaign to shift paradigms has not yet had a strong impact on the strongholds of post-structuralist theory in the Anglo-American academy, where names like Manent, Gauchet, Lipovetsky, Kriegel, Bouveresse, or Renaut are still only distant rumors, it has enjoyed a certain modest success in the broader marketplace of ideas. Lilla and Judt, both at NYU (until Lilla's recent move to Chicago) and well connected in the world of New York intellectuals, appear regularly in the pages of *The New York Review of Books* and *The New York Times Book Review.* When, for example, the latter recently sought a commentator on the translation of François Furet's *The Passing of an Illusion: The Idea of Communism in the Twentieth Century*, it was Lilla who was chosen to admonish its readers that the need for a "world beyond the bourgeoisie and beyond Capital, a world in which a genuine human community can flourish" is "a need that no society can ever satisfy."[12] Lilla's role as intellectual impresario was enhanced still further in early 1999, when he took over from Daniel Bell the role of editor of *Correspondence: An International Review of Culture and Society*, the offspring of a new cooperative venture between the Wissenschaftskolleg zu Berlin, the Suntory Foundation of Japan, and the American Academy of Arts and Sciences.[13] This lively digest of intellectual coming and goings around the world, inevitably filtered through the ideological lens of its editor, is, we are told, to be "distributed free-of-charge to leading figures in intellectual and cultural life in the Americas, Europe, and Asia."[14] Clearly, this is an intellectual movement with a game plan for success.

Benefiting from a certain fatigue with the linguistic challenges and conceptual inaccessibility of much post-structuralist theorizing as well as a sense of diminishing returns from its more widely applied lessons, the defenders of the new paradigm have been able to reoccupy some of the territory taken by successive waves of avant-garde thinkers, at least in the popular media. Their *rappel à l'ordre* has been, however, like other such efforts in the past: more of a negative critique of previous theoretical positions, whose political implications they see as less emancipatory than intended, than the promulgation of a genuinely new and positive alternative. Hammering away at Heidegger, Hegel, and Marx, resisting the lure of psychoanalysis, explaining "why we are not Nietzscheans,"[15] they remain little moved by the ways that feminism, queer theory, or postcolonial thought have taken positive sustenance from those "masters of suspicion" in their critiques of the hidden exclusions in ideologies of universalism.

The result is a focus almost entirely on the tradition of liberal Western political theory, whose universalist claims they hope to redeem. Except for Lipovetsky's ruminations on the virtues of consumerism, they do not celebrate unconstrained market capitalism or denounce state intervention in the manner of their neo-liberal cousins in the Anglo-American world. Blandine Kriegel's book, in fact, is an impassioned defense of the lawful state against those who identify it entirely with despotism, normalization, or bureaucratic constraint. If they have any common denominator—and it should not be assumed that they agree on everything—the likeliest candidate would seem to be a desire to revitalize the tradition of human rights as a fundamental dimension of a liberal polity, rights understood, that is, as more than the specific ones bestowed by positive law on the citizens of one state or another. As Lilla puts it, "nowhere has the break with postwar modes of French thought been more apparent than in the new interest, both theoretical and political, in human rights."[16] In what follows, I want therefore to concentrate on the arguments they marshal on behalf of those rights, bracketing of necessity many of the other themes that emerge in their work (and refraining as well from any serious engagement with the enormous literature in English that already has been devoted to this vexed question).[17]

There can be no doubt that the issue of human rights was largely neglected by the thinkers loosely grouped under the post-structuralist umbrella, as it was by many of their predecessors such as Nietzsche.[18] Their attention was more often directed at questions of justice, law, freedom, and what might be called the agonistic dimension of the political, but rarely did they concentrate explicitly on the discourse of rights, whether preceded by the adjective natural or human. Typical of their position was the disdain shown by Derrida in *Of Spirit* for "human rights" as an "axiomatic . . . which, directly or not, comes back to th[e] metaphysics of subjectivity."[19] Frequently intrigued by the antinormativity of political theorists like Carl Schmitt, they stepped gingerly around the unpleasant consequences that could be drawn from it, and historically often were. An exception such as Lyotard's short and relatively thin essay "The General Line" of 1990, which claimed that most basic and absolute of human rights, subtending all the others, is the right to personal separateness from the polity in the region he calls "no man's land," only proves the rule.[20] Although they frequently denounced humanism broadly speaking for its essentialism and transcendentalism and called into question many of the premises of the so-called human sciences, the claim that inalienable rights somehow inhere in the human condition is one that post-structuralist thinkers—perhaps because of the political fall-out from the Blanchot, de Man, and Heidegger scandals—have generally avoided tackling head on.

And yet, they have mounted an indirect attack that is not hard to discern. Although less explicitly scornful than traditional Marxists who decry such rights as bourgeois fictions serving to legitimate the status quo, the post-structuralists have nonetheless tacitly adopted some of their historicist disdain for the transcendental and universalist rhetoric normally underlying rights talk. Although not as celebratory of communal solidarity as neo-Aristotelians like Alasdair MacIntyre, communitarians like Michael Sandel, devotees of republican virtue like J. G. A. Pocock, or antifoundationalist pragmatists like Richard Rorty, they share some of their distrust for abstractions that pretend to transcend cultural contexts. Without restoring premodern notions of duties as prior to rights or hopeful of resurrecting a teleological notion of the common good, they often feel more comfortable evoking asymmetrical obligations, such as those imposed by the face of the other in Levinas's "hostage" philosophy, than reciprocal rights. Railing against the privileging of the present, they nonetheless remain skeptical of the search for ultimate origins, the alleged *archēs* and legitimating foundations that generally subtend rights talk.

If we have to unpack the implicit critique of human rights in the post-structuralist camp, allowing for all of the homogenization that such a task requires, its members present primary challenges to the resurrection of that tradition by the thinkers promoted by Pavel and Lilla. The first concerns the boundaries around and definition of the "human" whose rights are at issue. This means confronting the issue of abstracting the generic category of "man as such" from the concrete cultures in which each of us is to some degree embedded, as well as raising the question of the obliteration or at least marginalization of gender distinctions within that overarching category. It also implies resisting the abjection of the "other" that must be expelled before a fully "proper" notion of the human is realized, as well as reflecting on the permeable demarcation lines between humans and both animals and machines, which are by no means self-evident in an age of increasing cyberization. And perhaps most troubling of all, it means casting doubt on the integrity and self-sufficiency of the individual human subject who is the counterpart of the species category of humanity, the empirical doublet of the transcendental subject of knowledge Foucault famously identified as characteristic of the modern episteme.

The second challenge flows from the post-structuralist suspicion about strategies of legitimation employed to defend rights prior to those conveyed by a specific culture or polity. Here the post-structuralist distrust of absolute origins as points of departure, epitomized by Foucault's genealogical method and Derrida's infinite deferral of closure both backwards and forwards in time, translates into a deep uneasiness with a rhetoric that says something called nature ' "self-evidently" conveys rights on all individuals in whatever historical or cultural context. Acknowledging the performative power of acts of founding and declaration, which provides a way to jump-start a tradition without a prior source of legitimacy, helps to explain how a specific polity might get launched without a recognition of the violence at its origin, but it does little to explain the ground of rights that are alleged to exist prior to such a specific tear in the fabric of history. As in the case of the putative social contract moving us out of a state of nature, the questions arise: Can human rights be simply declared as self-evident when the uncertainty of their provenance is widely acknowledged? Can we plausibly claim that they have been bestowed upon us by our Creator, when we have a sneaking suspicion that no such actual bestowal ever really took place?

The final implicit post-structuralist challenge to the revival of human rights derives from the frequent recognition of what Lyotard calls "differends," those regimes of phrases that are incommensurable and lack any ability to be adjudicated by a higher authority.[21] In the case of human rights, this might mean looking at specific rights and asking how compatible they may be, and if they prove to be at odds, how their competing claims on us can be reconciled. For any serious theory of human rights has to descend from the lofty position of defending them in the aggregate, as if they were a coherent package, and ask hard questions about which rights are included and which are not, as well as explain how they fit together as equally powerful claimants on our protection or, failing that, as elements in a clear hierarchy of value.

In what follows, I want to explore the main answers that the New French Thinkers have given to these troubling questions. On the question of establishing the generic category of the human whose rights are to be defended, their most explicit strategy entails a debunking of the dangers of both historicist relativization and the Hegelian deification of the historical process as a whole. In this battle, they sometimes find an ally in an unlikely place: the philosophy of Leo Strauss. In the American context, where the school founded by Strauss is normally placed on the right, he is considered an elitist conservative with scorn for the egalitarian values of modernity. In Holmes's *Anatomy of Antiliberalism*, Strauss is typically denounced as a bedfellow of such scourges of the liberal tradition as Joseph de Maistre and Carl Schmitt.[22] In France as well, Renaut and Ferry have no patience for his Platonist defense of hierarchy and hostility to the modern age.[23]

But unexpectedly and in tension with the liberal labeling of the series' editors, a more sympathetic appreciation of Strauss's defense of natural rights against historicist and positivist relativism can be found elsewhere in New French Thought. One of its progenitors, Claude Lefort, long since past his days as the Marxist militant of *Socialisme ou barbarie*, had already signaled the change in 1980 when he called Strauss "one of the most penetrating thinkers of our time" and argued that "we can learn from his book, *Natural Right and History*, that the question of human nature was in no way settled by the abandonment of classical thought, that it has continued to haunt modern thought and has become more complicated as a result of the contradictions engendered by positive science and historicism."[24] It is, however, in the work of Pierre Manent, who has the distinction of two translations in the Lilla-Pavel series, where Strauss's influence is most apparent. Manent rehearses Strauss's praise for the wisdom of ancient political theory, based on a positive notion of virtue, and laments the decline of ontological and substantialist notions of human nature, which transcend the merely empirical self.

But when it comes to modern notions of human rights, which he traces to Hobbes and Locke, Manent reveals contempt for what he sees as their lowly origin in fear and defensiveness, based on the purely animal desire for self-preservation. "Preserving one's life, then, is the first human right; it is the matrix of human rights," he observes, "In spite of the rapid growth and diversity of the 'new rights,' the right to self-preservation remains their subterranean and sovereign source."[25] Even when a more positive notion of respect is understood as the basis of human rights, say by Kant, Manent protests that "respect is not far removed from fear, that it is, shall we say, only a refined and superior form of fear; a person is intimidated by what he respects."[26] The danger in this reduction of the good to a question of right, he concludes, is that it allows the alienation of the right to self-preservation to a representative, the absolute sovereign, whose power is then unlimited, as Hobbes showed. The allegedly autonomous individual of the liberal tradition is thus the potential source of a totalitarianism that was unthinkable in ancient times.

Manent, in short, proves to be a very odd defender indeed of the liberal notion of human rights. In fact, other New French Thinkers take him to task for his Straussian excoriation of everything modern, although sharing certain of his other premises.[27] Blandine Kriegel, for example, claims that the ultimate origin of human rights is in the ancient world, or more specifically in the biblical tradition that bestowed value on every member of the species. This tradition, she argues, ultimately supported what she calls the *status libertatis*, which defends the right to life and the security of the individual body. Its legitimation by classical notions of natural law was crucial. She notes, however, that the modern doctrine in its more elaborated form also drew from a later source: the *status civitatus* rooted in private contracts and feudal privileges, which became translated into the rights of free opinion, assembly, property, and association. Philosophically, this second tradition was grounded not in natural law, but in subjective idealism and a voluntarist notion of calculating will, which she claims can be traced back to Descartes and Pufendorf.

Rather than privileging this second concept of human rights, however, Kriegel claims that attempts to assert the importance of the latter over the former are misguided: "To ascribe a feudal origin to individual liberty and its legal recognition is to mistake a part for the whole, the part being *independence* in contrast to *liberation*, *autonomy* in contrast to *emancipation*, *liberties* rather than *liberty*."[28] In fact, "human liberty and civil liberties are not identical, either logically or chronologically. Logically, because they are governed by different legal logics. Human liberty arises from the modern and antidominial conception of power, and it is tied to a notion of a social contract and to a conception of rights as law. Rights are guaranteed by the form of the state. By contrast, civil liberties, most clearly those declared in the eighteenth-century declarations of rights, are derived from the purely individualist notion of contract and from private law."[29]

How then, we might wonder, does Kriegel mount a defense of modernity against Manent's Straussian critique? The answer is that although the *status libertatis* has an older source than the *status civilitatis* and is on firmer ground because of its root in natural law rather than voluntarist contract, she argues that it was not fully affirmed until the modern state gave it juridical status. Even Hobbes's illiberal version of that state did not, she argues implicitly against Manent, assert that the right to one's own self-preservation could be alienated to a sovereign who could dispense with it at will. Thus a fully realized notion of human rights—in particular, the fundamental rights to one's own life and body that prevents arbitrary death, slavery, and concubinage—is a modern phenomenon based on the existence of the rule of law in a constitutional state, even though its roots go back to premodern religious notions of the self. Rather than pitting human rights against the state, as was fashionable when something called "society" was seen as inherently oppressed by statist tyranny, it is only in a state of laws (a *Rechtstaat*) that they mean anything.

The ultimate foundation of human rights for Kriegel remains, however, in the past, in particular in a tradition of natural law arising from religious sources. Such a claim would be difficult to sustain against the post-structuralist suspicion of origins, except as an act of faith, and indeed gives pause to anyone unpersuaded by the logic of secularization as simply the pouring of old wine into new bottles.[30] Ferry and Renaut, to turn to the final consideration of human rights among the New French Thinkers, recognize this problem and acknowledge that "the present renewal of a certain juridical discourse in politics ('rights talk') would gain by clarifying its transcendental conditions of possibility, thus subjecting itself to philosophical interrogation."[31] For an answer they turn to Kant and Fichte, ironically revealing that like post-structuralism, New French Thought more often finds its inspiration across the Rhine than at home.[32]

Against Kriegel's pitting of "emancipation" against "autonomy" and her assimilation of the latter to a problematic emergence of individualist subjectivism, they—especially Renaut in his *Era of the Individual*—attempt to make a crucial distinction between the autonomous subject, to whom rights adhere, and the desiring individual. In so doing, they hope to answer the homogenizing, wholesale critique of the "metaphysical subject" promulgated by Nietzsche and Heidegger and so influential in French post-structuralist thought. They also explicitly distance themselves from Lipovetsky's celebration of the narcissistic and hedonist independence expressed in consumerist choice, which they distinguish from the genuine concept of autonomy on which a solid foundation of human rights can be built. The modern notion of the individual they trace to Leibniz's monadology, in which the self is understood as a windowless, self-contained, desiring being with no dependence on anything outside of itself and thus inherently antisocial. Leibniz's theodicy provided a way to harmonize monads, which was then abandoned with the radical atheism of a Nietzsche. More recent thinkers like Louis Dumont, who invidiously contrast premodern holistic societies with modern individualist ones, are thus following Leibniz's lead in failing to distinguish autonomy, properly understood, from individualism.

Autonomy, Ferry and Renaut claim, is not the opposite of dependence, nor is it absolute self-sufficiency without relation to others. The self-rule of autonomy, its willing dependence on lawful constraint, is contrasted instead with heteronomy, the coerced acceptance of laws imposed from without. "For autonomy is indeed in a sense a form of dependence—but in the sense that its valorization consists in making humanity itself the foundation of (sic) source of its norms and laws, since these are received neither from the nature of things, as the ancients supposed, nor from God, as in the Judeo-Christian tradition. It is no less true that autonomy in the sense of *dependence with regard to self-grounded human laws* is a *form* of independence . . . , but *only in relation to some radical Otherness that seeks to impose Law*."[33]

The Cartesian rather than Leibnizian notion of the subject, albeit containing a confusing mixture of universalist and particularist elements, was the starting point for this concept of autonomy, which came into its own in Kant and Fichte.[34] Their position was not based on the naive metaphysics of dominating subjectivity attributed to them by Heidegger and his disciples. The hedonistic self who seeks happiness, they understood, was inferior to the moral self who is guided by the precepts of practical reason. That self, moreover, entailed a notion of intersubjectivity that was absent from the monadic individualism derived from Leibniz, a notion that Kant developed in the *Critique of Judgment* in his discussion of aesthetics and Fichte elaborated in terms of mutual education in his *Science of Rights*.[35] Critics of modern autonomy, like Levinas, who claim that it fails to honor the other are mistaken, for "*the subject that gives itself its own law must, in order to rise to the level of this auto-nomy, have transcended the self-identity of the desiring subject (individuality) and opened itself up to the otherness of the human species. Transcendence-in-immanence is by definition what autonomy means*."[36]

The upshot of this claim is that human rights are not parasitic on a naive, metaphysical notion of man as such, derived from religious or classical models of human nature, but rather on a teleological idea of a future possibility. "The notion of humanity," "Ferry and Renaut write, "is retained as a regulative idea, with a value of meaning, or as Kant also says, as a symbolic value."[37] In the discourse of human rights, in other words, man is "homo noumenon," an ideal moral being, who is a horizon of ideal meaning, not an object in the world. If there is any foundation to this humanism, it is in a possible future, not an ahistorical present or allegedly presocial past.[38]

Seeking to get beyond the palpable inadequacies of a natural law tradition that is impossible to defend in the modern world and recognizing that a secularized version of religious notions of man smuggles back in precisely the heteronomy that rights discourse seeks to deny, Ferry and Renaut provide perhaps the most intriguing defense of the subject of those rights in the New French Thought literature.[39] But they fail to give us much guidance on the vexed question of precisely which rights are to be defended as species wide and capable of trumping local customs. For if "humanity" is a symbolic vessel to be filled with real substance only in the future, it is impossible to know which rights the "homo noumenon" will feel obliged to defend in the here and now. In fact, by moving away from the happiness of the phenomenal individual in favor of his or her noumenal double, they tacitly relegate the right to self-preservation that other New French Thinkers call the primordial human right to a more marginal position, for mere life is subordinated to obeying the moral law in the Kantian tradition. And ironically, in so doing, they run the risk of producing precisely what Claude Lefort has bemoaned in the Marxist critique of bourgeois rights: "the temptation to exchange the present for the future."[40]

The dilemma of identifying and prioritizing specific rights is, in fact, explicitly acknowledged by the Straussian Manent in *The City of Man*, when he cautions that "all the desires of nature, like all the commandments of the law, can, it seems, be looked at without violence or artifice in terms of human rights. . . . There is nothing under the sun or moon that is not susceptible of becoming the occasion and matter of a human right. This verifies the expansive force of the tautology linking man to the rights of man."[41] Although perhaps an exaggeration, this charge does direct our attention to the often ignored problem of disaggregating human rights into their component parts, which then would require a specific justification for each one. For if one glances at the history of rights discourse, beginning with the great declarations of the American and French Revolutions (including Olympe de Gouges's feminist version), and culminating in the thirty articles of the United Nations Universal Declaration of Human Rights in 1948, it becomes quickly apparent that no complete consensus has ever been achieved about what is a fundamental right and what is not, certainly not across cultures and in many cases not within them as well. The "right to work" in article 23 of the UN Declaration, for example, or the "right to a standard of living adequate for the health and well-being of himself and his family . . . and the right to security in the event of unemployment, etc." of article 26, sit uncomfortably with the free market orthodoxy of neo-liberalism. These so-called "social rights" can easily conflict with an allegedly absolute right to private property. That right has historically been invoked by owners of corporations to deny workers their right to unionize. At other times, segregationists have claimed a natural right to keep the races apart and critics of hate speech have invoked a right not to be offended. And as the endless debate over the right to life versus the right to choose in the abortion debate shows, the Lyotardian notion of an incommensurable "differend" does sometimes accurately describe the conflict between allegedly universal human rights (although luckily not always). It is this outcome that has frustrated commentators like the American literary critic Wai Chee Dimock, who complains that in the "concessionless" universe of human rights, "the adversarial language so crucial to rights turns out to be a language incapable of anything other than a categorical verdict, one that divides the adversaries into those with 'reason' and those with 'no reason,' absolute winners and absolute losers."[42]

Ironically, one implication of this absoluteness, which is at odds with the liberal agenda of the editors of the New French Thought series, is that appeals to human rights often buttress revolutionary movements, which eschew compromise with a corrupt status quo. In fact, as Lynn Hunt has recently reminded us in an essay on "The Origins of Human Rights in France," in which she takes issue with the fashionable attack on the French Revolution launched by Furet, "the intimate connection between rights and revolution (both in their establishment and their most obvious annihilation) has not been properly recognized and the consequences not fully explored."[43] The Marxist critique of bourgeois rights notwithstanding, rights talk has often functioned as a legitimation for violent resistance to oppressive authority, even if some of its defenders, such as Kant, have sought to head off precisely that implication.[44]

Be that as it may, in our own time, the appeal to human rights seems just as easily to be invoked to legitimate interference in the affairs of other countries, as in the case of Kosovo. It is very difficult to dismiss the power of that appeal, even when the cultural integrity and political sovereignty of the offending nation-state are violated. To the extent that New French Thinkers have redirected our attention to the question of human rights, which was never satisfactorily addressed by their post-structuralist predecessors, they should be taken seriously. But the concrete help they have given us in responding to the challenges of those predecessors—the uncertain boundaries of the category of the "human," the difficulty of finding a foundational *point d'appui* for transcendent rights, and the possible incommensurability of some of those alleged rights—is, as I have tried to show in this brief overview of their contribution, relatively modest. Even Richard Wolin, himself a vociferous critic of French Nietzschean and Heideggerian thought, has conceded that "the neoliberal attempts to base democratic politics on the rights of 'man,' separation of powers, and individualism, have, in truth, added very little to the time-honored catalogue of liberal nostrums . . . they have shown little sensitivity to the problematics of those thinkers who have legitimately called into question the viability of the traditional conception of the subject from the standpoint of contemporary intellectual and cultural needs."[45] Perhaps it is time to stop looking to French thought, new or otherwise, for guidance in such matters, and begin to rely more on our own conceptual resources and traditions.[46] Perhaps we don't need to cut our intellectual clothes to the latest Paris fashion or expect new master tailors to replace the ones whose brilliance is now fading. And perhaps in refusing to do so, we can begin to realize the promise in what is arguably the most fundamental human right, albeit one which no governmental code can guarantee: the right to be allowed to think for oneself.

14

SOMAESTHETICS AND DEMOCRACY
John Dewey and Contemporary Body Art

Perhaps no twentieth-century philosopher was as favorably inclined towards the role of aesthetic experience in building a democratic culture as was John Dewey, the preeminent public intellectual in America during the first half of the twentieth century. His vision of democracy necessitated a robust commitment not only to an open-ended process of unimpeded free inquiry, which emulated that of the scientific community, but also to the self-realization that came through active participation in the public sphere. The model of that self-realization he saw best expressed in the sensually mediated, organically consummated, formally molded activity that was aesthetic experience. "That which distinguishes an experience as esthetic (sic)," he wrote, "is conversion of resistance and tensions, of excitations that in themselves are temptations to diversions, into movement toward an inclusive and fulfilling close."[1] As such, it was the quintessential exemplar of what is meant when we say we "have *an* experience," rather than merely register an ephemeral sensation. In the words of Thomas Alexander, the foremost commentator on Dewey's aesthetics, "in the idea of art we find the moment in which human alienation is overcome and the need for the experience of meaning and value is satisfied. Through art, in the aesthetic experience, the rift in the world that frustrates our primordial desire for encountering a sense of meaning and value is healed."[2]

Because aesthetic experience has as its telos consummation, closure, fulfillment and inclusion, it can function as the model of a democratic politics that goes beyond a thin proceduralism to a more substantive form of life. "Art is a mode of production," Dewey wrote, "not found in charts and statistics, and it insinuates possibilities of human relations not to be found in rule and precept, admonition and administration."[3] Thus, as one of his most eminent recent biographers, Robert Westbrook has correctly noted with reference to Dewey's great work of 1934, "*Art as Experience* was not incidental to the radical politics that absorbed Dewey in the 1930's. Indeed, it was one of the most powerful statements of that politics, for it clearly indicated that his was not a radicalism directed solely to the material well-being of the American people but directed as well to the provision of consummatory experience that could be found only outside the circulation of commodities"[4] Or as another recent student of Dewey, David Fott, puts it, "For Dewey aesthetic experience is the paradigmatic form of meaningful experience, occurring when the controlling concern in experience is the immediately felt relation of order or fulfillment. That relation may obtain in political matters as well as in any other sort; in fact, we can consider aesthetic experience the goal of our attempts to solve our political problems, which arise when disorder is felt to occur."[5]

For Dewey, the full potential of aesthetic experience and of its political counterpart would be realized only if three fundamental changes were effected. First, art had to leave the elite world of museums and private galleries behind and become part of the everyday life of the masses. Life lived aesthetically would overcome the gap between means and ends and abet the inclusion of the many in the pleasures heretofore enjoyed only by the few. What Peter Bürger has seen as the historical mission of the avant-garde as opposed to that of the modernists, the infusing of life with the redemptive power of art, was thus also shared by Dewey.[6]

Second, aesthetic experience had to wean itself from the Kantian notion that it was inherently contemplative and spectatorial. The claim in the *Critique of Judgment* that disinterestedness was the hallmark of the aesthetic had to be abandoned, and the rights of need, desire, and yearning acknowledged as just as inherent in aesthetic experience as in experience in general. In fact, to the extent that the term "aesthetic" had contemplative connotations, Dewey preferred to speak of artistic experience instead. For whereas the former suggested perception, pleasure, and judgment, and was thus relatively passive in implication, the latter connoted production and action, making rather than merely enjoying or judging what others had made. Both, Dewey argued, should be acknowledged as complementary dimensions of politics as well as art.

Third, aesthetic or rather artistic experience involved the whole body and not just the mind and imagination or even the senses as receptors of stimuli from without. Dewey thus resisted the time-honored hierarchy that still subtended contemporary taste, which, so he charged, "tends to reckon as higher the fine arts that reshape material, where the product is enduring rather than fugitive, and is capable of appealing to a wide circle, including the unborn, in contrast with the limitation of singing, dancing, and oral story-telling to an immediate audience. But all rankings of higher and lower are, ultimately, out of place and stupid. Each medium has its own efficacy and value."[7] For politics, it was therefore perhaps the performative arts that were even more important than those devoted to building permanent objects for posterity, an insight that anticipated Hannah Arendt's well-known distinction in *The Human Condition* between man as *homo faber* and as political performer.

Although in eclipse for a generation after his death in 1952, pragmatism in general and Dewey in particular have enjoyed an extraordinary renaissance of interest in the past two decades. One of reasons for that renewed interest is precisely his theory of aesthetic experience and its larger implications.[8] Building on Dewey's argument, the contemporary pragmatist philosopher Richard Shusterman has proposed an ambitious project of what he calls "somaesthetics."[9] Hoping to efface the distinction between the fine arts and mere craftsmanship and undermine the exclusivity of art as an autonomous institution, Shusterman praises Dewey for his willingness to "exchange high art's autocratic aura of transcendental authority for a more down-to-earth and democratic glow of enhanced living and enriched community of understanding."[10] Noting Dewey's fascination for the body therapeutics of F. Matthias Alexander, whose system of upper torso exercises were designed to enhance breathing, posture, and motion, he argues that essential to aesthetic experience is prediscursive corporeal development.[11] Resisting the recasting of pragmatism in entirely linguistic terms urged by Richard Rorty, Shusterman insists on repairing the breach between mind and body. "The most radical and interesting way for philosophy to engage somatics," he writes, "is to integrate such bodily disciplines into the very practice of philosophy. This means practicing philosophy not simply as a discursive genre, a form of writing, but as a discipline of embodied life."[12]

Looking around for a current example of realized somaesthetics, Shusterman hit on rap and hip-hop music as embodiments of a democratic and inclusive practice that resists the purist claims of aesthetic autonomy. "Hip-hop repudiates such purity," he writes. "It wants to be appreciated fully through energetic movement and impassioned dance, not immobile, dispassionate contemplation."[13] The politics of this music, an aggressive burst of outrage and protest against social and racial injustice, belies the stereotype of popular art as inherently conservative and conformist. What its performers call "message" or "knowledge rap" is intended to integrate aesthetic with ethical and political concerns. "Though few may know it," Shusterman argues, "rap philosophers are really 'down with' Dewey, not merely in metaphysics but in a non-compartmentalized aesthetics which highlights social function, process and embodied experience."[14]

Whatever one may think of Shusterman's celebration of rap as a successful realization of the Deweyan ideal—he himself recognizes its distance from the irenic telos of consummation and order—it raises the question of the relationship between contemporary artistic practices, broadly defined, and the realization of democracy. Rap and hip hop are, to be sure, popular phenomena, which have introduced oppositional politics of a sort into the culture industry. At times, however, that politics has expressed itself in blatantly misogynist and homophobic terms, which Shusterman does not fully confront, although he acknowledges its dangerous rhetoric of violence. And to the extent that is has been commercially successful, it has perhaps lost some of its critical impetus.

It might therefore be useful to turn elsewhere for evidence of the plausibility of Dewey's ideas. We don't really have far to look. For a much more explicit attempt to combine somaesthetics with a critique of these impediments to democratic culture has, in fact, been made over the past forty years by artists who are not treated by Shusterman, perhaps because of their still esoteric appeal (if appeal is the right word).[15] I am speaking of a loose international community of performance artists who have experimented in often transgressive and provocative ways with their own bodies. With the recent publication of Tracy Warr and Amelia Jones' lavishly documented and graphically illustrated survey of what they call *The Artist's Body*, we can perhaps see for the first time the full extent and variety of this still vibrant movement.[16]

Although anticipations can be found in the performative impulse in Futurism, Dadaism, and Constructivism in the first decades of the last century and Antonin Artaud's Theater of Cruelty—perhaps they can even be spotted as early as the ancient Cynic philosopher Diogenes of Sinope—it was not really until the waning of High Modernism in the 1960s that it could fully develop. Inspired by the action painting identified with Jackson Pollock, which had drawn attention away from the canvas to the vigorous gesture of putting paint on its surface, and taking their cue from the foregrounding of the artist's complicated, often theatrically contrived identity advanced by Marcel Duchamp, artists in a number of countries in Europe, Asia, and the Americas began to turn attention to their own bodies as sites of artistic expression. Rejecting the high modernist fetish of formal purity—which had still tacitly informed Dewey's aesthetics of consummation[17]—and impatient with the worship of art objects functioning as embodiments of value in both the economic marketplace and canonical history of art, they turned to ephemeral performances, which were site-specific, often outside of the gallery or museum, and designed to leave no permanent residue beyond the recording of their appearance on film, video, or photographs. Hostile to traditional notions of authorial sovereignty, they often worked collaboratively or anonymously, refusing the heroic, normally male-gendered version of artistic genius still so powerful in modernist movements like abstract expressionism. No less distrustful of conventional notions of beauty or sensual pleasure, they disdained, as had Duchamp, mere "retinal painting" in favor of an art based on ideas, theories, linguistic reflexivity, and social critique, while all the time using their bodies as the material on which these conceptual projects were realized. Or more precisely, they paradoxically realized the dematerializing ambitions of conceptual art through the medium of bodies that were understood in terms of what Bataille would have called "base materialism," the body as a site of creaturely vulnerability, even abasement and decay, rather than ennobling beautification. In so doing, they intensified the antioptical theatricalization of the aesthetic experience, that addressing of the body of the beholder in real time that formalist critics like Michael Fried were vigorously, if unsuccessfully, condemning in the Minimalist art of the 1960s.[18]

During the earliest phases of body art, there was often an ecstatic sense of release from normal constraints, sexual in particular, which expressed the celebration of polymorphous perversity characteristic of the sixties at their most utopian. Works like Carolee Schneeman's *Meat Joy* of 1964, described by Warr and Jones as "an orgiastic happening in which male and female performers grappled with one another an a variety of fleshy, messy materials in close proximity to the audience,"[19] sought to liberate the body from the constraints imposed by moral, aesthetic, and social conventions. That the artist was a woman willing to perform naked in public was itself a radical departure, although male artists like Yves Klein had already used nude female models writhing on a canvas covered in his trademark blue paint to produce what he called "anthropometric" paintings in 1960. The Italian artist

Piero Manzoni, whose all-white canvases called *Achromes* registered the exhaustion of painting, had taken the process one step further by eliminating canvases entirely. In 1961, he exhibited what he called *Living Sculpture* in which nude models were signed by the artist and given a certificate of authenticity certifying that henceforth they were to be considered as genuine works of art.

Schneeman and other female performance artists who exhibited their unclothed bodies radicalized these gestures by wresting control of the aesthetic process from male artists. They explicitly sought the reversal of the sublimation of the naked, lust-inspiring body into the elevated nude, which had been a feature of Western art and the ideology of aesthetic disinterestedness for centuries. Following Duchamp, they urged the nude to descend the staircase from her pedestal and reveal herself, as she had done in Duchamp's final work, his infamous installation *Étant donnés (Being Given)*, as an explicit object of a voyeuristic gaze. Or rather, they sought to challenge the objectification of women through that gaze by pushing it to its limit and seizing control over the conditions of display and titillation.

Not only the objectification of women's bodies but the reification of their essence came under attack, as body artists anticipated the breakdown of gender boundaries later advocated by queer theorists like Judith Butler. In 1970, the New York artist Vito Acconci performed a piece called *Conversions* in which he pulled at each of his nipples to produce women's breasts, burned off his body hair and hid his penis between his legs in order to subvert his masculinity. The heady capacity to live beyond given gender categories, long a feature of drag queen self-fashioning, had been enacted by Duchamp in his celebrated self-image as Rrose Sélavy and then imitated by Andy Warhol's "Forged Image" a generation later. It inspired body artists like Paul McCarthy to masquerade both as a female sex object with a blond wig, mascara, and black panties and a randy male sailor who has sex with hamburger meat and mayonnaise in a 1975 performance called "Sailor's Meat." A year before, Lynda Benglis photographed herself nude with an immense rubber penis protruding from her body in an advertisement for a gallery that she placed in the art journal *Artforum*, thus ridiculing the imperative to decide whether she was a male or female artist.

From virtually the beginning, however, body art evinced a darker, more troubled side, which went beyond merely calling into question conventional gender categories. It increasingly moved away from the wholesome vision of integrated, consummatory artistic experience defended by Dewey and still informing Shusterman's somaesthetics, a telos that perhaps with some license could still be seen underlying the androgynous experiments of artists like Acconi, Benglis, and

McCarthy. Take, for example, the trajectory that led from Pollock's hyper-masculinist action paintings with their unavoidable evocation of ejaculatory frenzy to the Fluxus artist Shigeko Kubota's 1965 "Vagina Painting," in which she used a brush tacked on to her panties to smear red, menstrual-like paint on a canvas, to Rachel Lachowicz's "Red Not Blue" of 1992, in which men rather than Klein's women applied the color red, the color of menstrual blood, instead of his signature blue to a canvas via paint on their bodies and lipstick affixed to their penises, and finally to Keith Boadwee's 1995 "Untitled (Purple Squirt)," in which the artist somehow contrived to expel purple paint from his anus while lying on his back, in a gesture that mixed homoerotic anal-eroticism with excremental aggression. Instead of the heroic expression of the male creative body, whose inspired actions left traces of their presence on canvases that were meant to be hung vertically on museum walls, the results were resolutely horizontal in implication, fully opposed to the elevating sublimation of the raw body, and explicitly hostile to conventional standards of heteronormativity. Those who watched these performances or their video records were thrust into the world of the *informe*—formlessness—and base materiality celebrated by Georges Bataille, rather than the realm of art as cultivation of the senses and elevation of the sensibility.

At the same time as the gender assumptions and formalist purism of high modernism was being challenged by artists like Schneeman, Kubota, Lachowicz and Boadwee, even more transgressive performances with highly charged political and religious implications were mounted by the group calling themselves Actionists in Austria, led by Hermann Nitsch, Günter Brus, Rudolf Schwarzkogler, and Otto Mühl.[20] Here the dominant emotional effect was less lust than disgust, with meat not a source of joy, but of anguish. Nitsch's "Orgies-Mysteries Theater," which took place in the Schloss Prinzdorf in 1984.

> accommodated large numbers of performers and spectators for a three-day long Dionysiac orgy of blood and gore. Participants could come and go at will: activities included ritual disembowelments of bulls and sheep, stuffing entrails back into hacked-open carcasses, the treading of huge vats of grapes mixed with entrails, blood and wine, blood-letting on to actors representing Christ and Oedipus, and night-time processions around the castle with pigs, goats, sheep, horses, dogs and cattle and actors bearing flaming torches. Finally, buckets of blood, slime and entrails were dropped from helicopters on to military tanks, which then drove away.[21]

Contra Nietzsche, this was art as all Dionysus and no Apollo, a far cry from the glittering ornamentalism and precious elitism of the Viennese *fin-de-siècle* then being restored to its previous glory by the art establishment in the Austrian capital. Inevitably it provoked the strong reactions it so desperately sought, both from the state and from a confused and unsettled public, which worried about its dangerous identification with the regressive and nihilistic impulses it brought to the surface. Perhaps the most disturbing moment in the Actionist assault on bourgeois sensibilities, and as it turned out not on them alone, came in 1968 at the University of Vienna when Brus and his colleagues were asked to join a political meeting called "Art and Revolution," devoted to the role of art in late capitalist society. In what became know as "Action 33," Brus, standing naked on a chair, cut his body with a razor blade, urinated into a glass from which he then drank, defecated on the floor and smeared himself with his own excrement, masturbated while singing the Austrian national anthem and the university song "Gaudeamus Igitur," and capped it all off by inducing himself to vomit. Not only did this earn him an arrest by the state, whose still fascist essence he hoped to reveal, and exile to Germany, but also the wrath of the student militants, who thought he was mocking their pretensions to revolution.

However one interprets the highly ritualized spectacles of sacrifice and redemption staged by the Viennese Actionists with their echoes of German Expressionist pathos and violent reversal of everything held sacred in the traditional notion of *Kultur*, they foreshadowed powerful trends in the body art of the next two decades, in which masochistic self-mutilation, loss of boundaries between the interior and exterior of the artists' body, and a confusion of spectator and participant were all pursued with ferocious ingenuity. What was perhaps missing in the later work, however, was the attempt to create an ecstatic community, a communal festival rather than an alienated spectacle, a utopian goal that was a casualty of the post-1960s turn against redemptive politics and counter-cultural solidarity. What did remain, however, was the emphasis on the body in pain, to use Elaine Scarry's celebrated phrase, not the body in ecstatic pleasure.

Although it is dangerous to generalize about so heterogeneous a range of work, the body artists of the 1980s and 1990s seemed intent on foregrounding and even reveling in trauma, in both its physical and psychological senses, rather than trying to suppress or work it through. Self-abuse ran the gamut, metaphorical to literal, from Vito Acconci's *Seedbed* of 1971, in which he masturbated under a ramp in the Sonnabend gallery in New York, to the self-inflicted cuts to her hands, face and back by the French artist Gina Pane in 1972, or the Yugoslav Marina Abramovic's *Rhythm O* of 1974, in which she provided instruments of torture to her audience and asked them to use them on her for six hours (after three, apparently, a fight broke out among the torturers, who had done a frighteningly thorough job of hurting and humiliating her, and the ordeal ended). In 1976 and a performance called "Event for Stretched Skin," the Australian artist Stelarc pierced his own back with meat hooks and suspended himself over various sites such as a street in New York or a gallery in Tokyo. In works like her live video operation-performance of 1993 entitled *Omnipresence*, the French artist Orlan showed plastic surgeons cutting into and rearranging her face to conform to traditional Western ideals of feminine pulchritude. Revealing how detachable and malleable the face can actually be in our increasingly posthuman world of prostheses and cyberization, she both mocked conventional standards of beauty and compelled the horrified viewer to share her self-inflicted pain. In many of these examples, in fact, the extraordinary discomfort of the audience, scarcely able to look at the horror before them in the face, was deliberately intended, thus evoking in a very different register Dewey's appeal to overcome the distinction between artistic and aesthetic experience.

Whether the intention was highlighting violence to women, the evils of political torture, the plight of the insane, or the ravages of AIDS, these works were meant to shock their audiences out of the anaesthetic complacency into which they had fallen. Mobilizing aesthetics against anaesthesia restored the original meaning of the term coined by Alexander Baumgarten in the eighteenth century, when it sought to draw philosophy's attention to the body and the senses. But now it was not the sublimated body, the beautiful body, the body of grace and proportion, but rather the abject body, the body of base materiality, the body invaded by technology, ravaged by disease, and unable to maintain its normal boundaries.

Whether or not the results were what can be called "great art" or even "art" by any normal definition of the word is not an issue I want to raise; there are obvious distinctions of quality, originality, and efficacy among the many exemplars of body art that have accumulated over the past forty years. But if we take an institutional approach to the issue of what is or is not art, that pioneered by philosophers like George Dickie and sociologists like Pierre Bourdieu, there can be little doubt that this work has passed the test and is now included in the canon broadly conceived. It is also clear that as in all projects of intended radical transgression, here too there are contradictions that vitiate the intentions of the artists. As I have tried to argue elsewhere in connection with the embrace of abjection as a term of approbation in the 1990s, the impulse to undermine the institution of art and privilege desublimation as an end in itself can court bad faith when it leads to the deliberate creation of abject objects for display in the very museums they are supposed to subvert.[22] Most body artists resisted leaving behind more than photographic records of their ephemeral events, but these too have found their way into the canonical embrace of the all-devouring art machine. It is also not always certain whether or not the willingness to challenge taboos is inherently liberating or simply a kind of acting out that demands ever more radical manifestations, thus duplicating the logic of incessant innovation and search for means to astonish the bored masses that is so much an engine of the capitalist production of desire. Herbert Marcuse may have been an inspiration to the body art of the 1960s, but it is important to recall his warning against what he called "repressive desublimation," in which apparent liberation produced its opposite.

What is in any case abundantly clear is that we have moved a long way from Dewey's sunny vision of an art that presents attractive "possibilities of human relations" prefiguring a utopian form of realized life in the future. Even the hip hop music extolled by Shusterman as an example of a liberating somaesthetics seems bland in comparison; rapping and sampling are, after all, pretty tame when set against the self-mutilation of an Orlan, Chris Burden, or Bob Flanagan. But it may nonetheless be arguable that the body art of the past generation, for all its remaining outside the mainstream, does have something useful to tell us about democratic culture, or at least the challenges to it. Without wanting to make inflated claims about its importance, let me suggest at least a few possible ways in which it can be understood in these terms.

Most obviously, body art does so by continuing and deepening that long-standing trend to expand the subject matter thought fit for aesthetic appropriation. By overturning any remaining hierarchical residues of aesthetic value and rejecting an organic notion of the integrated artwork, it also works against any residual belief in the body politic as an organic metaphor of naturally legitimated super- and sub-ordination. On questions of gender and sexual identity, body art has clearly been aggressively forcing us to confront on a visceral level issues that that the most advanced thinkers in these areas have only been able to raise in theoretical terms. Moreover, what Arthur Danto famously called the "transfiguration of the commonplace" has now been extended to those dimension of human experience that were below all previous thresholds of respectability and suitability, except in the feverish imaginations of the dark writers of the Enlightenment like Sade or their twentieth-century descendents like Bataille.[23]

But rather than producing a problematic "aestheticization" of what should be confronted in moral or political terms, that danger against which Walter Benjamin famously warned in the case of fascist spectacle, this art refuses to beautify the hideous or sweeten the unpalatable in the service of formal pleasure (with certain exceptions aside like the coldly beautiful photographs of Robert Mapplethorpe, which make their way into the Warr and Jones anthology). Instead, it forces those with the stomachs to watch unflinchingly to realize that art need not transfigure or sublimate everything it touches, but rather can find ways to preserve its raw power and disturbing exigency. This is an art that resolutely resists the contemplative stance of disinterestedness associated with aestheticization at its furthest remove from moral and political problems, an aestheticization that paradoxically can have the anaesthetic function of numbing us to the real pain outside. It makes us aware, as Dewey would have hoped it would, that the interests of life break through the frame of art, no matter how fierce the attempt to keep them at bay.

In a less obvious sense, the transgressive body art of the past three decades has also opened important questions about the limits and composition of the public sphere, which is taken to be the site of democratic will-formation. Against the assumption that there is a single public sphere in which citizens come together to argue about the great issues of the day, a modern version of the Athenian agora writ large, it shows us how fragmented and plural public spheres are in contemporary democracies. For there can be no doubt that this is art by and for a minority audience, an art that cannot even pretend to mass appeal. Unlike the rap and hip hop musicians and wordsmiths celebrated by Shusterman, this is a body art without obvious roots in popular culture and very little ability to make its mark in the commercial market place. Although as shown by the dubious entanglements of the Brooklyn Museum of Art's infamous "Sensation" exhibition with its business sponsor, body art is not entirely safe from the lure of the marketplace, by and large, most of it has been able to avoid the temptations of commercial cooptation.[24]

When it does intersect with the more general public sphere, as it did when that show came under fire from the Giuliani administration for its alleged blasphemous implications, it was precisely its challenge to the reigning assumptions about decency, artistic value, and the role of state sponsorship of controversial art that had a democratizing effect. That is, by introducing ideas and artistic practices that could only have been nurtured in the permissive climate of an enclave public, a public that existed below the radar screen of the mass media, could it bring new issues to the more general public sphere, which could then make a start in sorting out their implications. Democracy, we might say, works best if such enclaves are allowed relative autonomy and allowed to serve as laboratories for unorthodox and even offensive ideas and practices, which can then invigorate, outrage, and provoke the general public, whose pieties need to be challenged from time to time. Although the more general public can easily dismiss what it finds objectionable as self-indulgent and exhibitionist acting out rather than anything worthy of the honorific title of art, and often has, in time, a kind of learning process can take place in which at least some of the provocations produce more general reflections on the cultural and political issues raised by the offenders.

There is also a powerful link between body art, indeed performance art of all kinds, and the fostering of a democratic culture. That is, the very gesture of resisting the reification of art objects and insistence on the transience and site-specificity of body art reminds us that democracy itself is a process, not a state of being, and a perpetually uncompleted project at that. To paraphrase Kant's famous description of the *Aufklärung,* we do not live in a democratic age, but in age of democratization. Contrary to Dewey's stress on the consummatory quality of artworks, it is precisely the open-ended, unfinished quality of body art, its refusal to leave a fixed residue behind, that best serves democratic culture. If, as Habermas has famously argued, the goal of perfect consensus is an ideal telos of intersubjective communication, which is only asymptotically realized, the performativity of body-art, its insistence that even the body is a process, not a fixed object in the world, powerfully instantiates the way in which democracy is always in front of us, never fully achieved. The illocutionary promise of a consensus based on rational deliberation and the victory of the better argument is always just short of being cashed in, even as we may strive to attain it. One might even argue that the confrontational impact of this art pays homage to the agonistic moment in democratic practice, which allows, indeed nurtures, creative dissensus rather than forcing a homogenizing consensus.

A similar conclusion follows from the complexity introduced by body art into the time-honored question of representation, which presents, of course, both a political and an aesthetic conundrum. By using the artist's body as a site of aesthetic experimentation, often taking real risks in so doing, the distinction between presence and representation is tacitly called into question. Although at times what seemed real was not—Nitsch and the Viennese Actionists dismembered only dead sheep, not live ones, and the legendary death by self-castration of

Rudolf Schwarzkogler was just that, only a legend—at others the knife did really cut flesh and the blood was real. Some body artists did have themselves shot in the arm and did sleep with corpses and did nail their foreskins to boards. The result has been to undermine the privilege and self-sufficiency of the represented image over the actual activity, thus working against the extraordinary power that images have in the media-saturated mass democracy of the modern world.

Instead of providing a positive representation of the sovereign people, this art reflects the insight of recent political theorists like Claude Lefort and Jean-Luc Nancy that at the center of the political realm there is an absence, a void, a lack, which is filled only at our peril. In resisting sublimation, metaphorization and representation, body art thus helps us avoid trying to construct a mythical embodiment of "the people," an embodiment that can only be simulacral and deceptive because it covers over the inevitable distinctions, even conflicts, which always subtend it. It reminds us that the "demos" in democracy is only a fictional or counterfactual notion, never perfectly equal to an ontologically real object in the world.

Another way to make this point is to note the foregrounding of trauma in body art, which refuses to sugarcoat the violence that was so much a feature of the terrible twentieth century. It may not be accidental that both Nitsch and Schwarzkogler's fathers were killed fighting for the Nazis, while Mühl himself fought in the war and was a POW.[25] Their ritualistic orgies of mayhem and redemption were, it seems, designed in part to remind Austrians of a past they were not anxious to register. If, as Cathy Caruth has argued, trauma involves a kind of "unclaimed experience" in which the wound doesn't heal, but remains still festering beneath the scar, then the deeply troubled art we have been discussing expresses the belatedness of a traumatic event or events that have not yet been assimilated or reconciled.[26] As such, it brings to the surface those moments of founding violence that even the most democratic polity has difficult fully acknowledging. Much of the body art we have been discussing can thus be called, *pace* Dewey, art as unclaimed experience, in which the temporal fragmentation of belatedness and repetition go hand in hand with the disintegration of spatial integrity and the permeability of boundaries.

Yet another way that body art might be seen as potentially in tandem with democratic impulses is through its explicit resistance to the disciplining and normalization of the docile body—whether through the harsh regulations of factory labor or the soft inducements of mainstream conventions of beauty—of which Foucault has made us all so aware. This hope has recently been expressed in Michael Hardt and

Antonio Negri's provocative new book *Empire*, which explicitly cites body artists like Stelarc as models of a new "posthuman" refashioning of the body.[27] Although acknowledging its problematic colonization by mass culture in the service of the status quo, Hardt and Negri also manage to give it a positive potential. "Today's corporeal mutations," they write, "constitute an *anthropological exodus* and represent an extraordinarily important, but still quite ambiguous, element of the configuration of republicanism 'against' imperial civilization. The anthropological exodus is important precisely because here is where the positive, constructive face of the mutation begins to appear: an ontological mutation in action, the concrete invention of a first *new place in the non-place*."[28]

Whatever one thinks of Hardt and Negri's tentative mobilization of transgressive somaesthetics for positive purposes—Stelarc's performances may perhaps be best seen as instances of ascetic self-discipline rather than expressions of bodily vulnerability—it brings us almost full circle back to John Dewey's *Art as Experience*. But the detour has certainly complicated the assumptions that underlay it. Dewey's aesthetics, it has been often been noted, lacked any sense of the sublime.[29] It was inspired by a desire to make the world more and more available for sensual appropriation and aesthetic mastery, more and more a home for lives of beauty and meaning, and thus lacked an acknowledgment of the limits to representation presented by the sublime. Although there are, of course, obvious dangers in a politics that is based entirely on the experience of sublime horror and awe, it may be the case that a certain humility when it comes to our power to remake the world in the image of beauty is a valuable dimension of a democratic politics that knows it is perpetually falling short of the absolute realization of its goal. And while there may well be questions raised about the compatibility between the human rights discourse that is now so much a part of democratic culture, a discourse that has one of its foundations the inviolability of the human body, and an art that seems so intent on demonstrating its antithesis, there is sufficient warrant in much—albeit not all—of the work to read it as protesting rather than celebrating the pain it so powerfully evokes. And perhaps in so doing, it serves as a negative instantiation of the more substantive notion of democratic culture that we've seen Dewey contrast with its thin proceduralist twin. In short, for all its aggression against the mainstream *sensus communis*, for all its willingness to flirt with the violence and irrationality that would seem to be the antithesis of democratic politics, the body art so tenaciously performed in the enclaves of avant-garde culture over the past forty years may be a version of somaesthetics that has something to teach democracy after all.

15

THE PARADOXES OF RELIGIOUS VIOLENCE

Of the many ironies that characterized the recent presidential campaign—Gore, the master debater, losing the debates; Bush, the dissolute frat boy, winning the character issue; Clinton, the impeached liar, looking increasingly presidential in comparison to his would-be successors, all topped off by the winner of the popular vote declared the loser of the election—none was as poignant as the spectacle of the first Jewish candidate for high office, Joseph Lieberman, extolling the virtues of religious morality against the backdrop of the escalating violence in the Middle East. For despite all of the high-minded claims he made on behalf of religion's civilizing function, the evidence in front of our eyes is of how poisonous religious conflicts can be in undercutting what most civilizations call moral norms. However one judges the arguments on both sides of the Middle East conflict, an incontrovertible fact at its heart is the willingness, even eagerness, of each party to resort to violent means to reach ends that are often explicitly religious in nature. Whether one sees Ariel Sharon's ill-fated visit to the Temple Mount as a cynical provocation or as the assertion of a justifiable right, the fact that it could produce such a horrific outcome speaks volumes about the thinness of the veneer of mutual tolerance that keeps these different religions from each other's throats.

To an outside observer unmoved by the call of faith—and that, let it be said at the outset, is where this writer stands—perhaps the most perplexing question concerning religion is its radical proximity to the very violence it so often purports to lament. Recent works by Mark Juergensmeyer, *Terror in the Mind of God: The Global Rise of Religious Violence*, and John R. Hall, *Apocalypse Observed: Religious Movements and Violence in North America, Europe and Japan,*[1] have focused attention on the troubling explosion of religiously legitimated violence on the fringes of the organized great religions. One need only list some obvious examples to make the point: the Branch Davidians of Waco, Jim Jones's People's Temple, Heaven's Gate, Japan's Aum Shinrikyo, Meier Kahane's Kach movement, and the Order of the Solar Temple in Switzerland and Quebec all manifested deadly violence, whether aimed at external foes or against themselves. In the guise of religious warfare against enemies imagined or real, collective martyrdom manifesting the intensity of their faith, or the alleged realization of apocalyptic prophecies, such movements raise profound questions about the deep and abiding link between religious belief, practice, and institutionalization, on the one hand, and violating the putative sanctity of human life and the inviolability of the human body, on the other.

Although it might be possible to dismiss these groups as aberrations with little to tell us about a fundamental dimension of religious life, characterize them as paranoid cults rather than genuine religions, or even attribute the upsurge of violence to millennial fantasies soon to be left behind as we move into the twenty-first century, an alternative response is more compelling. What do they reveal, we should ask, about the unfinished business that ties together the sacred and the violent? Is religion, understood broadly, part of the problem or part of the solution (or perhaps in different ways both)? Can the resources to combat violence come from within religion or do we need to examine other strategies to deal with its threat? Without trying to uncover the essence of all religions, an inevitably futile task, or even to speculate on the full spectrum of historical and cultural variations that tie one form or another to sanctified violence, it is certainly worth seeking answers to these highly fraught, and alas increasingly timely, questions.

In the great Western religious traditions, founding acts of violence have, of course, played a central role. If Rudolf Otto is right, the inexplicable and amoral "wrath of God" is a fundamental moment in the "mysterium tremendum" that helps to define the idea of the holy.[2] Greek paganism, despite attempts by the classicist tradition to whitewash its origins, was rooted in frequent acts of sacrificial piety—slaughtering and eating rams or bulls—to Olympian gods. Animal sacrifice, following highly codified rituals of preparation, consecration, purification, and restoration, was a staple of Jewish life before the destruction of the Temple. Abraham's willingness to slaughter Isaac in obedience to God's command showed how the shedding of human blood could also be an act of profound religious faith. Circumcision rites, some would argue, testify to its persistence into our own time. In certain cases, the motivation for sacrifice was to propitiate divine forces and win in return some favor, such as good crops, political stability, or long life, while in others, it expressed a noninstrumental logic, giving something to God with no quid pro quo. As such, sacrifice can be said to duplicate the dual function of prayer as either request or praise. But in both cases, it meant a willingness to sanctify the shedding of innocent blood, and thus challenge one of the most frequent and fundamental moral imperatives espoused by religion itself.

Although the Crucifixion could be interpreted as an extraordinary sacrifice designed to end the need for future sacrificial violence, the symbolic residue in the Mass, conducted at an altar whose sacrificial function could not be entirely forgotten, left a vivid reminder of the original deed. The brutal murder of God's son, a self-sacrifice unique and universal in its intentions, could nonetheless serve as the model for an infinity of subsequent mimetic, figurative reenactments. And if it were hoped that it would somehow end a cycle of sacrificial violence, the history of the Church—or rather the many churches that claim descent from Christ—certainly suggests it has yet to produce this result (with the same ironic implication that historians draw from World War I as "the war to end all wars").[3]

How to explain this welter of associations between the sacred and the violent has, of course, exercised many students of religion, such as Walter Burkert, René Girard, and Georges Bataille.[4] Speaking for them all, Burkert wrote, "sacrificial killing is the basic experience of the 'sacred.' *Homo religiosus* acts and attains self-awareness as *homo necans*."[5] Their ruminations on the possible links between the creation of religious communities and the sacrificing of scapegoats, animal or human; the erotic underpinnings of the dissolution of individual selfhood shared by religious ecstasy and sexual abandonment; the abjection of base materiality through cultural sublimation; and the dialectics of purity and impurity, homogeneity and heterogeneity, and obeying and transgressing the law, all would be fruitful points of departure, however speculative they may seem.

But one would have to investigate other linkages as well. For setting aside the founding act of sacrifice and its repetitions, symbolic or not, faith and bloodshed have often found themselves unhappily intertwined. Monotheism's jealous exclusion of other gods, secured in a covenant that binds together a community, may well abet the violent exclusion of those outside its limits.[6] The boundaries within religions, separating orthodoxy from heterodoxy, have also been flashpoints of hostility that often explode into violence. Understood in a metaphorical as well as literal sense, violence can also be discerned in many of the stigmatizing and disciplining practices of organized religions. Internalized, such violence can often manifest itself in the familiar forms of asceticism and mortification of the flesh considered marks of spiritual distinction by religious virtuosi. One need not accept all of Freud's ideas to acknowledge his insight into the self-directed aggressive impulse that so often accompanies the formation of punishing superegos.

It might, of course, be argued in response that religion at its best has the ability to defuse, master, and defer violent human inclinations that antedate its origin. Nor should we ignore, some would claim, the external triggering factors that create the conditions for the reversal of those processes, producing a desublimation of the violence that religion generally seeks to keep under control. Even paranoid cults, we might willingly concede, have real enemies in a world that is dominated by organized religions, fearful of losing their followers, or the secular state anxious to maintain order. It would therefore be insufficient to look for the sources of contemporary expressions of violence in religion alone, for a more contextual approach might alert us to the ways in which the tensions of modern life find a displaced expression in the idiom of religion. When, for example, class struggle is no longer on most agendas, but injustices of all kinds are still rife, religious conflict may be a surrogate locus for working out the conflicts that result. And certainly, the mess in the Middle East must be understood as an overdetermined tangle in which religious animosity is only one thread.

But whether or not we see religion as expressing violence or containing it, the inescapable conclusion is that its potential to do both, a potential that has been realized throughout history, calls into question the easy assumption, embraced by Senator Lieberman and so many others, that morality has its basic roots in religious experience. For there is ample evidence to suggest that sometimes the two are deeply at odds. No better exploration of this profound and troubling truth can be found than in Kierkegaard's celebrated account of the Abraham and Isaac story in *Fear and Trembling* of 1843, in which he introduced the idea of the "teleological suspension of the ethical."[7] The willingness to kill a son, Kierkegaard knew, was inherent in the submission of the individual to a God whose reasons were outside of human ken, but whose will had to be followed. Targeting Hegel's assumption that ethical life was embodied in the universally valid mores of a community (*Sittlichkeit*), as well as Kant's claim that God Himself was bound by moral law, Kierkegaard understood that Abraham's terrible decision was an individual expression of obedience to an Absolute that was above any human sociability. Abraham was willing to follow what he took to be a divine command because he believed that somehow he would be given his son back by a merciful God. And of course, he was rewarded for his faith by precisely this outcome just before he took the fatal step.

Although Abraham's suspension of the ethical does provide powerful testimony of his faith, his willingness to shed innocent blood has nothing to do with realizing the good—certainly not from Isaac's point of view, nor that of his loving father, nor that of the community as a whole. It expresses instead the inexplicable paradox of faith, which can somehow persuade a believer to transgress the universal ethical commands laid down by God. Or rather, to be more precise, because he acted prior to the promulgation of the Ten Commandments on Mount Sinai, Abraham's action suggests that faith both antedates moral obligation and indeed trumps it when there is a subsequent conflict. It is a faith, moreover, that exceeds human ken. Abraham, Kierkegaard tells us, "believed on the strength of the absurd, for there could be no question of human calculation, and it was indeed absurd that God who demanded this of him should in the next instant withdraw the command."[8] Thus he is the model of a true "knight of faith," willing to ignore the universal law, however secure or comfortable he might feel in following its precepts, in favor of following the particular command, which leaves him isolated and alone, but bearing witness to his love for God. Sacrifice in the service of a universal law, Kierkegaard argued, is typical of a tragic hero, whereas an Abraham knows that he cannot escape from the agony of his absurd situation. Even those who think they are acting in the name of their particular community—say, a religiously motivated assassin like Yigal Amir, who shows no repentance for his murder of Yitzak Rabin—do so in violation of universal laws; not even a formalist categorical imperative can be invoked to justify their amoral acts of pious violence.

No less absurd was the risk that the voice heard by Abraham might well be that of an imposter, a demonic rather than divine commander. Only a paper thin difference separates the individual in absolute relation with the Absolute and the individual who is seduced by the devil, a threat Kierkegaard acknowledges in *Fear and Trembling* in his discussion of the parable of the merman and Agnete, but does not satisfactorily resolve. Antinomianism, the belief that faith can transcend law, has always been a temptation that can lead in either direction: sainthood or damnation.

Perhaps even more troubling is the possibility that the very contrast between ethical law and violence may itself be difficult to sustain. In his provocative 1921 "Critique of Violence," Walter Benjamin argued that underlying the normative order was a legally sanctioned violence, whose origins he detected in myth. What Kierkegaard's knight of faith had resisted, he implied, was thus a universal ethical code that claimed universality, but was itself no more than the residue of a prior system of irrational belief. The knight's acceptance of divine violence, which Benjamin called "sovereign" and opposed to the "executive" or "administrative" counterparts subtending the current ethical and legal system, could thus ultimately be justified on a higher level:

> If mythical violence is lawmaking, divine violence is law-destroying; if the former sets boundaries, the latter boundlessly destroys them; if mythical violence brings at once guilt and retribution, divine power only expiates; if the former threatens, the latter strikes, if the former is bloody, the latter is lethal without spilling blood. . . . Mythical violence is bloody power over mere life for its own sake, divine violence is pure power over all life for the sake of the living. The first demands sacrifice, the second accepts it.[9]

Benjamin's apocalyptic embrace of a divine violence that accepts sacrifice, brings about expiation, and is somehow lethal without shedding blood, which he followed Georges Sorel in giving a social reading in terms of the General Strike, carries with it obvious risks. Beginning with Derrida's ambivalent consideration of it in his 1990 "Force of Law: 'The Mystical Foundation of Authority,' " a lively discussion has been generated by Benjamin's essay, which cannot be rehearsed here.[10] What is important to note now is his bold assertion of the liberating function of divine violence in challenging the other violence—mythical in origin and legislative in form—that subtends ethical systems, an assertion that once again highlights the tension between religion and morality rather than their full compatibility.

But for those of us who lack a belief in the cleansing role of divine violence, however "nonlethal," or worry that the voices people hear are more likely to be demonic than godly, even the most successfully realized teleological suspension of the ethical is hard to endorse. For the history of devout justifications of violent means to bring about holy ends inspires little confidence in the outcome. It is indeed hard to avoid the conclusion that, *pace* Senator Lieberman, religion has no monopoly over moral behavior, however much it may moralize about how we should behave. Let it not be forgotten, after all, that once God spared Isaac's life and stayed the hand of his father, He still demanded that an innocent ram be slaughtered in his place. Even an act of grace was covered in blood.

16

FEARFUL SYMMETRIES
9/11 and the Agonies of the Left

Alone in a restaurant in Santiago de Chile this past November, I attempted to order dinner in my rudimentary Spanish. Taking pity on me, a well-dressed man of about thirty at the next table offered to help, and soon a lively conversation began. He was, it turned out, an ophthalmologist with a strong interest in international affairs. Although he had only been to the United States once, for a short and not terribly pleasant trip to Miami, he assured me that he had warm feelings for the American people. But then he added, politely hoping I would take no offense, that he thought we had the events of September 11th coming to us. Eyes narrowing, he asked if I knew what that date meant in the history of his own country. When I confessed ignorance, he explained that it was on that very day in 1973 that the bloody coup of General Pinochet against the democratically elected government of Salvador Allende had taken place, a coup that had been fully supported by Richard Nixon and Henry Kissinger. It was only fitting, he concluded grimly, that the chickens would finally come home to roost on another September 11th.

Overwhelming my best efforts to respond, he doggedly insisted that the legacy of American intervention in the rest of the world was so odious and American understanding of its magnitude so wanting that nothing short of a horrible and desperate act like the destruction of the World Trade Center towers was an appropriate response. And then he added that the true face of America was being revealed by its adoption of the very methods that Pinochet, under the tutelage of the sinister U.S. Army School for the Americas, had perfected during his regime: detentions without trial, suspects who "disappeared" without public accountability, military tribunals with minimal due process, and even torture (which he had heard was now openly being discussed as a potential expedient in the fight against terrorism).[1] There was therefore a distinct symmetry or at least mirroring effect in the September 11th he remembered with such bitterness and the one now so seared into the American consciousness.

I don't know if I was successful in convincing him to modify his position, but one thing he said got my own attention. For symmetry has indeed been an oddly persistent figure in our attempts to come to terms with the effects of the terrorist attack, as well as to respond to it. Although we have been repeatedly told that the war against terrorism is an asymmetrical conflict between a superpower and a conspiratorial, dispersed, faceless enemy with only unconventional weapons at his disposal, symmetry somehow manages to return. Not only has it appeared in the twin towers themselves, whose destruction was foreshadowed by the Taliban razing of the ancient statues of the Buddha, but also in little ways as well, for example, the cowboy rhetoric of Bush's demand that bin Laden be brought back "dead or alive" and the vain search of relatives of the victims for their loved ones, either living or not, in the aftermath of the attack. Both victims and perpetrators shared a common invisibility, which the best efforts to find both only partially alleviated. The posters pasted throughout Manhattan by desperate survivors still clinging to the hope that "missing" meant more than a euphemism for pulverization were echoed in the posters of Al Qaeda leaders broadcast by the government throughout the world. Similarly symmetrical has been the underlying religious characterization of the struggle, with Islamic Holy War counterpoised to Crusade—even if Bush was quickly forced to repudiate the term—and Satanic America versus bin Laden as "the Evil One," which he still staunchly defends. As Hal Foster observed, "the perfect symmetry of the name calling is chilling."[2]

But it is the unexpected symmetrical logic of some of the Left's response to the event that concerns me here. Often, it appeared under the rubric of dialectics, marshalling the old idea of thesis and antithesis. Take, for example, Fredric Jameson's argument in *The London Review of Books* symposium on 9/11 that "America created bin Laden during the Cold War (and in particular during the Soviet war in Afghanistan), and that this is therefore a textbook case of dialectical reversal."[3] What Chalmers Johnson only a short time before had called "blowback" in his denunciation of the new "American Empire," by which he meant the unintended consequence of actions whose impact reversed that sought by their initiators, was quickly adopted as a label for the ways in which history produced ironic, symmetrical inversions.[4]

From the perspective of those who suffered the consequences, however, it could be only the coldest of comfort to be told that their misery was somehow warranted by so lofty a logic of dialectical reversal. As a result, commentators who effortlessly moved to this level of analysis in the immediate aftermath of the events, paying only quick lip service to the innocent victims, brought upon themselves the reproach of callous indifference to the realities of personal trauma. For their *Schadenfreude* was hard to stomach when the penalty was being paid by ordinary Americans (as well as unlucky foreigners), who in no direct or meaningful sense were responsible for releasing the chickens that had allegedly come home to roost. As a result, impassioned denunciations of coldhearted intellectuals capable of fitting the events into their preconceived schemes of dialectical historical processes quickly followed.

Often, however, these understandable complaints were accompanied by the menacing implication that any criticism of American foreign policy at this time was an unpatriotic justification for the terrorists themselves. The policy of Fox News, which quickly became the most rabid cheerleader for the war, to insist on accompanying any report of "collateral damage" among Afghan citizens with a symmetrical recounting of the horrors of 9/11, showed the way this logic functioned. Compassion for our innocent victims was a bludgeon to stifle any mourning for those we victimized. When a rightwing media watchdog group began to publish lists of allegedly treasonous statements, many of them little more than expressions of doubt about the means of fighting terrorism, it was clear that the very possibility of critical discussion itself seemed endangered. And so a new symmetry was born between the intolerance of the Taliban and that of the "patriotically correct" defenders of my country, right or wrong, both of which had little patience with dissent of any kind.

Ironically, the arrival of this new intolerance, along with the governmental curtailing of civil liberties by Attorney General Ashcroft's Justice Department, helped get the Left off the hook, at least in terms of its once again being able to assume a posture of moral righteousness. For by embracing the cause of dissenting speech and civil liberties, traditionally more liberal than radical values, it was possible to suppress or forget the more problematic implications of its earlier reliance on a rhetoric of subversion, transgression and disruption, which had been picking up momentum in the struggle against globalization. Now that these terms had been hijacked by the hijackers, it was no longer possible to invoke them with a clear conscience. "Cultural terrorism" had given way to the real thing, giving pause to anyone who had once blithely applauded any sign of counterhegemonic subversion as inherently emancipatory.

In fact, those who still held on to this logic, including the dialecticians who gained grim satisfaction by invoking the pay-back argument, failed to register the existence of yet another symmetrical relation, which involved "blowback" itself. That is, the left too has had to face the unintended consequences of its well-intentioned actions, especially those which invested a patently problematic historical agent with the charisma of redemption. If there was a cardinal lesson for the Left in the fall of communism, it is that compromising ideals in the service of dialectical realism is likely to turn disastrous, some hands being just too dirty to escape from the muck in which they are immersed. No one who has absorbed this lesson can expect the dialectic to turn the enemies of global capitalism and American cultural imperialism who took down the twin towers into instruments of emancipation, however that vexed word may be defined. Here the enemies of your enemies are in no sense your friends. For the two narratives of anti-American feeling—the one symbolized by the memory of September 11, 1973 and the other by its counterpart in 2001—cannot be folded into one meaningful story.

Is there then any role left for dialectical thinking at all in this new context? Already a much abused word with only a handful of die-hard enthusiasts willing to give it a hearing, dialectics can only provide guidance if it loses its penchant for schematic overinterpretation of a world far too messy to conform to its precepts. It can survive only if it abandons its desire for positive resolutions finding something to salvage in competing positions or forces. It can still be of use if it resists its penchant for the subsumption of individuals under collective categories. It can, in short, still be meaningful only if becomes, to borrow the formula of Theodor Adorno, entirely negative.

What a negative dialectics teaches is an awareness that there is no formula that will overcome the tension between two radically opposed truths. In this case, it makes us, first of all, sensitive to the utterly unredeemable suffering of the victims on both sides—the innocent lives lost or shattered both in America and abroad—and the impossibility of turning them into martyrs for a meaningful cause, however Satanic the enemy may seem. It helps us resist imitating the grotesque abuse of the concept of martyrdom by suicidal Islamic fundamentalists justifying their slaughter of innocents. It also makes it much harder to utter hard-hearted statements like the one the British academic Mary Beard made immediately after 9/11: "The United States had it coming. That is, of course, what many people openly or privately think."[5] For the individual lives effected by the events were never equivalent to "the United States," never simply subsumable under the generic category of a nation-state. One of the most insidious assumptions of terrorism in general is precisely to blur this distinction and turn guiltless victims into metonyms for governmental policies or economic trends like globalization. Only a dialectics that resists this form of displacement and honors the irreducible value of individual lives can hope to have any emancipatory effect.

The second lesson of a negative dialectics, however, is that remaining only on this level of individual analysis can prevent a more abstract and distanced understanding of the underlying causes for historical events and movements. If American foreign policy or globalization warrant serious rethinking, it is not simply "caving into the terrorists" to criticize those policies responsibly and carefully. When President Bush naively expressed his "amazement" at the hatred for America that is out there in the world—not only in the Middle East but also, it turns out, among Chilean eye doctors—he was revealing his inability to put himself in the place of people with different experiences of American power and its impact. By identifying only with the victims of our 9/11, he was foreclosing the knowledge of what I had learned in Santiago: that we are not all living by the same calendar and commemorating the same events. There is, in turns out, more than one September 11th in world history.

The final lesson of a negative dialectics is the necessity of keeping both these perspectives in play at the same time, refusing to reduce one to the other, while being fully aware that they cannot be easily reconciled, if at all. It means recognizing that blowback can happen to both those who run "the system" and those who think they are subverting it. It means, above all, being wary of the ways in which the logic of symmetrical reduction produces a chain of mirroring effects that is extremely hard to break, as the interminable reciprocal violence between Israel and the Palestinians makes abundantly clear. Unless that lesson is learned, the many symmetries that have characterized the attack and its aftermath will remain fearful for a long time to come.[6]

NOTES

Introduction

1. Georges Sorel, *Reflections on Violence*, trans. T. E. Hulme, intro. Edward Shils (London, 1970), p. 249. Italics in original.
2. Martin Jay, *Downcast Eyes: The Denigration of Vision in 20th-century French Thought* (Berkeley, 1993).
3. Jacques Derrida, "Violence and Metaphysics: An Essay on the Thought of Emmanuel Levinas," *Writing and Difference*, trans. Alan Bass (Chicago, 1978), 84. For further reflections on the theme, see Hent de Vries, *Religion and Violence: Philosophical Perspectives from Kant to Derrida* (Baltimore, 2002) and Beatrice Hanssen, *Critique of Violence: Between Poststructuralism and Critical Theory* (New York, 2000).
4. Paul Crowther, "Violence in Painting," in *Critical Aesthetics and Postmodernism* (Oxford, 1993), 97.
5. For an insightful account of the extension of the rhetoric of antipornography to discussions of the Holocaust and other violent episodes in history, see the forthcoming book by Carolyn J. Dean, *Human Dignity, Empathy, and the History of Suffering after 1950.*
6. W. J. T. Mitchell, "The Violence of Public Art: *Do the Right Thing*," in *Picture Theory* (Chicago, 1994), 375.
7. Derrida, "Violence and Metaphysics," 117. The word *vigilance* is derived from the Latin *vigilare*, to watch.
8. Jay Winter and Emmanuel Sivan, eds., *War and Remembrance in the Twentieth Century* (Cambridge, 1999). A slightly different version appeared as well in *Philosophical Designs for a Socio-Cultural Transformation: Beyond Violence and the Modern Era*, ed. Tetsuji Yamamoto (Boulder, Co., 1998).
9. I should add that efforts to bring the exhibition to America, including ones in which I participated for the San Francisco Bay Area, were derailed by the controversy and have not been renewed.
10. See, for example, Gillian Rose, *Judaism and Modernity: Philosophical Essays* (Oxford, 1993), 171–2.
11. *Ibid.*, 207.
12. For those interested in following the story, there are several websites devoted to it, including one designed by the victim's family at OurHolly.org., as well as hundreds of journalistic accounts on the Internet.

13. The conference was organized by Chungmoo Choi of UC, Irvine; my contribution was "Must Justice Be Blind?"
14. The proceedings appeared as *Law and the Image: The Authority of Art and the Aesthetics of Law*, eds. Costas Douzinas and Lynda Nead (Chicago, 1999). An earlier version of my essay also appeared in the Slovenian journal *Filosofski Vestnik* 2 (1996).
15. "Diving into the Wreck: Aesthetic Spectatorship at the *Fin-de-siécle*," *Critical Horizons* 1,1 (2000).
16. "The Speed of Light and the Virtualization of Reality," in *The Robot in the Garden: Telerobotics and Telepistemology in the Age of the Internet* (Cambridge, Mass., 2000).
17. The essay was subsequently published in several places, first in Slovenian translation in *Filosofksi Vestnik* 16, 1 (1995), then in English in *Definitions of Visual Culture 2, Modernist Utopias, Postformalism and Pure Visuality*, ed. Chantal Charbonneau (Montreal, 1996); *Perspectives in Embodiment*, eds. Gail Weiss and Honi Fern Haber (New York, 1999) and *Travelling Theory: France and the United States*, eds. Ieme van der Poel and Sophie Bertho (Madison, N.J., 1999). A German translation, following a presentation of the talk in The Depot in Vienna, appeared in *Privileg Blick: Kritik der visuellen Kultur*, ed., Christian Kravagna (Berlin, 1997).
18. "Lafayette's Children: The American Reception of French Liberalism," *Substance* 97, XXXI, 1 (2002).

Chapter 1

1. Gershom Scholem, *Walter Benjamin: The Story of a Friendship*, trans. Harry Zohn (New York, 1981), 12. Benjamin himself later wrote that he joined "without a spark of war fever in my heart." *Gesammelte Schriften*, vol. 6, 481.
2. *Ibid.*, 35.
3. Walter Benjamin, "A Berlin Chronicle," *Reflections: Essays, Aphorisms, Autobiographical Writings*, trans. Edmund Jephcott (New York, 1978), p. 18.
4. Scholem, *Walter Benjamin*, II. For accounts of the impact of his death, see John McCole, *Walter Benjamin and the Antinomies of Tradition* (Ithaca, 1993), 54, and Hans Puttnies and Gary Smith, *Benjaminia* (Giessen, 1991), 18. The fullest account of their friendship can be found in Rolf Tiedmann's Nachwort to Benjamin, *Sonette* (Frankfurt, 1986). They had, in fact, only met in the spring of 1913 and had gone through a period of some estrangement the following winter, but clearly the tie was strong.
5. Pierre Missac, *Walter Benjamin's Passages*, trans. Shierry Weber Nicholsen (Cambridge, Mass., 1995), 4.
6. Benjamin, *Sonette*, 6.
7. The will is cited in Scholem, *Walter Benjamin*, 187.
8. Werner Kraft saw them into print in *Akzente*, 31(1984). See his accompanying essay, "Friedrich C. Heinle," as well as his earlier piece, "Über einen verschollenen Dichter," in *Neue Rundschau*, 78 (1967).
9. Tiedemann writes, "Not only in his life but in his work was the war a caesura, but an even stronger one was the suicide of Heinle caused by it" (117). For accounts, see Richard Wolin, *Walter Benjamin: An Aesthetic of Redemption* (New York, 1982), chapter 1; McCole, *Walter Benjamin and the Antinomies of Tradition*, chapter 1. Before the war Benjamin had defended Heinle to Wyneken against the claim of Georges Barbizon that he was conspiring to take over the Youth Movement journal *Der Anfang*. See the letter of April 4, 1914 to Wyneken in Benjamin, *Gesammelte Briefe*, vol. 1, 1910–1918, eds. Christoph Gödde and Henri Lonitz (Frankfurt, 1995), 203.
10. Benjamin to Gustav Wyneken, March 9, 1915 in Benjamin, *Briefe*, 2 vols., eds. Gershom Scholem and Theodor W. Adorno (Frankfurt a.M., 1966), vol. 1, 120–1.

11. Herbert W. Belmore, "Walter Benjamin," *German Life and Letters*, 15 (1962).
12. For a discussion, see Julian Roberts, *Walter Benjamin* (Atlantic Highlands, N.J., 1983), 38.
13. For a discussion of the impact of the war on Benjamin's theory of language, see Anson Rabinbach, "Between Enlightenment and Apocalypse: Benjamin, Bloch and Modern German Jewish Messianism," *New German Critique* 34 (Winter 1985). He argues that "On Language as Such and on the Language of Man," of 1916 "must be read between the lines as an esoteric response to Buber's pro-war and pro-German position" (105). For a discussion of Benjamin in the context of a generational revolt against the German-Jewish fetish of *Kultur*, see Steven E. Aschheim, "German Jews beyond *Bildung* and Liberalism: The Radical Jewish Revival in the Weimar Republic," in *Culture and Catastrophe* (New York, 1996).
14. Peter Osborne, *The Politics of Time: Modernity and the Avant-Garde* (London, 1995), 227.
15. Walter Benjamin, "The Storyteller: Reflections on the Work of Nikolai Leskov," *Illuminations*, ed. Hannah Arendt, trans. Harry Zohn (New York, 1968), 84.
16. Walter Benjamin, "Theories of German Fascism: On the Collection of Essays *War and Warrior*, edited by Ernst Jünger," *New German Critique*, 17 (Spring 1979), 120–8.
17. See in particular his controversial essay "Critique of Violence," in *Reflections*. According to Irving Wohlfahrt, "Benjamin saw in pacifism no alternative to the cult of war but only its mirror image." From "No-Man's-Land. On Walter Benjamin's 'Destructive Character,' " *Diacritics* 8 (June 1978): 55.
18. According to Kai Erikson, "Traumatized people often come to feel that they have lost an important measure of control over the circumstances of their own lives and are thus very vulnerable. That is easy to understand. But they also come to feel that they have lost a natural immunity to misfortune and that something awful is almost *bound* to happen. One of the crucial tasks of culture, let's say, is to help people camouflage the actual risks of the world around them—to help them edit reality in such a way that it seems manageable, to help them edit it in such a way that the dangers pressing in on them from all sides are screened out of their line of vision as they go about their everyday rounds." From "Notes on Trauma and Community," in *Trauma: Explorations in Memory*, ed., Cathy Caruth (Baltimore, 1995), 194. Benjamin's disdain for culture as a means of camouflage was apparent in all of his subsequent work.
19. Kevin Newmark, "Traumatic Poetry: Charles Baudelaire and the Shock of Laughter," in Caruth, ed., *Trauma*, 238–9.
20. Benjamin, "On Some Motifs in Baudelaire," in *Illuminations*, 162 f.
21. On the issue of anaesthesia and Benjamin, see Susan Buck-Morss, "Aesthetics and Anaesthetics: Walter Benjamin's Artwork Essay," *October* 62 (Fall 1992).
22. For a suggestive discussion of the distinction between shock and trauma, see Hal Foster, "What is Neo About the Neo-Avant-Garde?," *October* 70 (Fall 1994). He stresses the delayed temporality in the trauma, which is "a complex relay of reconstructed past and anticipated future—in short, a deferred action that throws over any simple scheme of before and after, cause and effect, origin and repetition." The avant-garde, he goes on, was traumatic precisely in this sense: "a hole in the symbolic order of its time that is not prepared for it, that cannot receive it, at least not immediately, at least not without structural change" (30). Benjamin seems to have been anxious to resist symbolic recuperation of trauma for the same reason.
23. George L. Mosse, *Fallen Soldiers: Reshaping the Memory of the World Wars* (New York, 1990); Annette Becker, *La guerre et la foi: De la mort à la mémoire, 1914–1930* (Paris, 1994), and Jay Winter, *Sites of Memory, Sites of Mourning: The Great War in European Cultural History* (Cambridge, 1995). He was not, to be sure, the only critic of this culture of commemoration. See, for example, the chapter on "Anti-Monuments" in

Samuel Hynes, *A War Imagined: The First World War and English Culture* (New York, 1990), which discusses figures like the journalists C. E. Montague and Philip Gibbs and the painter Paul Nash.

24. Benjamin, "Theories of German Fascism," 126.
25. Susan Buck-Morss, *The Dialectics of Seeing* (Cambridge, Mass., 1989), 178. McCole notes that "behind the study of allegory, in turn, is the prologue to 'The Life of Students' written in the first months of the war." *Walter Benjamin and the Antinomies of Tradition*, 265. He discusses this apocalyptic and decisionist text on page 63 f.
26. According to McCole, "The desire to unmask the official monuments to progress, the stabilized totalities and transfigured appearances of the dominant culture, by casting them in the light of the petrified, primordial landscape created on the battlefields of the war—that gave Benjamin his eye for the coherence of the allegorical way of seeing." (*Walter Benjamin and the Antinomies of Tradition*, 139). I would emend this claim only slightly to include the monuments to the war dead produced by the dominant culture after 1918.
27. Benjamin, *The Origin of German Tragic Drama*, trans. John Osborne (London, 1977), 166.
28. For a discussion of the distinction between *Trauerspiel* and *Trauerarbeit*, see Philippe Lacoue-Labarthe, *Typography: Mimesis, Philosophy, Politics*, ed. Christopher Fynsk, intro. Jacques Derrida (Cambridge, Mass., 1989), 234. The same preference for a kind of play that resisted closure was evident in the scripts for Benjamin's radio plays of the 1930s. "What is significant," according to Jeffrey Mehlman, "is the author's insistence on repetition (*Wiederholung*) in opposition to imitation (*Nachahmung*) as the grounding virtue of play. For imitation (of parents) is the stuff of narcissism, the subjectivist psychologizing that Benjamin seems intent on keeping at bay. Whereas repetition, however oriented toward mastery, retains its traumatic or catastrophic valence to the end." *Walter Benjamin for Children: An Essay on His Radio Years* (Chicago, 1993), 5.
29. Benjamin, "Goethes Wahlverwandschaften," *Gesammelte Schriften*, vol. 1, eds. Rolf Tiedemann and Hermann Schweppenhäuser (Frankfurt, 1974). At times, to be sure, Benjamin had a more nuanced attitude towards myth, as a stage through which culture must pass before genuine *Erfahrung* could be achieved. See Winfried Menninghaus, "Walter Benjamin's Theory of Myth," in Smith, ed., *On Walter Benjamin*.
30. Benjamin, "A Berlin Chronicle," *Reflections*, 20.
31. Benjamin, "Linke Melancholie: Zu Erich Kästners neuem Gedichtbuch," *Die Gesellschaft* 8,l (1931): 181–4.
32. Winter, *Sites of Memory, Sites of Mourning*, 221.
33. Bernhild Boie, "Dichtung als Ritual der Erlösung. Zu den wiedergefundenen Sonetten von Walter Benjamin," *Akzente* 32 (1984): 30–1.
34. Theodor W. Adorno, "Benjamin the Letter Writer," in *On Walter Benjamin: Critical Essays and Recollections*, ed. Gary Smith (Cambridge, Mass., 1991), 330–1. Benjamin, to be sure, rejected the aestheticizing elitism and myth-mongering of the George Circle, as shown in his frequent criticism of Friedrich Gundolf. Tiedemann, in fact, argues that the sonnets to Heinle show an explicit rejection of the striving for redemptive form in Georg. See his *Nachwort*, pages 88–9. The link between ritual and other aspects of Benjamin's work is stressed by Andrew Benjamin, who argues that "it will be in relation to ritual that a conception of experience that involves allegory will emerge. Events are particularized and cannot be repeated. The continuity of ritual is the repetition of the storyteller." In "Tradition and Experience: Walter Benjamin's 'On Some Motifs in Baudelaire,' " in *The Problems of Modernity: Adorno and Benjamin*, ed. Andrew Benjamin (London, 1989), 127.
35. Benjamin, "A Berlin Chronicle," 27.

36. *Ibid.*, 26.
37. Benjamin, "The Destructive Character," *Reflections*. The last line of this piece, first published in 1931, shows what was still on Benjamin's mind: "The destructive character lives from the feeling, not that life is worth living, but that suicide is not worth the trouble" (303).
38. Benjamin, *Passagen-Werk* (Frankfurt a.M., 1982), 611.
39. Théodule Ribot, *Les Maladies de la mémoire* (Paris, 1881).
40. Stéphane Mosès, "The Theological-Political Model of History in the Thought of Walter Benjamin," *History and Memory* I,2 (Fall/Winter, 1989): 31.
41. Denis Hollier, *Against Architecture: The Writings of Georges Bataille*, trans. Betsy Wing (Cambridge, Mass., 1989).
42. On his fascination with Scheerbart, see Missac, *Walter Benjamin's Passages*, chapter 6. On Benjamin's general attitude towards modern architecture, including the work of Loos, see Michael Müller, "Architektur für das 'schlechte Neue'. Zu Walter Benjamins Verarbeitung avantgardistischer Positionen in der Architektur," *"Links hatte noch alles sich zu enträtseln . . ." Walter Benjamin im Kontext*, ed., Burkhardt Lindner (Frankfurt, 1978).
43. Benjamin, *Berliner Kindheit um 1900* (Frankfurt, 1989), 17. The translation is by Shierry Weber Nicholsen from the forthcoming English version of the book. I thank her for her letting me see it before publication.
44. For a discussion of Benjamin's thoughts on the metropolis, which highlights his rejection of *Gemeinschaft* as impossible to restore, see Massimo Cacciari, *Architecture and Nihilism: On the Philosophy of Modern Architecture*, trans. Stephen Sartarelli (New Haven, 1993), 92f. It is for this reason that Richard Terdiman's placement of Benjamin in the same camp as those nostalgic theorists influenced by Tönnies' classic distinction between *Gemeinschaft* and *Gesellschaft* is problematic. See his *Present Past: Modernity and the Memory Crisis* (Ithaca, 1993), 206.
45. Wohlfahrt, "No-Man's-Land," 63.
46. On the dialectic of remembering and forgetting in Benjamin, see Timothy Bahti, "Theories of Knowledge: Fate and Forgetting in the Early Works of Walter Benjamin," in *Benjamin's Ground: New Readings of Walter Benjamin*, ed., Rainer Nägele (Detroit, 1988).
47. Benjamin, "One-Way Street," *Reflections*, 93.
48. *Ibid.*
49. For a discussion of this phenomenon, which draws on Benjamin, see Jeffrey Herf, *Reactionary Modernism: Technology, Culture, and Politics in Weimar and the Third Reich* (Cambridge, 1984).
50. Benjamin, "Theories of German Fascism," 128.
51. See Winter, *Sites of Memory, Sites of Mourning*, chapter 6, for a discussion of the appropriation of the Resurrection by artists like Georges Rouault.
52. Benjamin, *The Origin of German Tragic Drama*, 152.
53. For a discussion, see Eric J. Leed, *No Man's Land: Combat and Identity in World War I* (Cambridge, 1979), chapter 3.
54. See Hollier, *Against Architecture*, 57–73, for the importance of the labyrinth in Bataille. On its role in Benjamin's work, see Mehlman, *Walter Benjamin for Children*, 63f. He comments on the parallel with Bataille.
55. Walter Benjamin, "Central Park," *New German Critique* 34 (Winter, 1985): 53.
56. Benjamin, *The Origin of German Tragic Drama*, 216–7.
57. Rey Chow, "Walter Benjamin's Love Affair with Death," *New German Critique* 48 (Fall 1989).
58. Winter, *Sites of Memory, Sites of Mourning*, 64f.
59. Benjamin, *The Origin of German Tragic Drama*, 182.

60. Gary Smith has argued that in the early 1920s Benjamin did share a certain rhetoric of spiritual esotericism with other heterodox Jewish thinkers of his day, including Oskar Goldberg, Erich Unger, Erich Gutkind, and Scholem. See Smith, " 'Die Zauberjuden': Walter Benjamin and Other Jewish Esoterics Between the World Wars," *The Journal of Jewish Thought and Philosophy* 4, (1995). However, he acknowledges that Benjamin always found Goldberg distasteful and ultimately came to dissociate himself explicitly from the other "Magic Jews." See Benjamin's letter to Scholem of December 24, 1934, where he uses the term derisorily. *The Correspondence of Walter Benjamin and Gershom Scholem, 1932–1940*, ed. Gershom Scholem, trans. Gary Smith and Andre Lefevre (New York, 1989), 148.
61. On the idea of apokatastasis in Benjamin, see Irving Wohlfahrt, "Et Cetera? De l'historien comme chiffonier," in *Walter Benjamin à Paris*, ed. Heinz Wismann (Paris, 1986), 596–609.
62. Gillian Rose, *Judaism and Modernity: Philosophical Essays* (Oxford, 1993), 209.
63. *Ibid.*, 207.
64. Peter Homans, *The Ability to Mourn: Disillusionment and the Social Origins of Psychoanalysis* (Chicago, 1989). He argues that the Nazis, "intolerant of chaos[,] . . . sought to reinvent with great rapidity and astonishing creativity a total common culture in which a sacred symbolic structure overcame time, the sense of transience and diachrony. . . . For them, the manic defense and persecutory activity successfully energized a new cosmology which abolished the ability to mourn and what I would also call 'the capacity to be depressed.' It was as if they had said, There has been no loss at all" (338). The larger argument of the book is that psychoanalysis, unlike Nazism, was based on a healthy ability to mourn the loss of cultural meaning produced by secularization.
65. Judith Lewis Herman, *Trauma and Recovery* (New York, 1992). For a critique of this argument, which comes close to Benjamin's position without drawing on it, see Ruth Leys, "Traumatic Cures: Shell Shock, Janet, and the Question of Memory," *Critical Inquiry* 20, 4 (Summer 1994): 623–62. She shows that for Pierre Janet, fully narrating the past was itself insufficient, as some liquidation of it as well was necessary to "cure" shell shock.
66. Mehlman, *Walter Benjamin for Children*, 80.
67. *Ibid.*, 94.
68. Mehlman hints at the end of his book that it is not so much the Marxist dream of a classless society that constitutes the fraudulent echo of Sabbatianism, but the Enlightenment dream of assimilation itself. The latter, he claims, leads to the " 'silent Holocaust' of Jewish self-denial which is the daily mode of ordinary Jewish life in the West." *Walter Benjamin for Children*, 97. In effect, Rose attacks Benjamin for his allegiance to a Jewish notion of repetitive, ahistorical memory, whereas Mehlman criticizes him for fostering the dissolution of Jewish particularity in the universal solvent of the Enlightenment.
69. "The cultic use value of art that Benjamin claims we have lost is actually an archaic version of the fascist use of art as he dramatically defines it in 'The Work of Art in the Age of Mechanical Reproduction': the aestheticizing of politics." Leo Bersani, *The Culture of Redemption* (Cambridge, Mass., 1990), 60.
70. For a consideration of the issue of origin in Benjamin, see John Pizer, *Toward a Theory of Radical Origin: Essays on Modern German Thought* (Lincoln, Neb., 1995). Pizer argues that the concept of *Ursprung* in Benjamin, derived in part from Karl Kraus, must be understood as more than a simple return to plenitudinous grace. But he rejects the deconstructionist reading of Benjamin as being entirely against all notions of origin.

71. According to Mosse, "the martyrs of the Nazi movement were identified with the dead of the First World War, and identical symbols were used to honor their memory: steel helmets, holy flames, and monuments which projected the Nazi dead as clones of the soldiers who had earlier fought and died for the fatherland." *Fallen Soldiers*, 183.
72. Benjamin, "On Some Motifs in Baudelaire," 165.
73. Cathy Caruth, "Introduction" to Caruth, ed., *Trauma*, 9.
74. According to Angelika Rauch's insightful gloss on Benjamin's position, "As memory of an experience, commemoration or remembrance must refuse the labor of mourning because such a *Trauerarbeit* aims at the representation of the *other*—the experience and affect—by turning it into what Benjamin had labeled 'a souvenir,' that is, an object in conscious memory that corresponds to an object in the history of events. Once the *other* has achieved the status of an object, the subject can dispose of it. If an experience in the sense of *Erfahrung* is, however, responsible for shaping the self, is part of the self, then it cannot so easily be split off, disposed of, and, in the end, forgotten. The mission of tradition is precisely *not* to make experience into an event or an object because only the power of feeling humbles us, sensitizes us to an *other*, and teaches us to live with what Kant had identified as the monstrosity of the sublime." From "The Broken Vessel of Tradition," *Representations* 53 (Winter 1996): 90.
75. Missac, *Benjamin's Passages*, 10. One might add that for Adorno in particular, Benjamin's suicide seems to have worked in the way that Heinle's had for Benjamin: as a never worked through trauma that came to emblematize the horror of the age. See the discussion in Susan Buck-Morss, *The Origin of Negative Dialectics: Theodor W. Adorno, Walter Benjamin, and the Frankfurt Institute* (New York, 1977), 165.

Chapter 3

1. *Der Spiegel*, 18 (April 29, 1996); see also the extended coverage in the *Hamburger Morgenpost*, April 27 and 29, 1996; the *Hamburger Bild*, April 27, 1996; the *Hamburger Abendblatt*, April 27/28, 1996; the *Süddeutsche Zeitung*, April 29, 1996; and the interview with Reemstma in *Die Zeit*, May 6, 1996.
2. Jan Philipp Reemtsma, *Im Keller* (Hamburg, 1997).
3. These are now available in English in *An Unmastered Past: The Autobiographical Reflections of Leo Lowenthal*, ed. Martin Jay (Berkeley, 1987).
4. The Frankfurt Institut had not, however, been keen on including Mitscherlich as a member three years earlier, for complicated reasons discussed in Rolf Wiggershaus, *The Frankfurt School: Its History, Theories and Political Significance*, trans. Michael Robertson (Cambridge, Mass., 1994), 462. Reemtsma, who also asked the controversial Trotskyist Ernest Mandel to join the board of his institute, was not hampered by excessive anxiety about public perceptions of his enterprise.
5. A collection of accompanying essays edited by Klaus Naumann and Hannes Heer appeared as *Vernichtungskrieg: Verbrechen der Wehrmacht 1941–1944* (Hamburg, 1995). For a selection of documents detailing the controversy it aroused, see the exhibition's website.
6. It should be noted that this popular myth had already been questioned, if in passing, in the scholarly literature, at least as early as Raul Hilberg's monumental *The Destruction of the European Jews* (New York, 1961), 196–9. More recently, see Omer Bartov, *Hitler's Army: Soldiers, Nazis, and War in the Third Reich* (New York, 1991). Ironically, at the beginning of the war, the Nazis had been careful to avoid atrocities against civilians in the west, where their occurrence during the First World War had been a propaganda boon for the other side (current scholarship on the atrocity stories now verifies many of them, whereas during the interwar era, their veracity

was widely questioned). But after the invasion of Russia, no such scruples were in evidence.

7. For Reemtsma's own response, see his talk at the opening in Munich, "Krieg ist ein Gesellschaftszustand," *Mittelweg 36* 6,2 (April, May 1997): 55–60.
8. Jan Philipp Reemtsma, "Die Mörder waren unter uns," *Süddeutsche Zeitung*, August 24/25, 1996.
9. See, for example, Jan Philipp Reemtsma, "Gibt es eine besondere politsche Verantwortung der Wissenschaften?," *Mittelweg 36* 5,4 (August/September, 1996).
10. Cited in the *Hamburger Morgenpost*, April 27, 1996, 7.
11. Reemtsma, *Im Keller*, 45.
12. In an interview he gave to the *Frankfurter Rundschau* in the spring of 1997, which is included in the website for the Wehrmacht exhibition (http://www.afg_vk.de/bundeswehr/wehrma22.htm) he resists the claim that his institute was directly modeled on the Frankfurt one with the same name or that Adorno was a personal example for him.

Chapter 4

1. Wolfgang Kraushaar, ed., *Frankfurter Schule und Studentenbewegung: Von der Flaschenpost zum Molotowcocktail 1946–1995*, vol. 1, *Chronik*, vol. 2, *Dokumente*, vol. 3, *Aufsätze und Kommentare* (Hamburg, 1998).
2. The phrase is cited, for example, in Marshall Berman's influential *All That Is Solid Melts into Air* (New York, 1982), 126, and found its way into Annette Michelson's "Heterology and the Critique of Instrumental Reason," *October* 36 (Spring, 1986): 127, where it is mistakenly attributed to Horkheimer instead.
3. Adorno to Marcuse, March 15, 1969 in Kraushaar, *Frankfurter Schule und Studentenbewegung*, vol. 2, 579.
4. For an account of his unfortunate essay, which was a much too friendly review of Herbert Muntzel's *The Banner of the Persecuted: A Cycle for Male Choir after the Volume of Poems of the Same Title by Baldur von Schirach*, see Rolf Wiggershaus, *The Frankfurt School: Its History, Theories and Political Significance*, trans. Michael Robertson (Cambridge, Mass., 1994), 157.
5. Martin Jay, "Adorno and Kracauer: Notes on a Troubled Friendship," *Salmagundi*, 40 (Winter 1978); reprinted in *Permanent Exiles: Essays on the Intellectual Migration from Germany* (New York, 1985). Kracauer was so upset with Adorno that he left a special file in his *Nachlass* with letters, documents, and a copy of Adorno's essay on him, "Der wunderliche Realist," with the note attached "this emotionally laden, slanderous article of TWA who does not shrink from telling falsehoods."
6. Cited in Elisabeth Young-Bruehl, *Hannah Arendt: For Love of the World* (New Haven, 1982), 80.
7. Lotte Lenya to Kurt Weill, April 10, 1942 in *Speak Low (When you Speak Love): The - Letters of Kurt Weill and Lotte Lenya*, ed. and trans. Lys Symonette and Kim H. Kowalke (Berkeley, 1996), 322. Wiesengrund was Adorno's patronym, which he dropped in exile.
8. Friedrich Niewöhner, "Alles andere ist Schwindel," *Frankfurter Allgemeine Zeitung*, September 3, 1997, p. 6.
9. Leo Lowenthal, *Mitmachen wollte ich nie: ein autobiographische Gespräch mit Helmut Dubiel* (Frankfurt, 1980); translated with additional material as *An Unmastered Past: The Autobiographical Reflections of Leo Lowenthal*, ed. Martin Jay (Berkeley, 1987).
10. Lowenthal, *An Unmastered Past*, p. 68.
11. For the record, on page 24 of *The Dialectical Imagination: A History of the Frankfurt School and the Institute of Social Research*, 2nd ed. (Berkeley, 1996), I wrote that after they moved to Columbia in 1934, "articles in the *Zeitschrift* scrupulously avoided

using words like 'Marxism' or 'communism,' substituting 'dialectical materialism' or 'the materialist theory of society' instead. Careful editing prevented emphasizing the revolutionary implications of their thought. . . . These changes were doubtless due in part to the sensitive situation in which the Institut's members found themselves at Columbia. They were also a reflection of their fundamental aversion to the type of Marxism that the Institute equated with the orthodoxy of the Soviet camp. But in addition they expressed a growing loss of that basic confidence, which Marxists had traditionally felt, in the revolutionary potential of the working class."

12. Scholem to Benjamin, November 6–8, 1938, in *The Correspondence of Walter Benjamin and Gershom Scholem, 1932–1940*, ed. Gershom Scholem, trans. Gary Smith and Andre Lefevere (New York, 1989), 236. The letter is filled, however, with unflattering remarks about Horkheimer and his colleagues who are described as "*highly* intelligent and slightly unreliable."
13. "Politics of Translation: Siegfried Kracauer and Walter Benjamin on the Buber-Rosenzweig Bible," *Leo Baeck Yearbook* 21 (London, 1976); reprinted in Martin Jay, *Permanent Exiles: Essays on the Intellectual Migration from German to America* (New York, 1985).
14. Dominick LaCapra, "History and Psychoanalysis," in *Soundings in Critical Theory* (Ithaca, 1989).

Chapter 5

1. Yehuda Bauer, *Rethinking the Holocaust* (New Haven, 2002), 242.
2. Michael Brenner, "Displaced Persons" in *The Holocaust Encyclopedia*, ed. Walter Laqueur (New Haven, 2001), 154.
3. *Ibid.*
4. See, for example, Dominick LaCapra, *Representing the Holocaust: History, Memory, Trauma* (Ithaca, 1994), *History and Memory After Auschwitz* (Ithaca, 1998), and *Writing History, Writing Trauma* (Baltimore, 2001).
5. Peter Novick, *The Holocaust in American Life* (Boston, 1999). See also, Tim Cole, *Selling the Holocaust: From Auschwitz to Schindler, How History is Bought, Packaged and Sold* (New York, 1999). For a much more contentious and biased study, see Norman G. Finkelstein, *The Holocaust Industry: Reflections on the Exploitation of Jewish Suffering* (New York, 2000).
6. Cathy Caruth, *Unclaimed Experience: Trauma, Narrative, History* (Baltimore, 1996), 7.
7. *Ibid.*, 62.
8. Cited in Ernst van Alphen, "Symptoms of Discursivity: Experience, Memory, and Trauma," in Mieke Bal, Jonathan Crewe, Leo Spitzer, eds., *Acts of Memory: Cultural Recall in the Present* (Hanover, N.H., 1999), 35.
9. Caruth, *Unclaimed Experience*, 63.
10. Alexander and Margarete Mitscherlich, *The Inability to Mourn: Principles of Collective Behavior*, trans. Beverley R. Placzek (New York, 1975).
11. Bauer, *Rethinking the Holocaust*, 52. One can push this argument too far, as the dehumanization of the Nazis did not prevent many of them from taking up positions of honor and power after the war.
12. LaCapra, *Writing History, Writing Trauma*, 22.
13. Alain Finkelkraut, *The Imaginary Jew*, trans. Kevin O'Neill and David Suchoff (Lincoln, Neb., 1994).
14. LaCapra, *Writing History, Writing Trauma*, chapter 2.
15. For a discussion, see Bauer, *Rethinking the Holocaust*, chapter 6.
16. In a chapter of a forthcoming book called *Songs of Experience*, now in preparation, I explore the attempts by Dilthey and Collingwood to defend a sustainable notion of

experience and either reexperiencing or reenactment, as well as the criticisms of their detractors.

17. For an exceptionally sensitive attempt to address these challenges, see Mark Roseman, *The Past in Hiding* (London, 2000), which reflects on the discrepancies between the memory of a Holocaust survivor, Marianne Ellenbogen, and her diaries. He disputes Lawrence Langer's claim that Holocaust testimony is the result of "insomniac memory," arguing instead that: "Marianne's memory suggests that even those traumatic memories which were always with her were subject to change. Moreover, the alterations followed certain common patterns, adding to my sense that what was happening in her mind was no accident" (476).
18. Siegfried Kracauer, *History: The Last Things Before the Last* (New York, 1969).
19. Whether or not the new technologies of recording mass testimonials would undercut this point seems to me questionable. What is certain is that a single witness cannot be the basis for a broad generalization. For a discussion of this issue, see Carlo Ginzburg, "Just One Witness," and my response, "Of Plots, Witnesses and Judgments," in Saul Friedlander, ed., *Probing the Limits of Representation: Nazism and the Final Solution* (Cambridge, Mass., 1992).
20. Kracauer, *History: The Last Things Before the Last*, 134.
21. *Ibid.*, 136.
22. F. R. Ankersmit, "Representation and the Representation of Experience," *Metaphilosophy* 31, 1 and 2 (2000): 152.
23. *Ibid*, 159.
24. My own encounter with such an experience, which did in fact have a tactile more than visual character, is described in "The Manacles of Gavrilo Princip," in *Cultural Semantics: Keywords of our Time* (Amherst, Mass., 1998). It involved a visit to Theresienstadt and my unexpected encounter with the jail cell and rusting manacles of the boy whose murder of the Archduke Franz Ferdinand precipitated World War I.
25. Angelika Rauch, *The Hieroglyph of Tradition: Freud, Benjamin, Gadamer, Novalis, Kant* (Madison, N.J., 2000), 199.
26. *Ibid.*, 210.
27. *Ibid.*
28. I am following the account here in Roger Greenspan's essay on "Cinema and Television" in Laqueur, ed., *The Holocaust Encyclopedia.* He notes that much of the material did find its way into a later film called *Memory of the Camps* narrated by Trevor Howard.

Chapter 6

1. A posthumous collection, *Mourning Becomes the Law: Philosophy and Representation,* was published by Cambridge University Press.
2. Rose, *Love's Work* (London, 1995), 52.
3. Gillian Rose, *Judaism and Modernity: Philosophical Essays* (Oxford, 1993), x.
4. Rose, *The Broken Middle: Out of Our Ancient Society* (Oxford, 1992), ix.
5. Rose, *Judaism and Modernity*, x.
6. *Ibid.*, 156.
7. Rose, *The Melancholy Science: An Introduction to the Thought of Theodor W. Adorno* (New York, 1978).
8. *Ibid.*, 148.
9. *Ibid.*
10. Rose, *Hegel Contra Sociology* (London, 1981), 33.
11. *Ibid.*
12. *Ibid.*, 219.

13. Rose, *Dialectic of Nihilism: Post-Structuralism and Law* (Oxford, 1984), 210.
14. *Ibid.*, 170.
15. *Ibid.*, 209.
16. Rose, *The Broken Middle*, 18.
17. Rose, *Judaism and Modernity*, 171.
18. Rose, *The Broken Middle*, xii.
19. *Ibid.*, 151.
20. Rose, *Judaism and Modernity*, 207.
21. For discussions of Hegel's hostile towards the Jews, see Nathan Rotenstreich, "Hegel's Image of Judaism," *Jewish Social Studies* 15, 1 (January, 1953); and Stephen B. Smith, "Hegel and the Jewish Question: In between Tradition and Modernity," *History of Political Thought*, 10, 1 (Spring, 1991).
22. Howard Caygill, "Gillian Rose, 1947–1995," *Radical Philosophy* 77 (May–June, 1996); Kate Soper, "Love's Work," *New Left Review* 218 (July–August, 1996).
23. Rose, *Love's Work*, 36. It was not, however, an entirely isolated decision, as her sister Jacqueline, who later became a distinguished feminist critic, adopted the same new name.
24. G. W. F. Hegel, *Philosophy of Right and Law* in *The Philosophy of Hegel*, ed. Carl Friedrich (New York, 1954), 226.
25. Rose, *Love's Work*, 130.
26. Rose, *The Broken Middle*, 277.
27. Caygill, "Gillian Rose, 1947–1995," 56.
28. Rose, *Love's Work*, 126.
29. Hannah Arendt, *The Human Condition* (New York, 1959), 218.

Chapter 7

1. "The Conversion of the Rose," *Salmagundi* 113 (Winter 1997).
2. The most extensive coverage was, as might be expected, in Philadelphia. The scores of articles in the *Philadelphia Inquirer* can be accessed on the Internet. National interest has also been high; see, for example, the essay in the December 1999 *Esquire*.
3. The reference here is to the journal *Telos*, which was an important forum in the 1960s and 1970s for the transmission and evaluation of Western Marxism. In the past decade, its turn to the right was expressed in the embrace of such troubling figures as the Nazi "crown jurist" Carl Schmitt.

Chapter 8

1. For accounts and analyses of the massacre, see Donald N. Clark, ed., *The Kwangju Uprising: Shadows over the Regime in South Korea* (Boulder, Co., 1988).
2. See Roland Robertson, "Globalization or Glolocalization?," *Journal of International Communication* 1,l (June 1994).
3. For a trenchant analysis of the relationship between cultural globalization and the boom in cultural studies, see Simon During, "Popular Culture on a Global Scale: A Challenge for Cultural Studies," *Critique Inquiry* 23,4 (Summer 1997).
4. For a helpful analysis of economic globalization, see Saskia Sassen, *The Global City: New York, London, Tokyo* (Princeton, 1991).
5. See, for example, the opposing analyses in Walter Russell Mead, "At Your Service: The New Global Economy Takes Your Order" and Robert Reich, "Working Class Dogged," in *Mother Jones* (March/April, 1998).
6. The precise nature of the deal has been disputed. Arguing against the credit taken by Carter and Reagan advisers Richard Holbrook and Richard Allen for the release,

Bruce Cumings has argued that "this is rubbish; Chun could not have executed Kim without every campus, many factories and the entire southwest of Korea erupting. Instead, he shrewdly used Kim's death sentence as a bargaining chip to coax an early state visit out of the incoming Reagan Administration and thus shore up his (then-nonexistent) legitimacy." From "Korea's Other Miracle," *The Nation* (March 30, 1998): 17.

7. See, for example, David Held, ed., *Prospects for Democracy: North, South, East, West* (Stanford, 1993). Held's introductory essay, "Democracy: From City States to Cosmopolitan Order" examines the challenge of globalization to democracy.
8. Slavoj Žižek, "Multiculturalism or, The Cultural Logic of Multinational Capital." *97 Kwangju Biennale: Unmapping the Earth* (Kwangju, 1997), 369.
9. John Rajchman, "The Earth and the Globe," *97 Kwangju Biennale*, 442.

Chapter 9

1. O. E. von Möller, "Die Augenbinde der Justitia," *Zeitschrift für christliche Kunst* 18 (1905): 107–22, 141–52; Otto R. Kissel, *Die Justitia: Reflexionen über ein Symbol und seine Darstellung in der bildenden Kunst* (Munich: Beck, 1984); Dennis E. Curtis and Judith Resnik, "Images of Justice," *Yale Law Journal* 1727 (1987); Christian-Nils Robert, *La justice, vertu, courtisane et bourreau* (Geneva: Georg, 1993); Robert Jacob, *Images de la justice: Essai sur l'iconographie judiciaire du Moyen Age à l'âge classique* (Paris: Leopard d'or, 1994).
2. Herman Bianchi, "The Scales of Justice as Represented in Engravings, Emblems, Reliefs and Sculptures in Early Modern Europe," in G. Lamoine, ed., *Images et répresentation de la justice du XVie au XIXe siècle* (Toulouse, 1983), 8.
3. Robert, *La Justice*, 13.
4. Erwin Panofsky, *Studies in Iconology: Humanist Themes in the Art of the Renaissance* (New York, 1967), 109.
5. Jacob, *Images de la Justice*, 234f.
6. Andrea Alciati, *Emblemata cum Commentariis* (New York, 1976).
7. Robert, *La Justice*, 37f.
8. Bernard J. Hibbitts, "Making Sense of Metaphors: Visuality, Aurality, and the Reconfiguration of American Legal Discourse," *Cardozo Law Review* 16, 2 (December, 1994): 255–6. He interprets these changes in terms of the growing ascendancy of an abstract, Cartesian visuality over the more concrete variant that reigned in the Middle Ages.
9. *Ibid.*, 241. Hibbitts, however, acknowledges that in the early modern period, when most people were still illiterate, texts were meant mainly to be read aloud rather than silently (256).
10. Max Horkheimer and Theodor W. Adorno, *Dialectic of Enlightenment*, trans., John Cumming (New York, 1972), 16–7.
11. W. J. T. Mitchell, *Iconology: Image, Text, Ideology* (Chicago, 1986), 108f.
12. Vassilis Lambropoulos, "The Rule of Justice," *Thesis Eleven* 40 (1995): 18.
13. See the entry on *Dike* in F. E. Peters, *Greek Philosophical Terms: A Historical Lexicon* (New York, 1967). For more sustained discussions, see Eric Havelock, *The Greek Concept of Justice: From Its Shadow in Homer to its Substance in Plato* (Cambridge, Mass., 1978); as well as Michael Gagarin, *Early Greek Law* (Berkeley, 1986).
14. Robert, *La Justice*, 65f.
15. For a comparison, see Robert, *La Justice*, 92.
16. Carol Gilligan, *In a Different Voice: Psychological Theory and Women's Development* (Cambridge, Mass., 1982); Seyla Benhabib, *Situating the Self: Gender, Community and Postmodernism in Contemporary Theory* (New York, 1992).

17. Hibbitts cites certain feminist scholars who claim that the power of the gaze is inherently male, whereas women's culture is more aural, and uses their arguments to buttress his claim that at least the American legal order until only recently was both ocularcentric and phallocentric (267). I would qualify this generalization to the extent that a female gaze is not a contradiction in terms and it is precisely its occlusion that may be complicitous with the type of visual regime that he shows dominated American legal theory. That is, without essentializing the gender differences, there may be a link between realizing the abstracting potential in vision and patriarchal domination, which functions by repressing the more concretizing alternative latent in the "female gaze" denied Justitia.
18. Alan Wolfe, "Algorithmic Justice," in Drucilla Cornell, Michel Rosenfeld, and David Gray Carlson, eds., *Deconstruction and the Possibility of Justice* (New York, 1992). He criticizes it for lacking an appreciation for "the rule-making, rule-applying, rule-interpreting capacities of human beings and an emphasis instead on the rule-following character" (366).
19. Martin Jay, "Mimesis and Mimetologie: Adorno and Lacoue-Labarthe," in *Cultural Semantics: Keywords of Our Time* (Amherst, Mass., 1998).
20. This raises the question of the status of images or representations of violence (or threatened violence, as in the case of the brandished sword). If they are understood as more mimetic than conceptual, does this mean that the violence in them is modified or even cancelled? Or can images participate in another kind of violence beyond that of subsumption? For a consideration of this theme, see Paul Crowther, "Violence in Painting," in *Critical Aesthetics and Postmodernism* (Oxford: Oxford U., 1993).
21. Jacques Derrida, "Force of Law: The 'Mystical Foundation of Authority'," in Cornell et al., eds, *Deconstruction and the Possibility of Justice*, p. 5.
22. Friedrich Nietzsche, *The Birth of Tragedy and The Genealogy of Morals*, trans., Francis Golfing (Garden City, N.Y.: Doubleday, 1956).
23. For a classic account of the dilemmas of political justice, see Otto Kirchheimer, *Political Justice: The Use of Legal Procedure for Political Ends* (Princeton: Princeton U., 1961). For a more recent discussion, which considers Kirchheimer's position with relation to Carl Schmitt, see William E. Scheuerman, *Between the Norm and the Exception: The Frankfurt School and the Rule of Law* (Cambridge, Mass.: MIT, 1994).
24. Walter Benjamin, "Critique of Violence," *Reflections: Essays, Aphorisms, Autobiographical Writings*, ed. Peter Demetz (New York, Harcourt, Brace, Jovanovich, 1978), 297.
25. *Ibid.*
26. Derrida, "Force of Law," 56. At the end of his piece, Derrida acknowledges the frightening potential in Benjamin's attraction to divine violence, an annihilating, expiatory violence, to become a perverted justification for the Holocaust. For differing opinions of how successful Derrida himself has been in thwarting this potential, see Dominick LaCapra, "Violence, Justice, and the Force of Law," *Cardozo Law Review* ll, 5–6 (1990), Drucilla Cornell, *The Philosophy of the Limit* (New York: Routledge, 1992), chapter 6; and Gillian Rose, *Judaism and Modernity: Philosophical Essays* (Oxford: Blackwell, 1993), chapter 7.
27. Adorno, *Aesthetic Theory*, trans. C. Lenhardt, eds. Gretel Adorno and Rolf Tiedemann (London, 1984), 141.
28. *Ibid.*, 143.
29. This metaphor of blindfolded Justice walking cautiously is taken from M. Petitjean, "Un homme de loi semurois: l'avocat P. Lemulier," *Annales de Bourgogne* 62: 245, cited in Robert, *la Justice*, 130.
30. On this issue, see Michel Rosenfeld, "Restitution, Retribution, Political Justice and the Rule of Law," *Constellations* 2,3 (January 1996): 309–32.

31. Arthur J. Wheelock, Jr., and Ben Broos, *Johannes Vermeer* (New Haven, 1996), 141–42.
32. Jean-François Lyotard and Jean-Loup Thébaud, *Just Gaming*, trans. Wlad Godzich (Minneapolis, 1985).
33. Jelic Šumić-Riha, "Fictions of Justice," *Filozofski Vestnik*, 2 (1994): 80.

Chapter 10

1. Hans Blumenberg, *Shipwreck with Spectator: Paradigm of a Metaphor for Existence*, trans. Steven Rendell (Cambridge, Mass., 1997).
2. *Ibid.*, 10.
3. *Ibid.*, 17.
4. Hannah Arendt, *Lectures on Kant's Political Philosophy*, ed. Ronald Beiner (Chicago, 1982).
5. Blumenberg, *Shipwreck with Spectator*, 19.
6. Cited in *ibid.*, 69.
7. Adrienne Rich, "Diving into the Wreck," in *Diving into the Wreck: Poems 1971–1972* (New York, 1973), 23.
8. *Ibid.*, 24.
9. See for example, the relevant essays in *Adrienne Rich's Poetry: Texts of the Poems; The Poet on Her Work; Reviews and Criticisms*, eds. Barbara Charlesworth Gelpi and Albert Gelpi (New York, 1975). Whether or not the poem was endorsing some form of androgyny seems now in dispute, partly in the light of her later endorsement of a more radical lesbian variant of feminism. See the discussion in Craig Werner, *Adrienne Rich: The Poet and Her Critics* (Chicago, 1988), 174–6.
10. See Stephan Oettermann, *The Panorama: The History of a Mass Medium*, trans. Deborah Lucas Schneider (New York, 1997); and Lieven de Cauter, "The Panoramic Ecstasy: On World Exhibitions and the Disintegration of Experience," *Theory, Culture and Society* 10, 4 (November 1993).
11. De Cauter, "The Panoramic Ecstasy," 18.
12. Robert Cantrell, *The Incredible Scream Machine: A History of the Roller Coaster* (Bowling Green, 1987).
13. De Cauter, "The Panoramic Ecstasy," 20.
14. Anne Friedberg, *Window Shopping: Cinema and the Postmodern* (Berkeley, 1993), 90.
15. Jeffrey Schnapp, "Crash (Speed as an Engine of Individuation)," *Modernism/Modernity* 6, l (January 1999).
16. *Ibid.*, 24.
17. Tom Gunning, "The Cinema of Attractions: Early Film, Its Spectator, and the Avant-Garde," in *Early Cinema: Space, Frame, and Narrative*, eds. Thomas Elsaesser and Adam Barker (London, 1990).
18. James H. Johnston *Listening in Paris: A Cultural History* (Berkeley, 1995); Lawrence Levine, *Highbrow/Lowbrow: The Emergence of Cultural Hierarchy in America* (Cambridge, 1988), chapter 3. Levine reads the bifurcation of high and low culture partly in terms of the former's suppression of the unruly audience behavior that was tolerated in the latter.
19. Linda Williams, "Discipline and Distraction: *Psycho*, Visual Culture and Postmodern Cinema," in *"Culture" and the Problem of the Disciplines*, ed. John Carlos Rowe (New York, 1998), 103.
20. Thomas Schatz, *Old Hollywood/New Hollywood: Ritual, Art, and Industry* (Ann Arbor, 1983).
21. Williams, "Discipline and Distraction," 95.
22. Martin Jay, "Modernism and the Retreat from Form," in *Force Fields: Between Intellectual History and Cultural Critique* (New York, 1993).

23. Yve-Alain Bois and Rosalind Krauss, *Formless: A User's Guide* (New York, 1997).
24. Schnapp, "Crash (Speed as Engine of Individuation," 7.
25. Gunning, "The Cinema of Attractions," 59.
26. Julia Kristeva, *Powers of Horror: An Essay in Abjection*, trans. Leon S. Rudiez (New York, 1982).
27. For a discussion of the typical horror film's attack on visual pleasure—often literally hurting the eye with bursts of light and overly rapid movement—see Carol J. Clover, *Men, Women, and Chain Saws: Gender in the Modern Horror Film* (Princeton, 1992), chapter 4.
28. Kristeva, Powers of Horror, 154.
29. Raphael Montanez Ortiz, "Destructivism: A Manifesto," in *Theories and Documents of Contemporary Art: A Sourcebook of Artists's Writings*, eds. Kristine Stiles and Peter Selz (Berkeley, 1996). On Metzer, Ortiz, and the DIAS, see Kristine Stiles, "The Destruction in Art Symposium (DIAS): The Radical Social Project of Event Structured Art," Ph.d. diss. (Berkeley, 1987) and Gustav Metzger, *"damaged nature, auto-destructive art"* (Nottingham, 1993). On abject art and the controversies surrounding it, see my "Abjection Overruled," in *Cultural Semantics: Keywords of Our Time* (Amherst, Mass., 1998), which has references to the relevant literature.
30. Walter de Maria, "On the Importance of Natural Disasters" (1960) in Stiles and Selz, eds., *Theories and Documents of Contemporary Art*, 527.
31. Hal Foster, *The Return of the Real* (Cambridge, Mass., 1996), chapter 5.
32. Royal Academy of Art, *Sensation: Young British Artists from the Saatchi Collection* (London, 1997). When this collection came to the Brooklyn Museum of Art in 1999, it occasioned an even greater outcry than it had in London. Mayor Rudolph Giuliani demanded that the museum stop the exhibition or else face the withdrawal of public funds. In San Francisco, another show with similar works opened in September at the Haines Gallery, tellingly called "Now It's My Turn to Scream: Selections of Contemporary British Art from the Logan Collection."
33. Stevie Smith, "Not Waving but Drowning," in *Committed to Memory: 100 Best Poems to Memorize*, ed., John Hollander (New York, 1997), 184.
34. See the catalogue, Elisabeth Sussman, ed., *On the Passage of a Few People Through a Rather Brief Moment of Time: The Situationist International 1957–1972* (Cambridge, Mass., 1989).
35. Foster, *The Return of the Real*, 156.
36. Walter Benjamin to Gershom Scholem, April 17, 1931, in *Briefe*, eds. Gershom Scholem and Theodor W. Adorno (Frankfurt, 1966), vol. 2, 532.
37. I have tried to explore the implications of this argument in " 'The Aesthetic Ideology' as Ideology, or, What Does It Mean to Aestheticize Politics?," in *Force Fields*.

Chapter 11

1. The classic study of Roemer and his work is still I. Bernard Cohen, *Roemer and the First Determination of the Velocity of Light* (New York, 1944). It contains a facsimile of the article in the December 7, 1676 issue of the *Journal des Sçavans* in which Roemer published his findings. See also the essays collected in *Roemer et la vitesse de la lumière*, conference proceedings of a CNRS conference (Paris, 1978). For general background, see A. I. Sabra, *Theories of Light from Descartes to Newton* (London, 1967).
2. For the later refinements in the measurement of the speed of light, see P. Grivet, "Progrés récents dans la mesure de la vitesse de la lumière Co," in *Roemer and et la vitesse de la lumière*. At present, *c* is understood to equal 299,792,457.4 +/− 1.2 km/s, or about one billion feet per second, which is called a gigafoot. Huygens came up

with 48,000 leagues (or about 144,000 miles) a second, which was off, but close to the right magnitude.

3. James Bradley, "An Account of a New Discovered Motion of the Fix'd Stars," *Philosophical Transactions*, xxxv (1727–1728), 637–61. Bradley noted that the star called gramma Draconis varied at the zenith distance at which it crossed over the meridian, but that the variations could not be explained entirely by the relative positions of the earth and the star (parallax means the apparent difference in the position of a celestial body with reference to a fixed background—the more distant stellar universe—when seen from two different locations). The excess in the variation had to be due instead to the different time it took the light to reach each of the locations. See A. B. Stewart, "The Discovery of Stellar Aberration," *Scientific American* 210 (March 1964).
4. In fact, the decisive defeat of Descartes' physics by Newton's was made possible by the discovery of the speed of light, which discredited his assumption that the universe was a plenum. Newton's own claim that light was corpuscular rather than a wave and travelled through the medium of "ether" was itself later shown to be incorrect.
5. The first terrestrial experiment that confirmed the speed of light was done in 1849 by A. H. L. Fizeau, who used mirrors rather than lanterns that had to be manually operated. See the discussion in Enders A. Robinson, *Einstein's Relativity in Metaphor and Mathematics* (Englewood Cliffs, N.J., 1990), 22.
6. Hans Blumenberg, *The Genesis of the Copernican World*, trans. Robert M. Wallace (Cambridge, Mass., 1987), 391.
7. For a discussion, see Michael Hoskin, "The Principle Consequences of the Discovery of the Finite Velocity of Light for the Development of Astronomy in the Eighteenth and Nineteenth Centuries," in *Roemer et la vitesse de la lumière.*
8. Marie-Antoinette Tonnelat, "Vitesse de la lumière et relativité," in *Roemer et la vitesse de la lumière*; Robinson, *Einstein's Relativity in Metaphor and Mathematics*; and Sidney Perkowitz, *Empire of Light: A History of Discovery in Science and Art* (New York, 1996).
9. William Whiston, *Praelectiones astronomicae* (Cambridge, 1707); the lecture, dated 1702, is discussed in Hoskins, 234–5. It should be noted, however, that it was a long while before the enormity of the temporal distances were understood. As late as Nietzsche, it was still reckoned only in "centuries." See his *Beyond Good and Evil*, part 9, section 285, trans. Walter Kaufmann, in *Basic Writings of Nietzsche* (New York, 1966), 417.
10. For a recent account of its implications, see Catherine Wilson, *The Invisible World: Early Modern Philosophy and the Invention of the Microscope* (Princeton, 1995).
11. Perkowitz, *Empire of Light*, 50. It is true that microscopes discern minute spatial distances that can be measured only in terms of the passage of light—the measurement called a "light-fermi" is the time it takes for light to travel between one side of a proton to another—but there is no effect of gazing back into an earlier time.
12. According to the latest reports, astronomers now think that based on measurements made by the European Space Agency's satellite Hipparcos of pulsing stars, or cepheids, the oldest stars are some ll billion years old, while the universe as a whole may be as old as 13 billion years. See "New Data Hint that the Universe May be Bigger than Thought," *The New York Times*, February 15, 1997.
13. For a discussion of his attitude towards sight, see my *Downcast Eyes: The Denigration of Vision in Twentieth-Century French Thought* (Berkeley, 1993), 186–209.
14. Hans Jonas, "The Nobility of Sight," *The Phenomenon of Life: Toward a Philosophical Biology* (Chicago, 1982), 136.

15. Régis Debray, *Media Manifestoes: On the Technological Transformation of Cultural Forms*, trans., Eric Rauth (London, 1996), 148. Syncope means a sudden break in the temporal flow, like a swoon from consciousness.
16. See, for example, Claude Gandelman, *Reading Pictures, Viewing Texts* (Bloomington, 1990); and Norman Bryson, *Vision and Painting: The Logic of the Gaze* (London, 1983).
17. Edward T. Hall, *The Hidden Dimension* (New York, 1982), 40.
18. Jonas, "The Nobility of Sight," 151.
19. George Berkeley, *Essay Toward a New Theory of Vision, Philosophical Works* (London, 1975), 21.
20. René Descartes, *Discourse on Method, Optics, Geometry, and Meteorology*, trans. Paul J. Olscamp (Indianapolis, 1965), 67.
21. A similar conclusion was drawn from the microscope, which revealed layers of seemingly immaterial, minute reality that no touch could verify. For a discussion, see Barbara Maria Stafford, *Body Criticism: Imaging the Unseen in Enlightenment Art and Medicine* (Cambridge, Mass., 1993), 36.
22. Blumenberg, *The Genesis of the Copernican World*, 632.
23. Maurice Blanchot, *The Writing of the Disaster*, trans., Ann Smock (Lincoln, Neb., 1986), 2.
24. *Ibid.*, 133.
25. Blumenberg, *The Genesis of the Copernican World*, 97.
26. For a discussion of this awareness, see *Ibid.*, 642–3.
27. It should be noted that this process was already underway with the invention of the first reflecting telescope by Newton in 1669, which used mirrors rather than lenses to magnify distant objects. See Perkowitz, *Empire of Light*, 53.
28. See Karl Menges, " 'Moral Astronomy': On a Metaphor in Novalis and its Conceptual Context," in *Languages of Visuality: Crossings between Science, Art, Politics, and Literature*, ed. Beate Allert (Detroit, 1996).
29. Roland Barthes, *Camera Lucida: Reflections on Photography*, trans. Richard Howard (New York, 1981); Susan Sontag, *On Photography* (New York, 1978); René Dubois, *L'acte photographique* (Paris, 1983).
30. Barthes, *Camera Lucida*, 80–81.
31. Eduardo Cadava, *Words of Light: Theses on the Photography of History* (Princeton, N.J., 1997).
32. *Ibid.*, 30. He shows Benjamin's debt to Auguste Blanqui's *L'éternité par les astres: Hypothèse astronomique* (Paris, Ballière, 1872), in which the catastrophe of stellar death is reversed by an eternal return that reproduces what has been destroyed.
33. Jonathan Crary, *Techniques of the Observer: On Vision and Modernity in the Nineteenth Century* (Cambridge, Mass, 1990).
34. *Ibid.*, 98.
35. Martin Jay, "Scopic Regimes of Modernity," in *Force Fields: Between Intellectual History and Cultural Critique* (New York: 1993).
36. See Margaret Atherton, "How to Write the History of Vision: Understanding the Relationship between Berkeley and Descartes," in David Michael Levin, ed., *Sites of Vision: The Discursive Construction of Sight in the History of Philosophy* (Cambridge, Mass., 1997).
37. Blumenberg, *The Genesis of the Copernican World*, 103. The passage in question is from *Beyond Good and Evil*, and refers to the fact that contemporaries fail to recognize the really creative spirits among them: "What happens is a little like what happens in the realm of stars. The light of the remotest stars comes last to men; and until it has arrived man denies that there are—stars there." See note 9.

38. Sigmund Freud, *The Interpretation of Dreams*, trans. James Strachey (New York, 1969), 575. Freud says such an instrument might be a microscope or camera as well as a telescope.
39. Jacques Derrida, *Writing and Difference*, trans. Alan Bass (Chicago, 1978).
40. Timothy J. Reiss, *The Discourse of Modernism* (Ithaca, 1982).
41. See, for example, Paul Virilio, *L'espace critique* (Paris, 1984).
42. For an account of his relation to virtuality, see Mark Poster, "Theorizing Virtual Reality: Baudrillard and Derrida," in *Cyberspace Textuality*, ed. Marie-Laure Ryan (Bloomington, 1999).
43. Jean Baudrillard, *Les stratégies fatale* (Paris, 1983), excerpted as "Fatal Strategies," *Selected Writings*, ed. Mark Poster (Stanford, 1988), 192.
44. *Ibid.*
45. *Ibid.*, 194.
46. Perkowitz, *Empire of Light*, 76.
47. See, for example, his essay "Simulacra and Simulations," in which he argues that the most recent phase of the image is one in which "it bears no relation to any reality whatever: it is its own pure simulacrum." *Selected Writings*, 170.
48. N. Katherine Hayles, "Virtual Bodies and Flickering Signifiers," *October* 66 (Fall 1993); 72.
49. Poster, "Theorizing Virtual Reality: Baudrillard and Derrida," *What's the Matter with the Internet* (Minneapolis, 2001).
50. Pierre Lèvy, *Qu'est-ce que le virtuel?* (Paris, 1995).
51. *Ibid.*, 16.
52. Jacques Derrida, *Specters of Marx: The State of the Debt, the Work of Mourning, and the New International*, trans. Peggy Kamuf, intro. Bernd Magnus and Stephen Cullenberg (New York, 1994). On the more general implications of the notion of the uncanny, see Martin Jay, "The Uncanny Nineties," *Cultural Semantics: Keywords of Our Time* (Amherst, 1998).

Chapter 12

1. Martin Jay, *Downcast Eyes: The Denigration of Vision in Twentieth-Century French Thought* (Berkeley, 1993).
2. Jacques Lacan, *The Four Fundamental Concepts of Psycho-analysis*, ed., Jacques-Alain Miller, trans. Alan Sheridan (New York, 1981), 118–9.
3. W. J. T. Mitchell, "The Pictorial Turn," *Artforum* (March 1992).
4. Richard Rorty, *Philosophy and the Mirror of Nature* (Princeton, 1979). See also his *Consequences of Pragmatism: Essays, 1972–1980* (Minneapolis, 1982), especially chapter 3, "Overcoming the Tradition: Heidegger and Dewey."
5. J. J. Gibson, *The Perception of the Visual World* (Boston, 1950).
6. Their importance for the French debate is addressed by Andreas Huyssen, "In the Shadow of McLuhan: Jean Baudrillard's Theory of Simulation," *Assemblage* 10 (1990). In general, however, McLuhan and Ong rarely find their way into the French theorizing I have examined.
7. David Michael Levin, ed., *Modernity and the Hegemony of Vision* (Berkeley: University of California Press, 1993).
8. Serge Guilbaut, *How New York Stole the Idea of Modern Art: Abstract Expressionism, Freedom, and the Cold War*, trans. Arthur Goldhammer (Chicago, 1983).
9. For a discussion, see Yves-Alain Bois, "Painting: The Task of Mourning," *Endgame* (Boston, 1990), 35.
10. Clement Greenberg, *Art and Culture: Critical Essays* (Boston, 1961), 171. Greenberg went so far as to argue that even modern sculpture had lost its tactile associations to become almost purely visual (142).

11. It also has often been compared with the defense of high modernism by Theodor W. Adorno. Adorno's "debate" with Walter Benjamin over the implications of mass culture became available for appropriation by Americans only in the early 1970s. Benjamin's sympathy for the emancipatory potential in mass culture was pitted against the apparent elitism of Adorno and used to reinforce the new anti-Greenbergian consensus. Here, too, differing attitudes towards Surrealism, which Benjamin generally supported and Adorno disdained, played a role. For a recent defense of Breton, which explicitly draws on Benjamin's debts to Surrealism, see Margaret Cohen, *Profane Illumination: Walter Benjamin and the Paris of Surrealist Revolution* (Berkeley, 1993).
12. In "After Abstract Expressionism," in *New York Painting and Sculpture: 1940–1970*, ed. Henry Geldzahler (New York, 1969), he argued that the ultimate source of value in art is the artist's "conception" that dictates the essentializing reduction (369).
13. *Ibid.*, 7. More recently, the repressed debt of abstract expressionists like Jackson Pollock to the automatism of Surrealism has been recalled. See, for example, Peter Wollen, *Raiding the Icebox: Reflections on Twentieth-Century Culture* (Bloomington, 1993), 91.
14. For a comparison of Greenberg and Szarkowski, see Victor Burgin, *The End of Art Theory: Criticism and Postmodernity* (London, 1986), 66f.
15. Michael Fried, "Art and Objecthood," *Artforum* 5,10 (1967). This essay and Fried's other criticism of the 1960s has been republished with a long introductory essay as *Art and Objecthood* (Chicago, 1998).
16. See his "How Modernism Works: A Response to T. J. Clark," *Critical Inquiry* 9,l (September 1982) and his interventions in the discussion "Theories of Art after Minimalism and Pop," in *Discussions in Contemporary Culture*, 1, ed. Hal Foster (Seattle, Bay Press, 1987), 71f. In fact, in his series of later works on the dynamic of theatricality and absorption, Fried seems to privilege an almost tactile immersion of the painter's and the beholder's bodies in the canvas over the distance of a disinterested spectator. Or more precisely, he acknowledges an irreducible tension between the two impulses, which never allows one to triumph over the other for very long. For a reading of Fried that foregrounds his distance from an ahistorical attempt to find painting's optical essence and appreciates his debt to Derrida, see Stephen W. Melville, *Philosophy Beside Itself: On Deconstruction and Modernism* (Minneapolis, 1986).
17. There were, of course, other developments, such as the reintroduction of figural, often neoexpressionist painting by German artists like Baselitz, Kiefer, and Penck, which challenged the Greenbergian paradigm from another angle. For a debate over its significance, see Benjamin H. D. Buchloh, "Figures of Authority, Ciphers of Regression," and Donald B. Kuspit, "Flak from the 'Radicals': The American Case against German Painting," in *Art After Modernism: Rethinking Representation*, ed. Brian Wallis (Boston, 1984).
18. Daniel Herwitz, *Making Theory/Constructing Art: On the Authority of the Avant-Garde* (Chicago, 1993).
19. Joseph Kosuth, "Art after Philosophy," in *Art after Philosophy and After: Collected Writings, 1966–1990*, ed. Gabriele Guercio (Cambridge, Mass., 1991).
20. The celebrated attack on Minimalism as theatrical by Michael Fried in "Art and Objecthood" was directed precisely at the restoration of temporality. For a typical post-Greenbergian response to Fried on this issue, see Douglas Crimp, "Pictures," *October*, 8 (Spring 1979).
21. Burgin, *The End of Art Theory*, 21. The essay from which this citation comes, "Modernism in the *Work* of Art," was originally a talk given in 1976.
22. Rosalind E. Krauss, "Sculpture in the Expanded Field," *The Originality of the Avant-Garde and Other Modernist Myths* (Cambridge, Mass., 1985); originally written in 1978.

23. *Ibid.*, 289.
24. Krauss herself was taken to task for being too beholden to an ahistorical structuralist logic and not sensitive enough to rhetorical, institutional and ideological questions by Craig Owens in "Analysis Logical and Ideological" (1985), reprinted in his *Beyond Recognition: Representation, Power, and Culture*, eds. Scott Bryson et al. (Berkeley, 1992), 268–83.
25. W. J. T. Mitchell, *Iconology: Image, Text, Ideology* (Chicago, 1986).
26. Michel Foucault, *This Is Not a Pipe*, trans. and ed. James Harkness (Berkeley, 1983).
27. Norman Bryson, *Vision and Painting: The Logic of the Gaze* (New Haven, 1983). Bryson, to be sure, was skeptical of the earlier structuralist turn, sardonically commenting that "the misfortune of the French is not to have translated Wittgenstein; instead, they read Saussure" (77). But he uses Derrida, Barthes, and Lacan to buttress his larger argument.
28. Norman Bryson, *Word and Image: French Painting of the Ancien Regime* (Cambridge, Mass., 1981); *Tradition and Desire: From David to Delacroix* (Cambridge, Mass., 1984).
29. Bryson, *Vision and Painting*, 94.
30. Krauss, "Richard Serra, A Translation," *The Originality of the Avant-Garde and Other Modernist Myths* (Cambridge, Mass., 1985). Discussing Serra's 1970–72 sculpture *Shift*, Krauss interprets it as a tacit realization of the arguments of Merleau-Ponty's *Phenomenology of Perception*.
31. The absence of a strong psychoanalytic component in Merleau-Ponty's reflections on the body meant that he lacked an appreciation of the effects of desire in the visual field. His phenomenology could thus be important for Michael Fried as well as the minimalists. For a debate over who got him right, see "Theories of Art after Minimalism and Pop," 72–3. Denying that he ever privileged pure opticality, Fried argues that it was in fact minimalism that carried the Greenbergian reduction to an extreme of literalness rather than contesting it.
32. Laura Mulvey, "Visual Pleasure and Narrative Cinema," *Screen* 16, 3 (1975).
33. Burgin, "Tea with Madeleine," *The End of Art Theory*, 106. This essay first appeared in *Wedge* in 1984.
34. Mary Kelly, "Re-viewing Modernist Criticism," in Wallis, ed., *Art After Modernism*, p. 96. This essay first appeared in *Screen* in 1981. For a discussion of Kristeva's general importance for the recent interest in abject art, see my essay "Abjection Overruled," *Cultural Semantics: Keywords of Our Time* (Amherst, Mass., 1998).
35. Fried, for example, admitted, "Yes, I was aware of Duchamp; he just doesn't interest me a lot." "Theories of Art after Minimalism and Pop," 80.
36. Amelia Jones, *Postmodernism and the En-gendering of Marcel Duchamp* (Cambridge, 1994); Jerrold Seigel, *The Private Worlds of Marcel Duchamp: Desire, Liberation and the Self in Modern Culture* (Berkeley, 1995); Dalia Judavitz, *Unpacking Duchamp: Art in Transit* (Berkeley, 1995), and "The Duchamp Effect," *October* 70 (Fall 1994).
37. See in particular Andreas Huyssen's influential essay, "Mass Culture as Woman: Modernism's Other," in *After the Great Divide: Modernism, Mass Culture, Postmodernism* (Bloomington, 1986).
38. See, for example, Guy Debord's complaint in his 1956 "Methods of Detournement," "Since the negation of the bourgeois conception of art and artistic genius has become pretty much old hat, [Duchamp's] drawing of a mustache on the *Mona Lisa* is no more interesting than the original version of the painting." *The Situationist International Anthology*, ed. and trans. Ken Knabb (Berkeley, 1981), 9.
39. Thierry de Duve, "Echoes of the Readymade: Critique of Pure Modernism," *October* 70 (Fall 1994), 65f.
40. Fried, "Art and Objecthood," 142.

41. Krauss acknowledged in her 1990 essay "The Blink of an Eye," that "Lyotard has been alone, as far as I know, in pushing this notion of the carnality of vision deep into the heart of Duchamp's production, which is to say, onto the very surface, of the *Large Glass*." *The States of "Theory," History, Art, and Critical Discourse*, ed. David Carroll (New York, 1990), 182. Krauss's involvement with French theory and art criticism was deepened by her discussions with the group around the journal *Macula*, which published from 1976 to 1982, and included Yve-Alain Bois and Jean Clay. Along with Hubert Damisch, they are acknowledged in *The Originality of the Avant-Garde and Other Modernist Myths*.
42. Jones, *Postmodernism and the En-gendering of Marcel Duchamp*, 56.
43. Rosalind E. Krauss, *The Optical Unconscious* (Cambridge, Mass., 1993), for example on page 309.
44. *Ibid.*, 142.
45. Krauss, *Passages in Modern Sculpture*, 76.
46. *Ibid.*, 270.
47. Krauss, "The Blink of an Eye," 176.
48. Krauss, "The Im/pulse to See," in *Vision and Visuality*, ed., Hal Foster (Seattle, 1988), 63.
49. With Jane Livingstone, Krauss curated a very influential show of Surrealist art at the Corcoran Gallery of Art in Washington in 1985 entitled *L'Amour Fou: Photography and Surrealism* (New York, 1985).
50. See in particular, "The Photographic Conditions of Surrealism" in *The Originality of the Avant-Garde and Other Modernist Myths*. For more recent evidence of the general impact of Derrida's ruminations on vision, see Peter Brunette and David Wills, eds. *Deconstruction and the Visual Arts: Art, Media, Architecture* (Cambridge, Mass., 1994).
51. Krauss, "Notes on the Index: Part 2," *The Originality of the Avant-Garde*, 219. Here she is referring specifically to a work of Marcia Hafif, but her point is a more general one.
52. Krauss had the advantage of a close relationship with the foremost Bataille scholar, Denis Hollier, who became a major figure at *October*.
53. Rosalind E. Krauss, "No More Play," *Primitivism in 20th Century Art: The Affinity of the Tribal and the Modern* (New York, 1984); reprinted in her *The Originality of the Avant-Garde and Other Modernist Myths*, from which the following citations come.
54. *Ibid.*, 64.
55. Rosalind E. Krauss, "Antivision," *October* 36 (Spring 1986).
56. *Ibid.*, 147.
57. *Ibid.*, 154.
58. Krauss notes that whereas Benjamin uses the term to imply the expansion of visual experience through new technologies like the camera, she wants to stress its implication of something that normally remains below the threshold of consciousness. "If it can be spoken of at all as externalized within the visual field," she writes, "this is because a group of disparate artists have so constructed it there, constructing it as a projection of the way that human vision can be thought to be less than a master of all it surveys, in conflict as it is with what is internal to the organism that houses it." *The Optical Unconscious*, 179–80.
59. Jonathan Crary, *Techniques of the Observer: On Vision and Modernity in the Nineteenth Century* (Cambridge, Mass., 1990). His argument was already presented in his contribution to the *Vision and Visuality* conference at the Dia Art Foundation in 1988, "Modernizing Vision."
60. Other figures connected with *October*, most notably Benjamin H. D. Buchloh, also contributed to the political critique of Greenbergian high modernism. Buchloh championed artists like Michael Asher, Marcel Broodthaers, Hans Haacke, and

Daniel Buren, who intensified the Duchampian subversion of the institutions of art. Issues of power, gender, and sexuality were also featured in the work of the one-time *October* collaborator Craig Owens, who acknowledged a strong debt to Foucault in particular. One of his major complaints against Michael Fried's mourning the end of modernism concerned in fact the absence of any discussion of power. See his 1982 *Art in America* essay "Representation, Appropriation, and Power," reprinted in *Beyond Recognition.*

61. Crary, *Techniques of the Observer,* 19.
62. *Ibid.,* 24.
63. Hal Foster, *Compulsive Beauty* (Cambridge, Mass., 1993), chapter 8.

Chapter 13

1. Thomas Pavel, *The Feud of Language: A History of Structuralist Thought,* trans. Linda Jordan and Thomas G. Pavel (Oxford, 1989) and Mark Lilla, *G. B. Vico: The Making of an Anti-Modernist* (Cambridge, Mass., 1993)
2. From the statement before the titles listed at the front of each book in the series.
3. Mark Lilla, ed., *New French Thought: Political Philosophy* (Princeton, 1994); Gilles Lipovetsky, *The Empire of Fashion: Dressing Modern Democracy,* trans. Catherine Porter (Princeton, 1994); Pierre Manent, *An Intellectual History of Liberalism,* trans. Rebecca Balinski (Princeton, 1994); Jacques Bouveresse, *Wittgenstein Reads Freud: The Myth of the Unconscious,* trans. Carol Cosman (Princeton, 1995); Blandine Kriegel, *The State and the Rule of Law,* trans. Marc A. LePain and Jeffrey C. Cohen (Princeton, 1995); Marcel Gauchet, *The Disenchantment of the World: A Political History of Religion,* trans. Oscar Burge (Princeton, 1997); Alain Renaut, *The Era of the Individual: A Contribution to a History of Subjectivity,* trans. M. B. DeBevoise (Princeton, 1997); Pierre Manent, *The City of Man,* trans. Marc A. LePain (Princeton, 1998); and Marcel Gauchet and Gladys Swain, *Madness and Democracy: The Modern Psychiatric Universe,* trans. Catherine Porter (Princeton, 1999).
4. Jerrold Seigel (twice), Jean Bethke Elshtain, Alexander Nehamas, Richard Sennett, Vincent Descombes, Donald R. Kelley, and Charles Taylor.
5. For another account that does attempt a view of the French scene itself, see Charles Larmore, "Histoire et raison en philosophie politique," *Stanford French Review* 15, 1–2 (1991).
6. Lilla, "The Legitimacy of the Liberal Age," in *New French Thought,* 26. Why American are assumed to be more passionately dogmatic than other peoples is not very clear. Nor is it necessarily the case that the French have completely turned their backs on the "master thinkers" of the post-1968 generation, as shown by the examples provided by Alan D. Schrift in *Nietzsche's French Legacy: A Genealogy of Poststructuralism* (New York, 1995), 162.
7. Fritz Stern, *The Failure of Illiberalism: Essays on the Political Culture of Modern Germany* (New York, 1972); Stephen Holmes, *The Anatomy of Antiliberalism* (Cambridge, Mass., 1993). As Natalie Doyle notes in her review of Lilla, *New French Thought* and other like texts [*Thesis Eleven* 49 (May 1997): 119], "the notion of 'illiberalism' cannot sufficiently account for the European experience, which it can only define negatively, as lacking the crucial ferment of Anglo-American liberalism."
8. Tony Judt, *Past Imperfect: French Intellectuals, 1944–1956* (Berkeley, 1992) and *The Burden of Responsibility: Blum, Camus, Aron, and the French Twentieth Century* (Chicago, 1998). Precisely what constitutes "responsibility" for Judt is not self-evident. Trying to disentangle it from the claims of "commitment," he correctly notes that "engaged intellectuals" could just as easily support radical right as radical left positions. Instead, he seems to identify responsibility with the refusal of radical solutions of any

kind and a willingness to retreat into moral abstention from direct political involvement if the choices are unappealing. His definition is, however, elastic enough to include Aron, whom he calls neither an empiricist, nor a moralist, but an eighteenth-century rationalist, and Camus, whom he sees as a latter-day Jansenist, who put concrete values above abstract ones. The only common denominator to "responsibility" for Judt seems to be a principled and unyielding opposition to Marxism.

9. Luc Ferry and Alain Renaut, *French Philosophy of the Sixties: An Essay on Antihumanism*, trans. Mary H. S. Cattani (Amherst, Mass., 1990).
10. See Jean-Philippe Mathy, *Extrême-Occident: French Intellectuals and America* (Chicago, 1993). Some of their disdain can, however, still be found in one of the theorists promoted by Lilla and Pavel, Pierre Manent. See his remarks in *The City of Man*, where he attacks the fetish of human rights in America: "On the *tabula rasa* of the continent, the appeal to rights gets carried away and loses patience; bursts of strident indignation disperse the already thin topsoil of human tradition; and from one side to the other, all the elements of the human world are attacked in the name of human rights" (147).
11. Tocqueville, not surprisingly, is a patron saint of New French Thought. He is, for example, the culminating figure in Manent's *Intellectual History of Liberalism* and praised by Judt as "a kindred spirit" to Aron (*The Burden of Responsibility*, 146). A new translation of *The Old Regime and the Revolution* by Alan Kahan (Chicago, 1998), vol. 1 has an admiring preface by Furet. Although occasional qualms are expressed about aspects of his legacy, for example in Gauchet's essay on Tocqueville in *New French Thought* and Kreigel's *The State and the Rule of Law*, it is clear that he remains the most potent nineteenth-century predecessor of their position.
12. Mark Lilla, "An Idea Whose Time Has Gone," *The New York Times Book Review*, July 25, 1999, 13. The first sentence is Furet's, the second Lilla's. Perhaps Lilla's most influential essay in *The New York Review of Books* was "The Politics of Jacques Derrida," June 25, 1998. For a more generous view of the same issue, see Geoffrey Galt Harpham, *Shadows of Ethics: Criticism and the Just Society* (Durham, N.C., 1999), chapter 4.
13. Many of the short articles in the first issue of his editorship (Spring/Summer, 1999), for example mocking accounts of Roger Garaudy's conversion to Islamic fundamentalism and Régis Debray's ill-considered defense of Milosevic in the recent war in Kosovo, are written by Lilla.
14. Lilla's "A Report to Our Readers" in *Ibid.*, 44.
15. Luc Ferry and Alain Renaut, eds., *Why We are Not Nietzscheans*, trans. Robert de Loaiza (Chicago, 1997). See also their *Heidegger and Modernity*, trans. Franklin Philip (Chicago, 1990). For more general overviews of the postwar French reception of Nietzsche and Heidegger, see Schrift, *Nietzsche's French Legacy*, and Tom Rockmore, *Heidegger and French Philosophy: Humanism, Antihumanism and Being* (New York, 1995).
16. Lilla, *New French Thought*, 147. Curiously, Marcel Gauchet's important book *La Révolution des Droits de l'Homme* (Paris, 1989) has not yet been included in the series, which chose instead to translate his book on the decline of religion.
17. For one recent overview, see Michael Ignatieff, "Human Rights: The Midlife Crisis," *New York Review of Books* 46, 9 (May 20, 1999).
18. In *Human, All-Too-Human*, Nietzsche writes, rather cryptically: "*The only human right*—Whoever turns away from his inheritance becomes the victim of the exceptional; whoever remains in his inheritance is its slave. One will be led to one's perdition in either case." (1, 555).
19. Jacques Derrida, *Of Spirit: Heidegger and the Question*, trans. Geoff Bennington and Rachel Bowlby (Chicago, 1989), 40.

20. Jean-François Lyotard, "The General Line," *Political Writings*, trans. Bill Readings and Kevin Paul Geiman (Minneapolis, 1993).
21. In *The Differend: Phrases in Dispute*, trans. Georges Van Den Abbeele (Minneapolis, 1988), Lyotard has a brief discussion of the 1789 Declaration of the Rights of Man, in which he focuses more on the conflict between the national and international addressees of the declaration, the one legitimated by a specific narrative, the other by transcendental claims. But the idea of the "differend" might also be applied to the incommensurability of different rights themselves.
22. Holmes, *The Anatomy of Antiliberalism*, chapter 3. His version of Strauss's antiliberalism has not gone, however, unchallenged. See the discussion in Robert Howse, "From Legitimacy to Dictatorship—and Back Again: Leo Strauss's Critique of the Anti-Liberalism of Carl Schmitt," in David Dyzenhaus, ed., *Law as Politics: Carl Schmitt's Critique of Liberalism* (Durham, 1998). He cites other relevant literature.
23. See, for example, Luc Ferry, *Political Philosophy 1: Rights–the New Quarrel between the Ancients and the Moderns*, trans. Franklin Philip (Chicago, 1990), part 1.
24. Claude Lefort, *The Political Forms of Modern Society: Bureaucracy, Democracy, Totalitarianism*, trans. John B. Thompson (Oxford, 1986), 239. For a suggestive comparison with his work and that of Derrida on the question of human rights, see Philippe van Haute, "Lefort and Derrida: The Paradoxical Status of Human Rights," in Harry Kunneman and Hent de Vries, eds., *Enlightenments: Encounters between Critical Theory and Contemporary French Thought* (The Hague, 1993). He shows that Lefort also denies the existence of an eternally given body of rights, preferring instead to locate them in the paradoxical logic of a democratic sovereignty that is both prior to the law and constituted by it.
25. Pierre Manent, "The Modern State," in Lilla, ed., *New French Thought*, 129.
26. *Ibid.*, 130.
27. Ferry, *Rights—the New Quarrel between the Ancients and the Moderns*, 58–60.
28. Kriegel, *The State and the Rule of Law*, 36.
29. *Ibid.*, 42.
30. The classic critique of this assumption can be found in Hans Blumenberg, *The Legitimacy of the Modern Age*, trans. Robert M. Wallace (Cambridge, Mass., 1983). From a Jewish point of view, Levinas argues against the assumption that modern humanism should be understood as the realization of older religious ideas, which can then be left behind, in "Antihumanism and Education" in *Difficult Freedom: Essays on Judaism*, trans. Seán Hand (Baltimore, 1990).
31. Ferry and Renaut, "How to Think about Rights," in Lilla, ed., *New French Thought*, 149. Translation modified.
32. For a sampling of previous thinkers in the French liberal tradition, see W. M. Simon, ed., *French Liberalism: 1789–1848* (New York, 1972). Of the fourteen figures excerpted there, only Benjamin Constant finds his way into Renaut's book, and then only to be criticized for confusing modern liberty with independence (18–9).
33. Renaut, *The Era of the Individual*, 39.
34. Another starting point, the individualism of Hugh Grotius, they neglect to discuss. See the account of his importance, in J. B. Schneewind, *The Invention of Autonomy: A History of Modern Moral Philosophy* (Cambridge, 1998), Chapter 4.
35. Ferry, *Political Philosophy I*, chapter 4. Although the third *Critique* is invoked here, it is clearly the *Critique of Practical Reason* that inspires Ferry and Renault's return to Kant and Fichte. Another recent return to Kant has taken place in France, however, which stresses the importance of reflective judgment developed in aesthetic terms for political purposes. This argument, reminiscent of the later reflections on Kant in the work of Hannah Arendt, is discussed in Vincent Descombes, *The Barometer of Modern Reason: On the Philosophies of Current Events*, trans. Stephen Adam Schwartz

(New York, 1993), chapter 2. Although this is not the place to discuss Arendt's ideas about human rights, her stress on judgment goes against the idea of a priori principles, moral as well as cognitive, which can be used as an absolute standard. For a nuanced treatment of her thoughts about human rights, see Jean L. Cohen and Andrew Arato, *Civil Society and Political Theory* (Cambridge, Mass., 1992), chapter 4.

36. Renaut, *The Era of the Individual*, 165. In so arguing, they expressly contradict Manent's claim that for the man of rights, "there is no longer any differential tension between empirical and completed being, between potency and act, between what is fulfilled and desired. Whether rights are guaranteed or scoffed at, it is in any case the empirical being himself who owns and holds them." *The City of Man*, 136.
37. Ferry and Renaut, "How to Think About Rights," 152.
38. Ironically, in certain respects this conclusion reintroduces the ethical critique of essentializing ontology and the metaphysics of presence made by post-structuralists like Levinas. For a useful discussion, see Simon Critchley, "Prolegomena to any Post-Deconstructive Subjectivity," in Critchley and Peter Dews, eds., *Deconstructive Subjectivities* (Albany, N.Y., 1996).
39. For a similar argument, see Agnes Heller, "Rights, Modernity, Democracy," in Drucilla Cornell, Michel Rosenfeld and David Gray Carlson, eds., *Deconstruction and the Possibility of Justice* (New York, 1992), where she says of human rights "their ontological character is illusory. *They are ethical and political principles.* They are *not theoretical*, but rather pure practical principles." (351). Heller argues for the admixture of liberal principles with those of democracy, basing human rights not on outmoded notions of natural law, but on modern ones of symmetric reciprocity.
40. Lefort, "Politics and Human Rights," 272. Of course, the noumenal notion of man as morally valuable in the present, captured in the version of the categorical imperative that enjoins us to treat men always as ends, never as means, would contradict this conclusion. But the problem in Kant has always been how to reconcile noumenal with phenomenal versions of humanity. When he historicizes the reconciliation, as he does in his essay on "Universal History from a Cosmopolitan Point of View," the actual "phenomenal" man can be sacrificed to the potential "noumenal" man through the workings of "asocial sociability." For a discussion of the consequences for Kant's view of rights, see Kimberly Hutchings, *Kant, Critique and Politics* (London, 1996), chapter 2.
41. Manent, *The City of Man*, 139. The confusion over which rights were truly human has dogged the debate from the beginning. See, for example, the polemical, and only half facetious, use of rights talk by Edmund Burke in *Reflections on the Revolution in France*, ed. William B. Todd (New York, 1962), where he follows the claim that "Government is not made in virtue of natural rights" with the counterclaim that "Government is a contrivance of human wisdom to provide for human *wants*. Men have a right that these wants should be provided for by this wisdom. Among these wants is to be reckoned the want, out of civil society, of a sufficient restraint on their passions. . . . In this sense the restraints on men, as well as on their liberties, are to be reckoned among their rights" (71–2).
42. Wai Chee Dimock, *Residues of Justice: Literature, Law, Philosophy* (Berkeley, 1996), 188.
43. Lynn Hunt, "The Origins of Human Rights in France," *Proceedings of the Western Society for French History: Selected Papers of the Annual Meeting* 24 (1997): 11–2. See also her edited edition of *The French Revolution and Human Rights* (Boston, 1996). In *Past Imperfect*, Judt argues that "in the course of the Revolution, the language of rights underwent a rapid if subtle change; from a device with which to defend the individual person against the overpowerful ruler, it emerged as the basis for advancing the claims of the whole against the interest of its parts. Far from protecting the

citizen against the caprice of authority, rights became enshrined as the basis for legitimizing the actions and caprices of that authority against the very citizens for whom and in whose name it exercised power. The shift entailed here was that from the rights of man to that of the rights (and duties) of citizens. Abstract or natural rights were displaced in favor of positive and concrete rights that depended upon membership of (sic) a formal community and that could be forfeited in the event of a citizen's failure to perform the tasks assigned him in that community" (234). Ironically, Judt seems to be blaming the Terror on the adoption of precisely the type of concrete rights and liberties that a conservative critic of the Revolution like Edmund Burke had blamed the Revolution for destroying! The difference is between a corporatist notion of concrete rights and liberties and a republican one. But both are checks on the absolutist claims of individual human rights prior to any membership in a community. For other essays on the links between the Revolution and human rights, see Dale Van Kley, ed., *The French Idea of Freedom: The Old Regime and the Declaration of Rights of* 1789 (Stanford, 1994).

44. Kant, "Theory and Practice Concerning the Common Saying: This May Be True in Theory But Does Not Apply to Practice," *The Philosophy of Kant*, ed. Carl J. Friedrich (New York, 1993).
45. Richard Wolin, *Labyrinths: Explorations in the Critical History of Ideas* (Amherst, Mass., 1995), 207.
46. Or alternatively, we might also draw from other intellectual traditions, such as the German. See, for example, the very suggestive essay by Rainer Forst, "The Basic Right to Justification: Toward a Constructivist Conception of Human Rights," *Constellations* 6, 1 (March 1999). Building on Habermasian premises, Forst makes a strong case for the right to be given acceptable reasons and justifications for political decisions as the most fundamental human right in all cultures. See also, Karl-Otto Apel, "The Problem of Justice in a Multicultural Society: The Response of Discourse Ethics," in Richard Kearney and Mark Dooley, eds., *Questioning Ethics: Contemporary Debates in Philosophy* (London, 1999). He makes the important point that the multicultural or communitarian appeal to the integrity of specific cultures against the intrusion of a putative universal set of rights imposed by one culture is itself based on the tacit assumption of a universal right: the right of all individual cultures to their impermeable integrity.

Chapter 14

1. John Dewey, *Art as Experience* (New York, 1934), 56.
2. Thomas Alexander, "The Art of Life: Dewey's Aesthetics," in *Reading Dewey: Interpretations for a Postmodern Generation*, ed., Larry A. Hickman (Bloomington, Ind., 1998), 4.
3. Dewey, *Art as Experience*, 349.
4. Robert B. Westbrook, *John Dewey and American Democracy* (Ithaca. 1991), 401–2.
5. David Fott, *John Dewey: America's Philosopher of Democracy* (Lanham, M.D., 1998), 109.
6. Peter Bürger, *Theory of the Avant-garde*, trans. Michael Snow (Minneapolis, 1984).
7. Dewey, *Art as Experience*, 227.
8. See, for example, Philip W. Jackson, *John Dewey and the Lessons of Art* (New Haven, 1998). Perhaps the best general study remains Thomas M. Alexander, *John Dewey's Theory of Art, Experience and Nature* (Albany, N.Y., 1987).
9. Richard Shusterman, *Practicing Philosophy: Pragmatism and the Philosophical Life* (New York, 1997), 177. See also his *Pragmatist Aesthetics: Living Beauty, Rethinking*

Art (Cambridge, Mass., 1992); and *Performing Live: Aesthetic Alternatives for the Ends of Art* (Ithaca, N.Y., 2001).

10. Shusterman, *Pragmatist Aesthetics*, 21.
11. Dewey wrote the introduction to three of Alexander's books, *Man's Supreme Inheritance* (1918), *Constructive Conscious Control of the Individual* (1923) and *The Use of the Self* (1932). He credited the "Alexander Technique" for having relieved his own problems of bad posture and stiffness, even his poor eyesight. Shusterman is himself a practitioner of Feldenkrais therapy, which continues this tradition.
12. Shusterman, *Practicing Philosophy*, 176. For Rorty's rebuttal, see his "Response to Richard Shusterman" in *Richard Rorty: Critical Dialogues*, eds., Matthew Festeinstein and Simon Thompson (Cambridge, 2001).
13. Shusterman, *Practicing Philosophy*, 150.
14. Shusterman, *Pragmatist Aesthetics*, 212.
15. In a recent interview, "Self-Styling after the "End of Art," conducted by Chantal Ponbrian and Olivier Asselin in *Parachute* 105 (2002): 59, Shusterman does mention in passing several of the body artists discussed below. But he understands them as examples of "self-fashioning" and bodily discipline, rather than as challenges to normative notions of the self as active agent and the body as a fashioned aesthetic whole.
16. Tracy Warr and Amelia Jones, *The Artist's Body* (London, 2000). There have, to be sure, been earlier accounts, e.g., RoseLee Goldberg, *Performance Art: From Futurism to the Present* (London, 1988); Amelia Jones, *Body Art/Performing the Subject* (Minneapolis, 1998); and Amelia Jones and Andrew Stephenson, eds., *Performing the Body/Performing the Text* (London, 1999).
17. Dewey's friendship with the collector Albert Barnes, who was a resolutely anticontextualist formalist, seems to have influenced his own judgments about the importance of form. For a discussion of Barnes and Dewey, which treats this issue at some length, see Alan Ryan, *John Dewey and the High Tide of American Liberalism* (New York, 1995), 252–65.
18. Michael Fried, "Art and Objecthood," (1967) in *Art and Objecthood: Essays and Reviews* (Chicago, 1998). In fact, this essay became an inevitable target in many accounts of the genesis of body art, e.g. Jones, *Body Art/Performing the Subject*, 112–3; *idem*, "Art History/Art Criticism: Performing Meaning," in Jones and Stephenson, eds., *Performing the Body/Performing the Text*, 42–46; Christine Poggi, "Following Acconci/Targeting Vision," in Jones and Stephenson, *Performing the Body/Performing the Text*, 269; and Joanna Lowry, "Performing Vision in the Theatre of the Gaze: The Work of Douglas Gordon," in Jones and Stephenson, *Performing the Body/Performing the Gaze*, 276.
19. Warr and Jones, *The Artist's Body*, 60.
20. For an analysis, see Philip Ursprung, " 'Catholic Tastes': Hurting and Healing the Body in Viennese Actionism in the 1960's," in Jones and Stephenson, eds. *Performing the Body/Performing the Text.*
21. Warr and Jones, *The Artist's Body*, 93.
22. Martin Jay, "Abjection Overruled," in *Cultural Semantics: Keywords of Our Time* (Amherst, Mass., 1998).
23. Arthur Danto, *The Transfiguration of the Commonplace: A Philosophy of Art* (Cambridge, Mass., 1981). For similar analyses, see Murray Krieger, *Arts on the Level: The Fall of the Elite Object* (Knoxville, Tenn., 1981); and George J. Leonard, *Into the Light of Things: The Art of the Commonplace from Wordsworth to John Cage* (Chicago, 1994).
24. Perhaps one exception is the recent self-marketing of Orlan, who has decided her art is not "body art" but rather "l'art charnel." See her website www.orlan.net.
25. Ursprung, " 'Catholic Tastes,' " 150.

26. Cathy Caruth, *Unclaimed Experience: Trauma, Narrative, and Experience* (Baltimore, 1996).
27. Michael Hardt and Antonio Negri, *Empire* (Cambridge, Mass., 2000), 448.
28. *Ibid.*, 215.
29. Fott, *John Dewey*, 118.

Chapter 15

1. (Berkeley, 2000) and (New York, 2000).
2. Rudolf Otto, *The Idea of the Holy*, trans. John W. Harvey (London, 1958), chapter 4.
3. For an insightful account of this issue, see Bruce Chilton, *The Temple of Jesus: His Sacrificial Program within a Cultural History of Sacrifice* (University Park, Pa., 1992).
4. Walter Burkert, *Homo Necans: The Anthropology of Ancient Greek Sacrificial Ritual and Myth*, trans. Peter Bing (Berkeley, 1983); René Girard, *Violence and the Sacred*, trans. Patrick Gregory (Baltimore, 1977); Georges Bataille, *Visions of Excess: Selected Writings 1927–1939*, ed. and trans. Allan Stoekl (Minneapolis, 1985). Bataille's work was carried out in the context of the College of Sociology, whose texts are available in Denis Hollier, ed., *The College of Sociology 1937–1939*, trans. Betsy Wing (Minneapolis, 1988). On Bataille, see Jean-Luc Nancy, "The Unsacrificeable," Yale French Studies 79 (1991).
5. Burkert, *Homo Necans*, 3.
6. For a critique of religious violence stressing this legacy, see Regina M. Schwartz, *The Curse of Cain: The Violent Legacy of Monotheism* (Chicago, 1997).
7. Søren Kierkegaard, *Fear and Trembling*, trans. Alastair Hannay (New York, 1986).
8. *Ibid.*, 65.
9. Walter Benjamin, "Critique of Violence," *Reflections: Essays, Aphorisms, Autobiographical Writings*, ed, Peter Demetz (New York, 1978), 297.
10. Jacques Derrida, "Force of Law: The 'Mystical Foundation of Authority," *Cardozo Law Review* 11, 5–6 (1990). For responses, see Dominick LaCapra, "Violence, Justice, and the Force of Law," *Cardozo Law Review*, ll, 5–6 (1990); Drucilla Cornell, *The Philosophy of the Limit* (New York, 1992), chapter 6; Gillian Rose, *Judaism and Modernity: Philosophical Essays* (Oxford, 1993), chapter 7 and Beatrice Hanssen, *Critique of Violence: Between Structuralism and Critical Theory* (London, 2000), chapter 1.

Chapter 16

1. My attempts to verify this charge have been unsuccessful, as the Pinochet regime is not normally mentioned in the literature on the School for the Americas. Nonetheless, its over 60,000 graduates since its founding in 1946 have had plenty of opportunities to violate human rights elsewhere in Latin America, thus earning its nickname "the school of assassins." A bill was introduced in 1996 by Congressman Joseph Kennedy to shut it down, but it has remained open under a different name, The Western Hemisphere Institute for Security Cooperation.
2. Hal Foster, contribution to the symposium on "11 September: Some *LRB* Reflections on the Reasons and Consequences," *London Review of Books* 23, 19 (October 4, 2001): 22.
3. Fredric Jameson, *ibid.* 23.
4. Chalmers Johnson, *Blowback: The Costs and Consequences of American Empire* (New York, 2000).
5. Mary Beard, *LRB* symposium, 20.
6. Recently, the virtues of what has been called "positive asymmetry" have been touted by American military planners, who want to use it as a weapon in the war against ter-

rorism. According to Todd Lappin in *The New York Times*, December 9, 2001, this strategy entails using food as way to show our humanitarianism, money to buy off some of the local warlords, and Hollywood to manipulate our image in a more favorable direction. What a "negative asymmetry" approach would do, however, is ask more fundamental questions about the direction of our foreign policy and monopolization of a disproportionate share of the world's resources. Our "humanitarianism" needs more serious demonstration than a few more food drops and the buffing of our image.

INDEX

41176967R00134

Made in the USA
Middletown, DE
10 March 2017